D1563941

THE FINAL FURY

PALMITO RANCH,
THE LAST BATTLE OF THE CIVIL WAR

PHILLIP THOMAS TUCKER

STACKPOLE
BOOKS

Published by
STACKPOLE BOOKS
5067 Ritter Road
Mechanicsburg, PA 17055
www.stackpolebooks.com

Printed in the United States of America

10 9 8 7 6 5 4 3 2 1

FIRST EDITION

Library of Congress Cataloging-in-Publication Data

Tucker, Phillip Thomas, 1953–
    The funal fury : Palmito Ranch, the last battle of the Civil War / Phillip Thomas
Tucker.—1st ed.
        p. cm.
    includes bibliographical references (p.) and index.
    ISBN 0-8117-0652-4
    1. Palmetto Ranch, Battle of, 1865. I. Title.

E477.8 T83 2001
976.7'38—dc21
                                                                    2001020151

To Will
Who patiently walked the forgotten field of
Palmito Ranch with me one last time
during the final month of the twentieth century

CONTENTS

ACKNOWLEDGMENTS

I WOULD LIKE TO THANK A GOOD MANY EXPERTS, ARCHIVISTS, AND HISTORIANS from the libraries and archives across the United States, and especially in Texas, for their gracious assistance on this project.

From beginning to end, Dr. Antonio N. Zavaleta, the vice president of External Affairs and professor of anthropology at the University of Texas at Brownsville, was most helpful. As the proud descendant of Ygnacio Trevino, the original owner of the land that would become Palmito Ranch, and the current owner of the officially designated "Historic Palmito Hill Ranch," located on the battlefield, Dr. Zavaleta offered both encouragement and expertise.

Dr. Zavaleta's late cousin, Praxedes Orive IV, and his widow and daughters are the present owners of "Rancho El Palmito." With a sense of dedication and reverence for the past, today's owners of the field of Palmito Ranch preserve and respect the pristine nature of the battlefield.

I would also like to thank Mr. Mark A. Warren, Bloomfield, Indiana, and Mr. Mark Weldon, Fort Wayne, Indiana, for their kind and timely assistance. Both of these gentlemen helped to secure the rare photographs of the 34th Indiana soldiers who fought at Palmito Ranch.

And I would like to thank the William Doan family of Paudling, Ohio, and Mrs. Jeanne Doan, who kindly allowed the publication of the rare photographs from the William Doan Collection. Mr. Doan was a descendant of a lieutenant colonel of the 34th Indiana killed during the Vicksburg campaign.

As always, the wise guidance and encouragement of Mr. William C. Davis continued to be invaluable to me. Leigh Ann Berry, one of Stackpole's best and brightest, also greatly assisted in the successful completion of this work. I owe a great deal of thanks to many people.

Phillip Thomas Tucker
December 31, 2000

PREFACE

ONE OF THE MOST FORGOTTEN AND LEAST UNDERSTOOD ENGAGEMENTS OF the Civil War was the battle of Palmito Ranch, May 13, 1865. Here, in a remote area along the Rio Grande River and the border between Texas and Mexico, the final shots of a Civil War land battle were fired on the coastal plain of Cameron County, Texas. The battle of Palmito Ranch was, however, fought nearly five weeks after General Robert E. Lee's surrender at Appomattox Court House, Virginia. Ironically, the final fighting at Palmito Ranch was also the last Southern victory of a conflict that began with Rebel success more than four years before at Fort Sumter, Charleston, South Carolina. Like the first major engagment of the war at Manassas, Virginia, in July 1861, the battle of Palmito Ranch was also a Southern victory.

Many years after the Civil War, the symbolism that embraced the battle of Palmito Ranch was not lost to Jefferson Davis, the former chief executive of the Confederacy. In his *The Rise and Fall of the Confederate Government,* Davis wrote from Beauvoir, his Mississippi Gulf Coast home, that the battle of Palmito Ranch "was . . . the last armed conflict of the war, and, though very small in comparison to its great battles, it deserves notice as having closed the long struggle—as it opened—with a Confederate victory." Perhaps more than any other single battle of the Civil War, the last flurry of fighting at the isolated and lonely ranch called Palmito was characterized by an unusual mixture of irony, symbolism, and paradox.

The story of the battle of Palmito Ranch has been lost in obscurity for more than 135 years. To historians, writers, and Civil War buffs alike, the name of Palmito Ranch has little, if any, meaning or significance. Quite simply, the battle has been ignored and forgotten since the last shot was fired in anger. Partly because of its obscurity and absence in the annals of Civil War historiography, the battle of Palmito Ranch remains one of the last, good untold stories of the Civil War.

Other factors explain why the final engagement of the Civil War deserves to be analyzed and interpreted by today's historians: the role of African American troops who symbolically fired the last volley of the war; the brilliant tactical plan employed by an old Indian fighter and Texas Ranger, Col. John Salmon Ford, who won his greatest battlefield success on May 13, 1865, even though Jefferson Davis mistakenly believed that a Confederate general deserved credit for the Confederacy's final victory; a handful of French soldiers fighting for the Confederacy north of the Rio Grande; Hispanics in blue battling Hispanics in gray on their home soil of Texas; a lengthy, running fight along the level flood plain of the Rio Grande and within sight of Mexico; a controversy over responsibility for the Federal defeat resulting in a bitter court-martial proceeding; an unnecessary engagement that violated a truce along the Rio Grande, which only resulted in the deaths of additional young soldiers for little reason; a battle initiated by an overly ambitious Federal officer who lusted for glory but found defeat instead along the Rio Grande; the battle fought on one of the southernmost corners of U.S. soil and in one of the most remote sections of the Confederacy; Texans in gray meeting Texans in blue on the battlefield to settle old scores during their own fratricidal conflict on the border; a one-sided victory won by outnumbered Texas cavalry over a larger number of Yankee infantry; and perhaps a forgotten battlefield atrocity.

In addition, the untold story of the Civil War's concluding chapter—Palmito Ranch—is also about the little-known players of the Western war along the Rio Grande border, including Colonel "Old Rip" Ford and his top lieutenants, and the Mexicans, Tejanos, Irish, Germans, and other European immigrants, and African Americans who fought at Palmito Ranch. These various ethnic groups went to war for a variety of personal reasons and motivations, in a brothers' war being waged not only within the American nation but also within the state of Texas.

Because of the mystery surrounding the last land engagement of the Civil War, some enduring myths still shroud the truth of the battle of Palmito Ranch. One of these has been the fiction that the African American soldiers of the 62nd U.S. Colored Infantry fought without discipline, skill, or distinction on May 13, 1865. For instance, one account emphasized that the "negro troops ran, and ran well." Other Texan and Southern accounts also highlighted this alleged "cowardice" of African Americans in blue. In truth, the role and performance of these black troops during the battle was as distinguished as that of their white Union counterparts.

Another myth surrounding the struggle at Palmito Ranch was that the number of casualties was few. While not large, the actual number of losses was higher than generally recognized by historians. Quite possibly, the number of fatalities was underreported for a variety of reasons, including the fact that the Federal leadership feared political and military repercussions from the Union "disaster" at Palmito Ranch with the French presence in Mexico. Consequently, the story of the last Confederate victory of the Civil War has remained controversial for more than a century.

Controversy extends even to the battle's name. This final clash between blue and gray has been frequently identified as the battle of "Palmetto" Ranch by generations of historians. In addition, the battle also has been incorrectly described by historians and writers as Palmito "Hill." Since the war's end and continuing today, the name "Palmetto Hill" has been more frequently used for the battle than Palmito Ranch. Leading to additional confusion is the fact that a Palmito Hill, a slight elevation along the Rio Grande amid the broad coastal plain, is the highest ground on Palmito Ranch.

Much of the mythology surrounding the battle of "Palmetto Hill" developed around the turn of the last century. This grew indirectly as a result of the popularization of the battle of San Juan Hill during the Spanish American War. During the summer of 1898, Teddy Roosevelt's Rough Riders won fame for their much publicized and highly romanticized charge up San Juan Hill during the principal land battle of the war. The legend of San Juan Hill propelled the most famous Rough Rider and war hero, Roosevelt, into national prominence and eventually to the White House in 1901. In the national consciousness, the popularization of the battle of San Juan Hill played a part in transforming Palmito Ranch into the battle of "Palmetto Hill" in the annals of Civil War historiography.

A final reason the battle of Palmito Ranch deserves attention from today's historians: perhaps no single engagement of the Civil War witnessed a more diverse mixture or a larger percentage of ethnic participation on both sides. Along with the fact that Palmito Ranch is one of the most forgotten engagements of the Civil War, this factor also makes this first ever book-length study of the battle long overdue. Therefore, the forgotten roles of the various ethnic groups at Palmito Ranch have been explored in detail so that the key players at the battle of Palmito Ranch can be better understood and appreciated.

CHAPTER 1

Death of a Nation

WHAT LITTLE REMAINED OF THE DECIMATED BUT PROUD ARMY OF NORTH-
ern Virginia—the Confederacy's primary Eastern army—was in its final
death throes by the early spring of 1865. The Southern nation's capital at
Richmond, Virginia, had been evacuated after Gen. Ulysses S. Grant's Army
of the Potomac broke through the thin gray lines of Gen. Robert E. Lee's
army at Petersburg, Virginia. Pres. Jefferson Davis and his cabinet became
refugees from the infant nation's capital, fleeing into the countryside to escape. One realistic Georgia Rebel summarized how the last futile battles of
the doomed Army of Northern Virginia were little more than "the dying effort of an overpowered and discouraged people."[1]

Hoping to keep a fast-fading dream alive, the outnumbered men of Gen-
eral Lee's army limped westward in a futile bid to link with Gen. Joseph E.
Johnston's army near Raleigh, North Carolina. But it was already too late.
The Confederacy was dying a slow, agonizing death. On March 29, Sen.
Louis T. Wigfall of Texas declared with bitter resignation, "It is all over [and]
the game is up," before departing for Texas and then the safety of Mexico.

When General Lee's avenue of escape westward through the Appomattox
River country was blocked by the Army of the Potomac in the depths of the
Appomattox valley, the once invincible Army of Northern Virginia was all
but finished. While truce flags were raised along the lines, scattered firing
around the little village of Appomattox Court House broke the early "stillness" at Appomattox. Old habits were hard to break. Rearguard skirmishing
continued between blue and gray on the western outskirts of Appomattox,
before the cease-fire order reached all units on both sides. Meanwhile, a final
shot was fired from a Confederate artillery piece. The projectile spun through

the air to strike one unlucky young man, Lt. Hiram Clark of the 185th New York Volunteer Infantry.

As fate would have it, Lieutenant Clark earned the distinction as "the last victim" of the Civil War, dying on Palm Sunday, April 9, 1865. But in truth the last Federal fatality of the Civil War did not occur near Appomattox Court House, but on an obscure field at the southernmost tip of Texas, at Palmito Ranch nearly five weeks later.[2]

After four years of war the end of the Army of Northern Virginia came at last. Gen. John B. Gordon, one of General Lee's hard-fighting corps commanders, described how "during these last scenes at Appomattox some of the paroled Confederates now hoped for an early exchange and release from the pledge, that they might continue the struggle with some organized force, operating in a different section of the Confederacy[; therefore] they were looking hopefully to the Trans-Mississippi" to continue fighting against the odds.[3]

Both General Grant and Pres. Abraham Lincoln realized that once General Lee's army capitulated, the remaining Rebel armies in the field would also surrender. Understanding as much, Gen. Edward Porter Alexander wrote how when "the Army of Northern Va. surrenders every other army will surrender as fast as the news reaches it [because] it is the morale of this army which has supported the whole Confederacy."[4]

Meanwhile, more of the fragile fabric of the Confederate nation unraveled with each passing day. In a conquered Richmond, Mary Chesnut described the hopelessness felt across the dying Southern nation: "Running is useless now [so] Why fly? They are everywhere, these Yankees—like red ants—like the locusts and frogs which were the plagues of Egypt."[5]

After the faint hope of uniting with the Army of Northern Virginia was no more, General Johnston had little choice but to follow General Lee's example. At the Bennett House near Bentonville, North Carolina, on April 26, he surrendered to General Grant's top lieutenant and his old antagonist during the Atlanta campaign of 1864, Gen. William T. Sherman.

Many Rebel die-hards continued to deny that the end was near and that the Confederate experiment in nationhood had failed. President Davis refused to concede defeat, believing that, "if, as now seemed probable, there should be no prospect of a successful resistance east of the Mississippi, I intended then to cross to the Trans-Mississippi Department [where Confederate commanders] would continue to uphold our cause." The vast Trans-Mississippi Theater now became a symbol of the last remaining hope for continuing the struggle to support a fading dream.[6]

More dramatic events at the war's end rapidly unfolded. On April 14 at Ford's Theater in Washington, D.C., President Lincoln was shot by John Wilkes Booth. Less than a week after Lincoln's burial and long before reaching the Trans-Mississippi, President Davis was captured by Wisconsin cavalry-men in Georgia. A shackled Davis, with his dreams of a new nation crushed forever, was imprisoned at Fortress Monroe, Virginia. So closed the final chapter on the two leaders from Kentucky, whom destiny had taken in different directions.[7]

All across the vanquished South, the curtain was descending rapidly on the expiring Confederacy. An Arkansas soldier felt that "the world had suddenly come to an end." Throughout the North, church bells rang and Northerners celebrated their great victory. As anticipated by Union leadership, the news of General Lee's surrender in Virginia shattered the morale of remaining Rebels in the field.

Despite General Lee's surrender at Appomattox Court House, however, the Trans-Mississippi region remained unconquered. In fact, General Grant had asked General Lee at Appomattox to expedite the surrender of remaining Rebel forces, including Trans-Mississippi troops. But the Virginian lacked the authority to do so. With the collapse of Southern resistance in the East and Richmond's fall, seemingly little now remained for the Rebels west of the Mississippi but to lay down their arms and go home. However, hundreds of Confederates of the far-flung Trans-Mississippi Theater, especially in Texas, were determined to continue fighting against the Yankee invader as long as possible.[8]

One Texas Rebel in the south of the state caught the representative spirit of Col. John Salmon Ford's remaining soldiers in the Lower Rio Grande Valley when he wrote, "If I can't have a confederacy I don't want anything else."[9]

THE LOWER RIO GRANDE VALLEY

Months before the surrender of Generals Lee and Johnston in the East, the war was already winding down in one of the least accessible sections of the Confederacy and in one of the most remote corners of the vast Trans-Mississippi Theater. Here, an informal truce between Union and Confederate leaders had already brought an early peace to the Lower Rio Grande Valley and the southernmost tip of Texas.

While blue and gray continued to fight and die in the Eastern theater, this truce had first begun to take shape during the early days of 1865. In mid-January, Maj. Gen. Lew Wallace, the Indiana commander of the Middle Department in the East, informed General Grant that recent intelligence indicated that "the rebel soldiery in Western Texas, particularly those at Brownsville [Texas]" were demoralized and ready to quit the war. General Wallace, consequently, obtained a leave of absence to embark on one of the most unusual secret missions of the Civil War.

Endorsed by President Lincoln and General Grant, General Wallace's secret mission was calculated to begin initiatives to end the war in one of the

southernmost corners of the Confederacy for a larger purpose: to set the stage
for a possible joint Union-Confederate expedition into Mexico against the
French forces of Ferdinand Maximilian, who had been established as the emperor of Mexico by France's Napoléon III. Hoping to revive imperial dreams
of a French empire in the New World, the French were attempting to create a
European monarchy in Mexico under the cover of a civil war south of the
border. Like the United States, Mexico was also engaged in a civil war, as the
French and their Imperialist allies waged war against Benito Juarez, the president recognized by the Lincoln administration.

In addition, General Wallace also wished to enhance a tarnished reputation. Wallace's position had been sullied during the battle of Shiloh, Tennessee, in early April 1862 because of his division's late arrival on the
battlefield, when General Grant's army was on the ropes after the Confederate
surprise attack. A successful mission now and the accompanying prestige
would bolster the prospects of General Wallace's postwar political ambitions.
So as not to arouse suspicions, General Wallace's mission to south Texas was
disguised as an inspection tour of the Federal garrison at Brazos Santiago. Brazos Santiago, or Brazos Island, was a narrow barrier island in the Gulf of Mexico immediately off the southeastern tip of the Texas mainland, just north of
the Mexican border and the mouth of the Rio Grande River.

In early March 1865, General Wallace, a masterful politician and nego-
tiator, arrived by steamboat at Brazos Santiago, around twenty-five miles
northeast of Brownsville, Texas. Because the mouth of the Rio Grande was
too shallow for the entry of ships, the water passageway at the north end of
Brazos Santiago, which linked the river traffic of the Rio Grande to the Gulf
of Mexico, was known as Brazos Santiago Pass. A natural harbor just north of
the mouth of the Rio Grande and extending inward from the sea, the Brazos
Pass was located at the southern tip of 150-mile-long Padre Island and at the
southern end of a wide, shallow bay known as Laguna Madre. Both Padre Island and the Laguna Madre ran parallel, or north-south, to the gulf coast.
Looking more like a lake than a bay, the lengthy Laguna Madre was a narrow
shallow waterway located between the Texas mainland and the barrier islands
of Padre Island and Brazos Santiago.

General Wallace originally formulated the details of his proposed peace
plan after first gaining intelligence from a former Texas schoolmate, Charles
Worthington. Worthington ascertained the Confederates' willingness to agree
to a possible truce and "a settlement of difficulties" in the lower Rio Grande
country. General Wallace was informed that General Slaughter, Confederate
commander of the West Subdistrict of Texas, would engage in discussions with
him at Point Isabel, on the eastern point of the Texas mainland.

Therefore, a 12:30 P.M. conference on March 9, 1865, between Generals Wallace and Slaughter "under a flag of truce" was scheduled at Point Isabel. Situated on the Texas mainland, Point Isabel was little more than a clay mound that jutted out into the waters of the Laguna Madre, standing only slightly higher than the water level. With the war's end drawing ever closer, General Wallace, a Mexican War veteran who had first fought under Sam Grant at Fort Donelson, Tennessee, during February 1862, now planned to "discuss measures looking to a permanent peace honorable to both parties" along the Lower Rio Grande Valley. A man of many talents, General Wallace later wrote the Biblical classic entitled *Ben Hur: A Tale of the Christ,* after serving on the court-martial of the Lincoln assassination conspirators.[10]

On March 9 at Point Isabel, a cold wind, "a 'norther,' sprung up, making it impossible on the part of both of us to fulfill the arrangement," wrote a disappointed General Wallace to General Grant. The following morning, General Wallace sent a letter under a flag of truce to General Slaughter. The Hoosier general now requested a new conference at Point Isabel. The true nature of the secret meeting was concealed from everyone except the Confederate and Union officers who planned to meet. A war-weary General Slaughter remained eager to meet with General Wallace. From his Brownsville headquarters, General Slaughter had written that General Wallace was "as anxious in the business as I am myself"—a hopeful sign of cooperation between blue and gray in the future.[11]

A small party of Confederate officers rode east along the dusty road leading to the Gulf Coast from Brownsville. Meanwhile, from the north end of the island of Brazos Santiago on March 11, General Wallace caught a glimpse of the prearranged signals from the Point Isabel lighthouse on the Texas mainland. The flashing lights that reflected off the dark waters of the expansive Laguna Madre told of General Slaughter's arrival at the point. General Wallace, with three Union officers and Charles Worthington, who was the collector of the port of Brazos, immediately departed Brazos Santiago by boat.

The Union officers pushed west across the placid waters of Laguna Madre, which separated the Texas mainland from Brazos Santiago, and landed at Point Isabel with high expectations. Anticipating a successful outcome, General Wallace was prepared for lengthy negotiations with the Confederates. Therefore, the general and his party came "carrying along supplies and tents," so that they could meet comfortably for an extended period if necessary.[12]

Such thorough preparations for a lengthy conference were wise because Point Isabel was little more than a barren stretch of windswept land. The only distinguishing feature of the stretch of sandy ground that thrust eastward toward the south end of Padre Island was the Point Isabel lighthouse. The lighthouse stood on a mound of clay that jutted eastward toward the waters of Brazos Santiago Pass. Completed in 1853, the towering brick structure was one of two lighthouses funded by Congress in 1850 to illuminate the harbor of Brazos Santiago and the pass. Located about ten miles north of the mouth of the Rio Grande on the west side of Brazos Santiago harbor at the lower, southern end of Laguna Madre, the Point Isabel Lighthouse, standing more than fifty feet high, was the harbor's principal beacon.

Besides his staff of young officers, General Slaughter brought to Point Isabel his top lieutenant and an old ex-Texas Ranger, Col. John Salmon Ford. The rough-hewn frontier cavalry leader was known as "Old Rip" by his hard-riding Texas cavalrymen.

The peace talks between the Union and Confederate leaders began in a cordial manner despite the years of vicious conflict. Such camaraderie was possible, wrote Colonel Ford, because these veteran officers in blue and gray understood that it was useless to fight on the Rio Grande, and that if the contending parties met and slaughtered each other it would have no effect on the final result of the contest.

In fact, the interaction among the Union and Confederate officers at Point Isabel was so cordial that General Wallace described in his report to his friend General Grant: "If you at any time hear in the way of complaint that I have been hob-nobbing and sleeping with the rebels in this region, please understand the matter and take care of me." General Grant had taken good "care of" General Wallace in the past. He had reinstated the general after his removal from command by Gen. Henry W. Halleck, chief of staff, who had also desired to relieve General Grant from command because of his too-rapid rise to prominence in the Western Theater.[13]

The conference among the Union and Confederate officers at Point Isabel progressed. General Wallace realized "very early in the interview . . . that both General Slaughter and Colonel Ford were not only willing but anxious to find some ground upon which they could honorably get from under what they admitted to be a failing Confederacy." The meeting began to pay additional dividends. Colonel Ford recalled the importance of the Point Isabel meeting, describing how "the matter of concluding a peace between the North and the South was discussed" at length. After the talks, both Union and Confederate officers bedded down to sleep beside each other on the night of March 11. Then, the Point Isabel conference continued into the next day.[14]

Later a hopeful General Wallace described to General Grant the mind-set of these Confederate officers who now worked on a peaceful settlement "upon the grounds of humanity and an unwillingness to see [Texas] invaded and ruined and the war decline into guerrilla murders. [General Slaughter] and Ford insisted that they could procrastinate the final result indefinitely, but at the same time frankly admitted that if that were done the North would ultimately conquer the South as a desert."[15]

Then, General Wallace explained to General Grant the disadvantageous situation the Texas Rebels found themselves in because they "could not reasonably hope for assistance from Richmond and their eastern armies; that they were practically isolated [and] that as a consequence their highest present obligations were to their Trans-Mississippi army and citizens, whose honor and welfare they were charged with and alone bound to regard." To this assessment of the political and military situation, General Slaughter and Colonel Ford, continued General Wallace, both "agreed with me without hesitation, and asked me to give them such propositions" for future negotiations toward a peaceful settlement to end not only the war along the Rio Grande but also throughout the Trans-Mississippi Theater.

Like a country lawyer back in his native Indiana, General Wallace drew up six propositions for consideration by the Confederate authorities commanding the Trans-Mississippi. This cartel spelled out the exact terms and requirements for the Trans-Mississippi Confederates to relinquish authority and to reestablish Union control, "to secure a speedy peace." Then, the Confederates had the option to either depart the United States "with [their] property [slaves]" or once again become U.S. citizens, after taking an oath of allegiance.

Basking in what he believed was a successful mission, General Wallace sent a copy of his six proposals to General Grant. Wallace's propositions were then dispatched by General Slaughter to Gen. John G. Walker, the district commander of Confederate forces in Texas. General Walker was then to forward the propositions to the commander of the Trans-Mississippi, Gen. Kirby Smith.

Respecting and trusting Colonel Ford, General Wallace was encouraged that this honest Texas frontierman was originally selected to personally deliver these proposals to his superiors. Wrote General Wallace, Colonel "Rip" Ford "is politically the most influential Confederate soldier in Texas." Evidently because of either illness or personal reasons, however, Colonel Ford was unable to undertake this mission.[16]

But the initiatives of the secret Point Isabel conference were ultimately thwarted by General Walker, a die-hard Missouri Confederate whose home state had groaned for years under Union occupation. General Wallace's proposals were never forwarded to General Smith's headquarters at Shreveport, Louisiana. General Smith, ironically, might well have accepted General Wallace's proposals had he received them.

From Houston, Texas, an infuriated General Walker instantly rejected General Wallace's proposals without contemplation. In reply, General Walker wrote angrily to General Wallace on March 27, declaring that

> your proposition is nothing less than that we of the Trans-Mississippi States are to lay down our arms, surrender at discretion, take an oath of allegiance to the United States Government, and in return to accept such terms as amnesty, pardon, or foreign exile as our conquerors shall graciously accord us [but] we will accept no other than an honorable peace. With 300,000 men yet in the field, we would be the most abject of mankind if we should now basely yield all that we have been fighting for during the last four years, namely, nationality and the rights of self-government. With the blessing of God, we will yet achieve these, and extort from your own Government all that we ask. Whenever you are willing to yield these, and to treat as equal with equal, an officer of your high rank and character, clothed with the proper authority from your Government, will not be reduced to the necessity of seeking an obscure corner of the Confederacy to inaugurate negotiations.

In short, an uncompromising General Walker planned to continue fighting to the bitter end.[17]

General Walker found many valid reasons for rejecting General Wallace's proposals. By way of this diplomatic initiative, the Grant-Wallace team had in effect attempted to finally put an end to the flood of supplies, medicines, and war munitions pouring from the busy port of Matamoros, Mexico, and across the Rio Grande to fuel the war effort in the Trans-Mississippi. Unlike the situation in the East, the Trans-Mississippi Confederates could yet continue fighting thanks to this steady flow of war matériel.

At the end of his March 14 report to General Grant, General Wallace revealed his concern for the massive volume of supplies streaming from Mexico to the Trans-Mississippi. He described an unbelievable sight at the mouth of the Rio Grande: "As to the rebel trade by way of [the twin cities of] Matamoros and Brownsville, I think it is only sufficient to say that I can stand on my boat and count at least 100 vessels of all kinds lying of[f] Bagdad [theoretically a neutral port of Mexico, where the Rio Grande entered the Gulf, but in reality a Confederate port like Matamoros]. Neither the port of New Orleans nor that of Baltimore can present to-day such a promise of commercial activity." Here, ships from Europe unloaded tons of war supplies on the south bank of the Rio Grande. Then, the goods were transported by land around twenty-five miles west to Matamoros from where they crossed the Rio Grande to Brownsville.[18]

As General Walker realized by this time, the Lower Rio Grande Valley was certainly "an obscure corner of the Confederacy" but one of considerable importance. And, ironically, it was this very obscurity that explained why this remote section had become so important not only to the Confederacy but also to the North. This isolated region along the Rio Grande was the vital back-door to the South. The munitions and supplies that passed through this door, bypassing the Union naval blockade, fueled the Rebel war machine in the Western Theater. For years, this back-door of the Confederacy remained wide open for the tons of resources, munitions, and war matériel which streamed like a flood into Texas from Mexico.[19]

Equally as important, another key factor explained why the secret Point Isabel meeting took place between Union and Confederate officers: urgent geopolitical realities and realpolitik. On March 14, General Wallace described to General Grant the political component of his secret mission, which revealed President Lincoln's foreign relations concerns near the war's end: "both Slaughter and Ford . . . entered heartily into the Mexican project [of fighting the Imperial French] . . . [but] it is understood between us that the pacification of Texas [against Indian and Mexican incursions] is the preliminary step to a crossing of the Rio Grande." This called for an advance of a joint Union-Confederate force into northern Mexico to drive the French from the southern border of the United States.[20]

At the two-day Point Isabel conference, General Wallace attempted to lay a foundation for an ambitious plan—his "Mexican Project"—calling for united Union-Confederate military action against the Imperial French forces under Emperor Maximilian, France's puppet ruler in Mexico. With the United States self-destructing in bloody civil war, Maximilian was attempting to defeat the Mexican Liberals, or Juaristas. Such a joint Union-Confederate force would assist Benito Juarez, the elected president of Mexico, in his struggle to drive the French from the Mexican homeland.

For such a military effort south of the border, more than just Federal forces would be needed. Veteran Texas Rebels who knew Mexico and how to fight on the border were essential to a successful expedition. At this time, the Texas horse soldiers under Colonel Ford's command were some of the finest light cavalry in the west. In addition, General Wallace also envisioned a joint expedition using the still-plentiful resources of the Confederate Trans-Mississippi, and the trade connections across the Rio Grande.

On March 14, Wallace described to General Grant in his written six-point proposal that "not a word is said about the arms now in the hands of the Confederates [but] we expect to get their use. Neither can they see any reason why that portion of the cotton now in Texas, and belonging to the Confederate Government, should not be diverted to the same purpose." Thousands of bales of cotton could be sold to fund a joint Union-Confederate invasion of northern Mexico. To further his plan, the Confederate officers at Point Isabel were offered amnesty in return for their services south of the border. Unlike other Southern troops fighting their last rearguard actions, the Texas Rebels of the Lower Rio Grande Valley were offered a chance to reenter the Union with honor and in the name of upholding the Monroe Doctrine weeks before General Lee's surrender at Appomattox.[21]

Clearly, with the war's end near, such an ambitious plan held potential for the splintered American nation. General Slaughter realized "that the best way for officers in [their] situation to get honorably back into the Union was to cross the river, conquer two or three [Mexican] States from the French, and ultimately annex them, with all their inhabitants, to the United States." Colonel Ford was also eager to strike into northern Mexico because he feared that his commander, General Smith, was negotiating with Maximilian to support the French.

If that was indeed the case, then Colonel Ford was prepared to "instantly bring about a counter revolution" against the Confederacy and General Smith. General Smith, who planned to flee to Mexico after the Confederacy's final collapse, believed that "our cause has reached [such] a crisis [as] to call for foreign intervention" from the French. If this plan succeeded, the French would gain a buffer against the United States by allying themselves with the Trans-Mississippi Confederates.[22]

By early 1865, the idea of annexing the northern Mexico states—shades of the Manifest Destiny of the 1840s—was nothing new in the volatile world along the Texas-Mexico border. Santiago Vidaurri, the rebellious governor of the northern Mexican province of Nuevo Leon y Coahuila, had proposed to Pres. Jefferson Davis that the Confederacy "annex northern Mexico" as early as 1861. In many ways, northern Mexico already more closely resembled Confederate Texas than the Mexican interior.[23]

Regardless of the refusal of General Smith to accept General Wallace's peace proposals, the shooting war came to an abrupt end along the Lower Rio Grande Valley, after the Wallace-Slaughter conference at Point Isabel. As Colonel Ford described the situation along the Lower Rio Grande frontier after mid-March 1865: "though nothing was decided of a formal nature, Ford and Slaughter [had] left General Wallace expecting the peaceful coexistence along the [Rio Grande] river to continue" throughout the remainder of 1865 and until the war's conclusion.

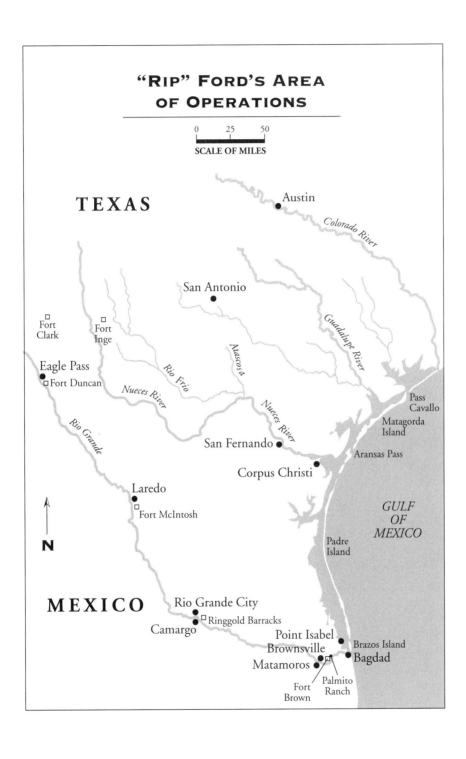

"RIP" FORD'S AREA
OF OPERATIONS

0   25   50

SCALE OF MILES

TEXAS

Austin

Colorado River

San Antonio

Fort
Clark

Fort
Inge

Guadalupe River

Eagle Pass

Fort Duncan

Atascosa

Rio Frio

Nueces River

Nueces River

Pass
Cavallo

Matagorda
Island

San Fernando

Aransas Pass

Rio Grande

Corpus Christi

N

Laredo

Fort McIntosh

GULF
OF
MEXICO

Padre
Island

MEXICO

Rio Grande City

Ringgold Barracks

Camargo

Point Isabel

Brazos Island

Brownsville

Bagdad

Matamoros

Fort
Brown

Palmito
Ranch

For one, this informal truce along the Lower Rio Grande Valley was beneficial to the Confederacy. Not only was the South not losing anything by adhering to the informal agreement, but the truce also allowed the Rebels of the Lower Rio Grande to continue accomplishing their primary mission. The informal truce along the Rio Grande ensured that the Confederates would continue to fulfil their principal mission of keeping tons of war supplies flowing unimpeded across the river from Mexico.

Even along the Lower Rio Grande Valley, the Rebels were so confident of a continuance of a "peaceful coexistence" that they relinquished their usual vigilance. With the countryside ravished by a record drought and years of border conflict, Colonel Ford was only too aware of the extent of unpreparedness among his Confederate cavalry in early 1865. After the informal Point Isabel truce, Colonel Ford described how the majority of his Texas horsemen were now "scattered between the Rio Grande and Arroya Colorado."[24]

Thanks to the independent agreement struck between Generals Wallace and Slaughter, a tranquil peace settled over the Lower Rio Grande Valley during the last months of the war, while the Confederate dream vanished at Petersburg, Richmond, Sailor's Creek, and Appomattox Court House. All the while, Colonel Ford's remote section of the Confederacy enjoyed a peaceful seclusion along the Mexican border throughout the early weeks of 1865.

Here, the Lower Rio Grande Valley lay just north of the Mexican border. Through this broad east-west valley ran the "Great River," the Rio Grande. The river separated the two neighboring republics of Mexico and the Confederacy, both of which were born in violent revolution. At the lowest, or southernmost end of the Lower Rio Grande Valley, where the river ended its 1,800-mile journey from Colorado's mountains to enter the Gulf of Mexico, were the arid borderlands of Cameron County, Texas. Cameron County bordered not only the Rio Grande and the Mexican State of Tamaulipas to the south but also the Gulf of Mexico to the east.[25]

Located at the southernmost tip of Texas, Cameron County stood between the Nueces River, about halfway between San Antonio and Mexico, and the Rio Grande. This troubled country was part of the coveted border region located between Texas and Mexico, which had sparked the border dispute that had helped begin the Mexican-American War that erupted in the spring of 1846.

Like much of Texas, Cameron County was thinly populated. Most of the county's inhabitants were settled primarily along the fertile lands bordering the Rio Grande. In 1850, the entire southern tip of Texas—consisting of Cameron and two other Texas counties—contained less than 8,500 persons, including many Tejanos, Texans of Mexican heritage. Partly indicating that these Texas Rebels were not fighting principally on behalf of slavery, only 7 slaves, along with 63 free blacks, resided in Cameron County in 1860. And almost all of these slaves were located in Brownsville, the county seat, and the largest city in the Lower Rio Grande Valley. Not a single slave worked on the prairie ranches outside of Brownsville.

During the Point Isabel conference both General Slaughter and Colonel Ford indicated that the value of slave property in Cameron County had simply "ceased to be of great importance," despite the fact that Texas slavery, thanks to limited Union invasions, remained relatively unscathed by the war compared with that in other Southern states.

Colonel Ford explained that at the time of the Mexican-American War, "the lower Rio Grande was a cotton growing country [as] cotton could be cultivated at a considerable profit [and] Peon [Mexican] labor was cheap, more so than that of the African slave [but] after the occupation of the valley of the Rio Grande from the mouth of that stream to Laredo by American troops, Mexican slaves commenced leaving their masters [and] this did much towards destroying the labor system prevailing on the lower Rio Grande. After the conclusion of the Mexican War in 1848, the culture of cotton ceased almost entirely." Ironically, in the twentieth century, cotton would become the leading crop in Cameron County in contrast with its position during the antebellum period when slavery thrived across the South.[26]

Despite the Wallace-Slaughter truce, the Confederates of the Lower Rio Grande Valley were anything but defeated by the late winter of 1864–65. As one conflict was coming to an inglorious end, and despite four years of fighting in vain, some Texas Rebels, unlike their Eastern Theater counterparts, now had their eyes on the possibility of yet another war, this time south of the border. For these Texans in gray, striking a blow against their ancient enemy—Mexico—now seemed far more preferable than a fratricidal conflict of Americans killing Americans. Such a conflict in northern Mexico would certainly help to take the sting out of the Confederate defeat for both Texas and the exhausted nation. The Texans' lengthy list of grievances against Mexico—and *vice versa*—went back long before sectional issues, including slavery, had torn the American nation apart.

While the Confederacy died a slow death to the east, in early 1865 the earlier tradition of the Texas Revolution remained alive among Colonel Ford's Texas Rebels. A reminder of the Texas Revolution, Cameron County had been named for Capt. Ewen Cameron, a Scotsman and immigrant Texan. He was taken prisoner during the ill-fated Texas thrust into Mexico during the Mier Expedition of late 1842. Thrown into captivity and herded deep into Mexico after failing to capture Mier, the hard-luck Texans under Cameron's leadership escaped from the Salado Prison but were quickly recaptured. In retaliation, seventeen Texans were executed by the Mexicans, including Captain Cameron.

To Colonel Ford and his Texans, the traditions of the Texas Revolution could yet be relived by a joint Union-Confederate operation south of the border. Hence, for the Texas Rebels, victories in northern Mexico and images of the flag of the Lone Star State flying on the south side of the Rio Grande would wash away the agony of Confederate defeat.

By mid-March 1865, the possibility of a combined Union-Confederate strike into northern Mexico made good sense to many men in both blue and gray. Such Rebels of the Lower Rio Grande Valley believed by this time that "such a step [soon would be] an immediate consequence of peace."[27]

Meanwhile, the Civil War continued to wind down in the East during the spring of 1865, fading farther away like the dream of Southern independence. In the West, however, Rebel forces remained in the field. Referring to the last crumbling remains of what little was left of Confederate forces east of Texas, a disillusioned Mary Chesnut wrote in her diary from Richmond in May 1865: "[T]hat fool [Gen.] Dick Taylor will not disband and let this nasty Confederacy smash and be done with it." But by this time, little remained of Gen. Richard Taylor's Western forces, which disintegrated with the war's conclusion east of the Mississippi.

On May 4, 1865, General Taylor, President Davis's brother-in-law and the only son of Zachary Taylor, who had won the first American victory of the Mexican-American War at Palo Alto in Cameron County, met with Union general Edward R. S. Canby, who had recently captured Mobile, to accept surrender terms. Commanding the Department of East Louisiana, Mississippi, and Alabama, General Taylor understood the futility of further resistance, after learning of General Lee's and General Johnston's surrender.

Soon thereafter, General Taylor surrendered his forces of the Cis-Mississippi at Citronville, Alabama, just northwest of Mobile. On May 8, General Taylor's remaining Confederates signed paroles and began their journeys home like the vanquished warriors of the Rebels' Eastern armies, while elsewhere the final curtain continued to fall upon the short-lived Confederacy. Now only the scattered Rebel forces in the sprawling Trans-Mississippi Theater remained in the field, determined not to surrender.[28]

Ten days after Appomattox, Gen. Edmund Kirby Smith, the Trans-Mississippi's commander, learned of General Lee's capitulation. General Smith remained defiant, as did the Texas governor, Pendleton Murrah. Determined to fight on against the odds, the governor now appealed to his fellow Texans not to forsake the struggle. He believed incorrectly that President Davis and the surviving Confederate troops from the Eastern Theater were now proceeding toward the Trans-Mississippi to link with forces in Texas to continue the fight to keep the dream of an independent Southern nation alive.[29]

By this time, the bulk of the Confederate forces in the Trans-Mississippi was disintegrating with each passing day. Many Rebel soldiers simply walked away from their units, fading away to return to homes that they had left in the heady days of the spring of 1861. Other disgruntled Trans-Mississippi troops mutinied in mid-May against their commanders, rebelling against the failed revolution. In fact, widespread discontent among both civilians and soldiers of the Trans-Mississippi had been simmering since the loss of the Mississippi River after the fall of Vicksburg and Port Hudson during the summer of 1863.

Therefore, with the balmy weather of mid-May 1865 drawing closer and with the Union already in the process of disbanding its armies, the principal Confederate authorities of the Trans-Mississippi were eager to end hostilities, though without having to "submit to ignominious terms." As fate would have it, Gen. Kirby Smith was destined to be the last general in command of a Confederate theater to surrender. As in the Eastern Theater, the final chapter of a long, futile struggle was rapidly closing in the Trans-Mississippi.[30]

CHAPTER 2

Undefeated Texans
in Gray

AFTER THE AGREEMENT OF MARCH 1865, GENERAL WALLACE AND THE EX-iled Yankees on the sun-baked island of Brazos Santiago probably desired to adhere to the informal truce for another reason. This isolated island was the last land possession of an extensive Union conquest that had earlier claimed most of the Rio Grande Valley. The Texas Rebel opponents of these idle Union garrison troops were some of the best Rebel horse soldiers in the Western Confederacy, and were commanded by Colonel Ford, the longtime cavalry leader of the Rio Grande Valley.

"Old Rip" was the most active and hardest fighting Rebel horse commander in the Rio Grande Valley during the war. In fact, Colonel Ford had been the border region's defender for decades, defeating interlopers, both Indians and Mexicans, whenever they invaded Texas from Mexico or the Indian territory. By this time, Colonel Ford was a legend not just to the people of the Rio Grande Valley but to all Texas.

Colonel Ford relied upon decades of experience in border and guerrilla warfare to vanquish any opponent bold enough to threaten Texas or Texans. Ford's lengthy record of military experience made him "a Texan among Texans." The colonel's role in Texas affairs began at an early date. Only months after the Alamo's fall in March 1836, the South Carolina–born Ford had migrated to Texas from Tennessee on his own.[1]

Colonel Ford first rose to prominence as a hard-hitting commander of cavalry on the Texas frontier. As early as 1836, he had departed his prior occupation as a physician to help organize a militia cavalry company from St. Augustine County, Texas.

Like other Texans along the troubled border, Ford feared taht an alliance between the Indians and Mexicans might reclaim Texas. In one frontier campaign after another, Ford led Texas volunteers and Rangers during "the continuing war" to defend their besieged homeland to prevent such an alliance. Then, in 1847, he joined the Texas Rangers in Mexico, embarking on yet another military campaign during the war with Mexico.[2]

Here, south of the border, Ford first acquired his sobriquet of "Rip" and "Old Rip." As the adjutant of Col. John C. Hays's wild Texans and as a member of the colonel's staff, he signed so many Texas Ranger death certificates with "May His Soul Rest In Peace" that he shortened this to simply "RIP," or "Rest in Peace." One day in the Rangers' encampment, a Texan shouted "there goes old 'RIP' Ford" when Adjutant Ford passed. Hence, the nickname of "Rip" and "Old Rip" was bestowed upon Adjutant Ford by his Texas Rangers, and it stuck.

With his medical background, Ford also served as the surgeon for the Texas Rangers. Not long after Gen. Winfield Scott's army successfully landed at Vera Cruz, Mexico, and began marching inland from the coast, Ford and the Texas Rangers, armed with .44 caliber Walker Colt six-shooters, engaged bands of Mexican guerrillas during the drive on Mexico City.[3]

It was also during the Mexican-American War that Ford rose to prominence as the captain of a Texas Ranger "spy company." Ford and his "spies" served as the eyes and ears of General Scott's invading army during the offensive that captured Mexico City.[4]

Despite often being sick with the malaria that would plague him for the remainder of his life, Ford and his "Los Diablos Tejanos" rode proudly into a conquered Mexico City, after fighting guerrilla-style across central Mexico. Thanks to skillful frontier leaders like "Old Rip" and because of their fighting prowess, the Texas Rangers acquired another well-desired nickname among the Mexicans, "Los Tejanos Sangrientes," or the Bloody Texans.[5]

Even after General Scott's capture of Mexico City, the war continued for Captain Ford and his Texas Rangers. Brutal guerrilla warfare was waged as the proud Mexican people refused to lay down arms to the hated "gringo" invaders from the north. In hard-hitting raids that swept across the Mexican countryside, Ford and the Texas Rangers battled guerrillas in the mountains of central Mexico.[6]

Mexican and Indian threats persisted long after the conclusion of the Mexican-American War, and likewise Ford continued to wage war, fighting for years to protect Texas and its people. In early 1849, Ford became the captain of Texas volunteers when another Indian threat surfaced. By the summer, he had organized a volunteer company of Colonel Hays's old Texas Rangers for U.S. service to protect the Rio Grande frontier against both Indians and Mexicans. Ford advocated a simple but effective philosophy that paid dividends on the untamed Texas frontier: the Indians "should be made to feel the iron hand of war upon their hunting-grounds, and within their lodges [therefore] Whip them and then talk of treaties."[7]

In 1850, more arduous campaigns against both the Indians and Mexican bandits followed, with Ford leading cavalry strikes into Mexico to hit the enemy's sanctuaries south of the Rio Grande.[8]

For years, Ford continued to parry Mexican and Indian threats whenever or wherever they appeared, acquiring a widespread reputation. For example, he sought to eliminate the escalating menace of the Indian raids that ravished the frontier in north Texas. The fierce Comanches were proving more than a match for both U.S. troopers and the state militia. At the state capital of Austin, Ford convinced Gov. Hardin R. Runnels to adopt his solution of striking deep into the Comanche homeland to eliminate the threat once and for all.

In consequence, Ford departed Austin with a new assignment and the rank of "Senior Captain" of all Texas Rangers. He realized that the solution to the frontier's Indian problems lay in taking the war to the Comanche heartland in the northern frontier, beyond the Red River and deep into the Canadian River country. Hundreds of miles north of the Rio Grande borderlands, the northern tip of the Texas panhandle, the Comanche country, was Captain Ford's objective.

During a bloody ten-hour battle in April 1858, Ford and his 200 Texas Rangers, with Indian allies, decisively defeated the Comanches under Chief Iron Jacket. During a frontier campaign in which Chief Iron Jacket was killed, Ford eliminated the greatest Indian threat on the northern Texas frontier, while demonstrating that "self-protection is the first law of Nature."

Despite facing warriors who fought a no-quarter "war to the knife," Ford was not the stereotypical frontier Indian hater. Whenever possible, he wisely utilized Indian allies. On one occasion, he saved a group of peaceful agency Indians who were falsely accused of committing deprivations on the Texas frontier. In overall terms, Ford's successful Indian campaigns proved the salvation to dozens of isolated settlements on the remote Texas frontier.[9]

After crushing the latest Comanche threat, Ford turned south to fight Mexicans along the conflict-torn border of Texas's southern frontier. Gen. Juan Nepomuceno Cortina, a Texan of Mexican parents, and his Mexican raiders, or liberators as many Hispanics saw them, struck across the Rio Grande. Motivated by racial and cultural animosities and, partly, to regain lands lost in the Mexican-American War, these Hispanic raiders hit the vulnerable border settlements with impunity, even occupying Brownsville. Leading a Hispanic revolt in a holy war of "liberation," Cortina attempted to push the Texans north to the disputed border of the Nueces River, and beyond.

After issuing a declaration that "the territory of Texas has been invaded," the Texas governor immediately turned to the one man who could save the day, "Rip" Ford. Consequently, the governor authorized Ford, now with a lieutenant colonel's rank, to take command of Texas state troops, and to organize a Texas Ranger company to chase down the Mexican invaders.

With the assistance of U.S. cavalry, Lieutenant Colonel Ford led sixty Texas Rangers in a two-month fight through the Rio Grande country during the fall of 1859. Employing frontier tactics and Indian-style fighting in punishing retaliatory strikes, he defeated Cortina in three consecutive battles.[10]

In March 1860, Ford was again battling Cortina, crossing the Rio Grande into Mexico to attack the secure guerrilla sanctuaries south of the border. During this campaign, Ford and his Texans earned yet another nickname from the Mexicans, "gringos apestosos," or stinking gringos. These raids proved decisive in driving Cortina deeper into northern Mexico.[11]

By the time of the outbreak of the Civil War, Ford was a veteran frontier commander with a widespread reputation, after having fought for decades on both Indian frontiers in north and west Texas and along the southern frontier of the Rio Grande country. He rose to the rank of senior captain of all Texas state troops before the war. When President Lincoln was elected in 1860, Ford was one of the first to call for a secession convention to take Texas out of the Union.

The people of Cameron County elected Ford as their secession delegate to the late January 1861 Secession Convention in Austin. He defeated a Rio Grande Valley resident who would soon become his adversary during the struggle for possession of the Lower Rio Grande Valley, Edmund J. Davis. Ford now believed in "the right of revolution to resist oppression and wrong" in the tradition of the Texas Revolution. At the Austin convention, Ford helped to draw up the resolutions for the state's secession. The ordinance of secession was adopted on February 1, 1861, and on February 8 Texas joined the infant nation called the Confederate States of America.[12]

The Texas Committee of Public Safety then ordered the seizure of all Federal property and the removal of 2,500 Federal troops from Texas soil. By this time, Ford was considered "unquestionably the best military man in Texas." He was authorized by the Committee of Public Safety to raise a cavalry regiment in the newly founded Army of Texas. Organized for southern frontier duty along the Rio Grande, this horse command later became the nucleus of the 2nd Texas Cavalry Regiment, C.S.A. This unit, with Colonel Ford at its head, together with another horse regiment, rode north to capture Union property in north Texas. By February 1861, Ford was active in Houston, enlisting additional volunteers to defend his home state. Here, he raised the horse companies to complete his regiment's organization and quota of ten companies.[13]

Many factors explain why Texans like "Rip" Ford sided against the U.S. government. For one, these men, who lived along the one thousand miles of sprawling Texas frontier, had suffered for years from the raids of Mexicans, Comanches, Kiowas, Shawnees, and Apaches without the protection of the U.S. government. With each attack, which left more men, women, and children dead, the ties of allegiance with Federal authority were gradually broken down and diluted.

Worst of all, these raids also fanned the fear of slave revolts. The greatest concern among the Texas frontiersmen was that the Indians, Mexicans, and African American slaves would unite in a holy and racial war against white Texans. With President Lincoln's election, these Texans believed that an abolitionist government would help to incite slave revolts in their midst and all across the South.[14]

Ford believed that civil war was preferable to living under a government that was sympathetic to abolitionists who promoted slave revolt. The Texas Rebels could easily envision slaves rising up and slaughtering their wives, parents, and children.[15]

In mid-February 1861, Colonel Ford and his 500 Texas Rebels were ordered to ride south from Houston with the mission of conquering the Lower Rio Grande Valley. From the port of Galveston, Ford led an amphibious strike—the South's first west of the Mississippi—to capture the barrier island on the Gulf Coast known as Brazos Santiago. After the journey south along Texas's east coast, he disembarked his cavalrymen on the island from a schooner and steamboat.

Ford and his Rebels landed on the windswept beaches of Brazos Santiago on February 21, swarming ashore to capture the fort, a depot with artillery, the diminutive Federal garrison, and its humbled lieutenant. The Brazos Santiago garrison surrendered weeks before Fort Sumter's capitulation. By unexpectedly striking first, Colonel Ford succeeded in capturing this strategic position that commanded the mouth of the Rio Grande River.[16]

Immediately after capturing "the Brazos," the energetic Colonel Ford was then off to win a string of successes in the Lower Rio Grande Valley. Turning west, Ford led his men along the river toward Fort Brown, the fortified position along the Rio Grande opposite Matamoros, Mexico, that protected Brownsville. Along the way, he passed through the borderlands of Palmito Ranch, situated along the Rio Grande.

Upon reaching Brownsville, and before Fort Sumter's surrender, Colonel Ford negotiated the capitulation of all Union outposts along the Rio Grande from Brownsville to El Paso, Texas, without a shot being fired. Along this sprawling stretch of territory spanning almost 1,200 miles, "Rip" and his Texans took possession of eight U.S. forts and outposts.[17]

Meanwhile, Ford's dream of commanding a Confederate regiment was finally realized on May 23, 1861. After enlisting in Confederate service, 1,200 Rebels under Colonel Ford's command organized to become the 2nd Texas Confederate Cavalry. Ford, however, was not offered a Confederate commission, thanks to political maneuvering at headquarters. This "insult" caused the independent-minded Ford to thereafter refuse to enter his name as a candidate for a Confederate colonel's commission. But he would be widely known and officially addressed as colonel by both superiors and subordinates throughout the war.

After driving the Federals out of the Rio Grande Valley, Colonel Ford's primary mission was now to protect the valley from Federal invasion. In addition, he negotiated with Mexican officials in Matamoros to ensure that Confederate ships, under the cover of both Mexican and British flags, could pass freely through the Union blockade to deliver tons of war matériel to Texas and the Trans-Mississippi.[18]

By this time, Colonel Ford's 2nd Texas troopers were the principal defenders of the Rio Grande border. Carrying Bowie knives and riding Mexican horses, Ford's long-haired and bearded frontiersmen presented a menacing appearance to both friend and foe. Their high black hats with wide brims were decorated with silver and brass "Lone Star" State insignias and pins. Large Mexican spurs completed the frontier uniform of these Rebel troopers.

Besides carrying braces of Colt and Navy six-shooters, Colonel Ford's horse soldiers also carried double-barrel shotguns. With almost every cavalryman armed with a shotgun, one of the colonel's troopers swore that "as our Regiment [the 2nd Texas] is called Texas Mounted Rifles, they [should] be called 'Texas Mounted Shot Guns'." This combination of shotguns and six-shooters provided formidable firepower to Colonel Ford's Texans.[19]

Col. Arthur James Lyon Fremantle, an aristocratic Englishman who was in Brownsville, recalled the unforgettable sight of Colonel Ford's Texas warriors. He described that "their dress consisted simply of flannel shirts, very ancient trousers, jack boots with enormous spurs, and black felt hats ornamented with the 'Lone Star of Texas.' They looked rough and dirty." Another observer wrote how these Texas Rebels "wore belts around the waist, suspending one or two revolvers and a bowie knife [and] were experts in the saddle, had a reckless dare-devil look and were always ready" for action.[20]

Most important for both political and military reasons, besides negotiating his vital trade agreement with Mexico, Ford also maintained good relations with the Confederacy's southern neighbor. The situation along the Rio Grande border remained volatile and sensitive during the war years, with civil wars raging on both sides of the border. Fortunately for the Confederacy, no Texas Confederate commander in the Rio Grande Valley was more adept at dealing fairly with the local Tejanos—who outnumbered Anglos in the Rio Grande Valley—than Colonel Ford.

Most importantly, Ford treated the Tejanos first as Southerners—or equals in this case—rather than as Mexicans. In addition, Ford respected the Hispanic people and culture. Tejano, the distinctive blend of Texas and Mexico, was very much Texan culture. In fact, a largely forgotten relationship of allies—Anglo and Hispanic—had endured since the earliest days of the Texas Revolution. During the struggle for Texas independence, many Tejanos had supported the Texan revolt with both manpower and resources, fueling the revolution from the beginning.

Thanks partly to Colonel Ford's diplomatic efforts with Mexican officials, the vital Confederate trade continued to pass unmolested through Matamoros and across the Rio Grande. To ensure that the flow of trade continued, Ford played a key role in maintaining the good relations between the Confederacy and the Mexican state of Temaulipas, and the port of Matamoros opposite Brownsville.[21]

Thereafter, Colonel Ford remained in the Lower Rio Grande Valley, commanding the District of the Rio Grande throughout 1861. This was an immense area of operations, spanning more than a thousand miles from the Rio Grande's mouth northwestward to above El Paso. With the Lower Rio Grande Valley now clear of Yankees thanks largely to his own military and diplomatic efforts, Ford dispatched seven companies of his 2nd Texas Cavalry up the Rio Grande to protect the border and to occupy positions around El Paso to defend the frontier against Indians and Mexicans.

In the fall of 1861, Colonel Ford was unexpectedly "relieved from duty." He was then ordered "to retire to San Antonio for a much needed rest"—an ill-timed decision by Confederate leadership based more upon politics than military realities. Consequently, from June 1862, Colonel Ford languished at a desk in his new assignment as the chief of the Texas Conscript Bureau, despite the popular opinion that he was the best "military man . . . in Texas." Such a leader would soon be needed for the Rio Grande Valley's defense.[22]

While the Confederacy turned its attention away from the Lower Rio Grande Valley, the North was preparing to reclaim it. By the summer of 1863 and after winning control of the Mississippi, President Lincoln realized that a

Union presence in Texas had become a strategic priority. First, he understood that the Union needed to stop the high volume of trade pouring across the Rio Grande. Additionally, with Federal troops stationed in Texas, Lincoln wished to demonstrate support for the Monroe Doctrine and stand up to the nearby French presence in Mexico. Troops in Texas would also secure cotton for the Union war effort, and facilitate the conquest of Louisiana.

Gen. Nathaniel Prentiss Banks was chosen for the assignment of raising the U.S. flag on Texas soil. He was a Massachusetts politician and three-time former governor of the Bay State whose star rose with his capture of Port Hudson, Louisiana, in July 1863. With a successful invasion of Texas, the politically minded General Banks planned to repeat the glories of Port Hudson by capturing Houston and Galveston. But Banks's winning streak was broken at Sabine Pass on September 8, 1863, when a handful of Irish Rebels of the Jeff Davis Guards—Company F, 1st Texas Heavy Artillery, under Ireland-born Lt. Richard W. "Dick" Dowling—thwarted the first phase of his offensive along the Texas coast.

To compensate for the Sabine Pass humiliation and to appease the Lincoln government's call for a Texas invasion, General Banks decided in late October 1863 to again "attempt a lodgement upon some point on the coast from the mouth of the Mississippi to the Rio Grande."[23]

Eager to prove himself, and with presidential aspirations in mind, General Banks then pinpointed the next target of his newly formed Rio Grande Expedition, the mouth of the Rio Grande. With confidence high, the mighty armada of Union ships with 6,000 troops steamed southwestward from New Orleans during the last week of October 1863, sailing for Brazos Santiago.[24]

Hundreds of Yankee troops splashed ashore on November 2, spilling onto Texas soil without a shot fired in anger. Above the windswept sand dunes of Brazos Santiago, "Old Glory" fluttered in the stiff November breeze sweeping off the waters of the Gulf of Mexico. General Banks wrote with pride that "the flag of the Union floated over [Confederate] Texas to-day at meridian precisely."[25]

The nearest Rebels to the Union landing at Brazos Santiago were stationed approximately twenty-five miles west at Brownsville. They were badly outnumbered and could do nothing. Brownsville was soon evacuated without a fight. After the Confederates withdrew westward up the Rio Grande Valley, Brownsville was captured by the Yankees in early November 1863.

Soon larger sections of the Texas coast were gobbled up by the blueclads, including the Gulf port of Corpus Christi north of Brazos Santiago, while the recently landed Union forces surged up the Rio Grande Valley. The invading Yankees captured one Texas town after another, including San Gertrudis,

Edinburg, Ringgold Barracks, and Rio Grande City, as they advanced along the Rio Grande in an attempt to stop the flow of trade from Mexico. Although the valuable port of Matamoros was denied the Confederacy, the heavy volume of goods merely shifted farther upriver to cross beyond the limit of Union control.[26]

Gen. "Prince John" Magruder, once one of General Lee's divisional commanders and now Confederate commander of Texas, attempted to belatedly muster an army to meet the invaders. Colonel Ford described that General Magruder, a West Pointer who had served in the Seminole and Mexican-American Wars, was "evinced [with] a determination to defend the State . . . [, and] Texas was again ready to do and die." One of General Magruder's smartest decisions was to give Colonel Ford a new field command.

A disgruntled Ford had resigned from his hated position as chief of the Texas Conscript Bureau in November 1862. He then became the superintendent of conscripts for General Magruder's district. "Prince John" knew that Colonel Ford was the "ablest field officer in Texas" and he made a popular decision by appointing the Texans' "most reliable troubleshooter" to reverse Confederate fortunes in the Rio Grande Valley. He ordered Ford to take the field in late December 1863.

In the frontier tradition of the citizen-soldier, Colonel Ford was busy raising a full cavalry brigade where none had existed before. Ford's new "secret" mission was to reconquer the Lower Rio Grande Valley and Brownsville in a repeat performance of 1861. The Yankees must be driven from the Texas mainland and their hold on Brownsville, which guaranteed their control of the mouth of the Rio Grande, broken. Thanks in part to incompetent Confederate leadership, Colonel Ford would have to reconquer the Lower Rio Grande Valley not once but twice during this war. With a good deal of understatement, the homespun Texas colonel admitted that he "was keen to make an effort to clear the Texas mainland of Federals." First, however, he asked General Magruder to provide him with 200 bales of cotton because this "was the only way to get funds for the expedition."[27]

Strategic developments now presented Colonel Ford with an opportunity. After he had conquered the Rio Grande Valley, General Banks set his sights on capturing the port of Galveston, Texas. But by this time, General Halleck, the Union chief of staff, embraced other strategic plans and new ambitions prevailed. Consequently, orders reached General Banks from headquarters in Washington, D.C., directing him to conquer Texas by way of the Red River— the avenue of conquest for east Texas and lower Louisiana. While General Banks embarked on his Red River campaign to slash through the heart of the Trans-Mississippi Department, the Rio Grande Valley was given secondary

priority. With the Union conquest of west Texas suddenly aborted, the Yankees consolidated their hold on the Lower Rio Grande Valley. Union troops,
consequently, retired to Brownsville, which was fortified along with Brazos
Santiago and Point Isabel. Union forces on Texas soil yet remained a threat because they could be reinforced by sea and launch a new invasion of Texas.[28]

The unexpected Yankee withdrawal toward the Texas coast coincided
with Colonel Ford's ambition to "clear the Texas mainland of Federals." General Magruder nevertheless now depended solely on Colonel Ford to recapture
Brownsville and win the victories that "might save the rest of Texas [and]
recapture the Rio Grande Valley and renew the invaluable trade through
Matamoros."

With the "secret" mission of reclaiming the Lower Rio Grande Valley,
Colonel Ford personally created and then molded the Rio Grande Expedition
into a fighting force. General Magruder ordered Colonel Ford to make "a sudden and rapid movement [that will] create a panic among the enemy; and, if so,
you will follow it up and gain every advantage you can." A confident Colonel
Ford informed General Magruder that "there is no doubt of success."[29]

By this time, the Texas Rebels were highly motivated. In Colonel Ford's
words, he and his men were determined to fight, because "for the sake of the
glorious memories of the past, the hopes of the future [were now at stake]."
Colonel Ford desired most of all "to wash out the stains of invasion by the
blood of your ruthless enemies."[30]

Colonel Ford employed innovative means in creating his new command
to "liberate" the valley. Despite fighting Mexicans along the border for years,
Colonel Ford saw the Texas Mexicans or Mexicans born in Texas as invaluable
allies. With the money gained from the selling of cotton, he "could secure the
services of many Mexicans [since] I am intimately acquainted with many of
that nation who could, and I think would, perform valuable service in our
cause." In fact, he dispatched recruiters into Mexico to obtain Mexican volunteers, deserters, and refugees in Rio Grande towns such as Matamoros, Camargo, and Reynosa.[31]

Unlike Colonel Ford, many Union leaders often held these same Hispanics in low esteem, maintaining less respect for the Tejanos. Much like the "experiment" of enlisting African Americans in Federal service, some Northerners
in high places felt that Hispanics were not worthy to wear Union blue.
Colonel Ford was inclined to agree, but only if they were to wear Confederate
gray instead.[32]

Ford took pride in the role of his Hispanic Confederates, like that of the
Tejanos who fought in the Texas Revolution. An estimated 3,000 Tejanos
fought for the Confederacy and served with distinction.

Colonel Ford was pleased to have in his command the Hispanic troopers of a cavalry regiment, the 33rd Texas Confederate Cavalry, under Col. Santos Benavides. The Tejano colonel commanded his Hispanic Rebels at Laredo, Texas, more than 250 miles northwest up the Rio Grande from Brownsville. A former Texas Ranger and descendant of Laredo's Hispanic founder, Colonel Benavides, age thirty-six, had served as major of the 33rd Texas Confederate Cavalry. In addition, he was Laredo's mayor and city lawyer, and was county judge before the Civil War.

In compiling "a brilliant record of border defense," Colonel Benavides was a skilled tactician. Like Ford, he learned the frontier fighting ways and tactics of the Texas Rangers. In this fratricidal border war, Benavides battled against fellow Hispanics in blue as if they were Yankees from Connecticut, New York, or Illinois. Before the war's end, this enterprising Hispanic Rebel would win a general's rank and become the highest ranking Tejano to serve the Confederacy. Colonel Benavides's horse regiment, mostly tough Tejano fighters who learned the art of war in battling Indians and Mexican banditos, "performed a record of border defense unprecedented in Texas history."[33]

Coincidentally, one of Colonel Ford's Tejano soldiers had stormed the Alamo with General Santa Anna's army in March 1836, while serving as a sergeant of the Matamoros Battalion. Ford himself swore the fifty-one-year-old Lt. Francisco Becerra into Confederate service. Becerra led a charmed life, escaping the Texans' slaughter of General Santa Anna's Mexicans at San Jacinto in April 1836. After his capture by the Texans, Becerra settled in Texas instead of returning to his native Mexico. Thereafter, he became a respected Tejano fighter. Becerra battled Indian raiders and then fellow Mexicans during the Mexican-American War before embarking upon a career as a Confederate under Colonel Ford's command.[34]

In addition, Colonel Ford also received the service of Arizona Rebels, who were in fact mostly Texans. These gray-clad troopers of the 4th Arizona Cavalry served under Col. Spruce M. Baird. Earlier, in February 1864, Colonel Baird had been in San Antonio on a recruiting mission when his 4th Arizona troopers were guarding the Indian frontier under Col. Daniel Showalter. Thanks to General Magruder's support, Colonel Ford incorporated the Arizona Rebels into his command despite Colonel Baird's indignation to the high-handed impressment.[35]

Meanwhile, additional numbers of Texas recruits filtered into San Antonio in response to Colonel Ford's call to arms issued in February 1864. The arrival of these recruits bolstered Ford's confidence that he could accomplish great things in the days ahead. Soon Colonel Ford's ever-growing cavalry brigade became known as the "expeditionary force" of "the Cavalry of the West."

Colonel Ford also secured a cadre of dependable officers, especially to serve on his staff. Ford asked General Magruder to send him Maj. Felix Blucher, a gifted German who knew the Rio Grande country intimately. Soon to become Colonel Ford's chief of staff, Blucher was a descendant of Field Marshal Blucher, who crushed Napoléon Bonaparte's dreams of future glory at Waterloo. In addition, Colonel Ford sought to employ the use of camels. These animals had originally been sent to Texas for military use in the 1850s by the then–secretary of war, Jefferson Davis.[36]

In short order, Colonel Ford organized the largest force that he would ever command, the Rio Grande Expeditionary Force. By early March 1864, Ford collected nearly 1,300 cavalrymen in San Antonio for his forthcoming effort to drive some 7,000 Yankees out of Texas. Because the prime of Texas manhood was lying in shallow graves at Vicksburg, Antietam, Gettysburg, and on the battlefields of the Trans-Mississippi, Colonel Ford was forced to rely on many conscription-exempt youths and older men.

One of Colonel Ford's officers noted that "fifty-seven children"—or teenagers—joined the frontier command. The boys were joined by rougher characters: volunteers, deserters, mixed-blood Indians, banditos, renegades, bushwhackers, drunks, and soldiers of fortune.

Leading his command from San Antonio despite the fact that his force was "not fully collected" by this time, the eager Colonel Ford finally embarked upon his mission of reclaiming the Rio Grande Valley in mid-March 1864. These self-proclaimed liberators were now led south toward Corpus Christi by a popular officer, Ford, who held no official Confederate commission or rank.[37]

Colonel Ford's "Expeditionary Force" then pushed west toward Laredo on the Rio Grande; he planned to link up with the Tejanos of Colonel Benavides's regiment and Lt. Col. George H. Giddings's battalion in the Rio Grande River country. Employing Texas Ranger tactics while moving swiftly across the parched grasslands to ensure the element of surprise, Ford concealed his ultimate destination by spreading word that the command was heading northeast to quell a new Yankee threat from western Louisiana.[38]

Colonel Ford realized that because of severe droughts in 1863 and 1864, the advance upon Brownsville had to be made along the Rio Grande, where good water and grass were available for his horses. In addition, by pushing down the Rio Grande, Ford could also ensure that the trade route across the river from Mexico to Texas remained open. Consequently, Ford led his men toward Laredo and the Rio Grande.[39]

Colonel Ford was fortunate to have under his command Lieutenant Colonel Giddings, who had a strong reputation leading Giddings's Texas

Cavalry Battalion of approximately 150 troopers. This cavalry unit had been lately stationed at Eagle Pass, Texas, some ninety miles up the Rio Grande from Laredo, before being ordered to report to Colonel Ford.[40]

While Colonel Ford hailed from the Upper South, Giddings had been born in Susquehanna County, Pennsylvania, in 1823. With his brother James L. Giddings, Henry migrated to Texas in 1846, following in the footsteps of his hero-brother, Giles A. Giddings, who had been one of the few Texans killed during the battle of San Jacinto. Settling in Washington County, Texas, George became a lawyer, and then county clerk and deputy of Washington County. But like Ford, defending the frontier soon became Giddings's vocation as well.[41]

Not long after his arrival in Texas, Giddings served against Indian raiders. Then, eager to emulate the example of his martyred brother, Giddings joined a mounted volunteer company during the Mexican-American War.[42]

Throughout the summer of 1846, Giddings and his comrades patrolled the Texas frontier from San Antonio to the Brazos River. Then, he served as the quartermaster and commissary officer of a volunteer company of Texas Rangers. Unlike the men with Ford, these Rangers initially remained in Texas to guard the frontier. But during the winter of 1846–47, Giddings and his Texas Rangers finally rode across the Rio Grande and into Mexico. Here, the young man learned important tactical lessons that served him and his Texas Rebels well during the Civil War.[43]

When the Civil War broke out in 1861, Giddings became the commander of an independent battalion of Texas cavalry: Colonel Giddings's Battalion. Despite two of his brothers having been killed before the war—one by Mexicans and the other by Indians—the surviving Giddings brothers served the Confederacy with distinction. Lt. Col. DeWitt Clinton Giddings, George's brother, led the 21st Texas Confederate Cavalry in the Trans-Mississippi and acquired a well-deserved reputation as an aggressive cavalry commander.[44]

It was on April 15, 1864, that Colonel Ford finally linked up with the Hispanic troopers under Colonel Benavides at Laredo. Here, Ford took diplomatic measures to placate the Juarez government in order to ensure the flow of trade from Mexico to Texas, while taking care to remain neutral in their conflict with the French Imperialists. When Colonel Ford heard that the Yankees had received permission to pass through Mexico to attack Laredo, he laid plans to cross into Mexico to launch a preemptive strike. He asked General Magruder: "[W]ould I not be justifiable in crossing the Rio Grande to meet the enemy?" As during Texas Ranger days, Ford was not hesitant to cross the border to fight an enemy on his own ground.[45]

At Laredo, Ford was positioned only 200 miles northwest of his Brownsville objective. Best of all, he still retained the element of surprise. Within days and without wasting precious time now that he had the jump on the Yankees, Ford was again on the move. Singing "The Yellow Rose of Texas," the Rebel troopers rode southeast down the Great River Road, which paralleled the Rio Grande. Located about halfway between Laredo and Brownsville, Rio Grande City and Ringgold Barracks fell to Ford's swift advance. About twenty-five miles northwest of Brownsville, Colonel Ford prepared to strike an advanced Union outpost guarding the approach to Brownsville at Las Rucias Ranch to catch the Yankees by surprise.

While the Federals anticipated Colonel Ford's approach from the north or upriver, Ford led his Rebels overland to strike the Yankees' rear from the south. As usual, Ford launched his attack with stealth. On June 25, 1864, easing forward out of sight through the dense chaparral and mesquite, the former Texas Ranger and his troopers caught the Yankees unawares. As so often in the past, the opponent who underestimated "Old Rip" or remained careless when he was nearby was in serious trouble.

The hot fight at Las Rucias Ranch, on the flatlands bordering the Rio Grande about a dozen miles west of Brownsville, quickly turned into an ugly grudge match as the Texas Rebels met the hated "renegades," or Texans in blue. Ford's men engaged Companies A and C, Col. Edmund J. Davis's 1st Texas Cavalry. Even for the opposing commanders, this clash involved the settling of old scores. Colonel Ford had defeated Colonel Davis as a Cameron County delegate to the state convention at the war's beginning.

After close-range fighting swirled across the Las Rucias Ranch, the Texas Rebels drove the Yankees from good defensive positions behind the cover of rocks, chaparral, and Mexican houses. The retreat turned into a rout. Ford's attackers scattered the blue-clad "renegades" like autumn leaves on a windy November morning. Almost forty Texas Yankees were captured and another thirty were killed or wounded.

It was at this point that Lieutenant Colonel Giddings's cavalry finally linked up with Ford's command to add momentum to the attack. Less than a dozen Texas Yankees escaped the sharp fight at the Las Rucias Ranch out of a total figure of more than one hundred. Some bluecoat survivors fled through the thickets and then swam across the Rio Grande to Mexico to escape. Colonel Ford lost only three killed and four wounded during the skirmish. One of the wounded attackers was a Hispanic Rebel, Hijenio Sanchez, of the Arizona cavalry regiment.

"Old Rip" now threatened the entire Lower Rio Grande Valley. General Magruder was justly proud of Colonel Ford's accomplishments in securing such a lengthy stretch of the valley for the Confederacy. Without exaggeration, the general wrote that "none could have conducted the operations with greater success" than Ford.[46]

Anticipating immediate retaliation from the Union garrison at Brownsville, a prudent Colonel Ford retired a short distance up the Rio Grande in case the Federals counterattacked. Here, he savored the lopsided victory and secured munitions from Matamoros for the fighting that he knew lay ahead. With no Federal retaliatory strike forthcoming, Colonel Ford then resumed his advance southeast toward Brownsville. He led his 1,500 Rebels carefully down the Great River Road, inching forward in the frontier manner to avoid getting caught by ambush.

Despite suffering from a bout of malaria so severe that he could hardly stay in the saddle, Colonel Ford continued to lead the advance. He again struck the Yankees, this time immediately before Brownsville. With his attacking Rebels screaming the "Texas yell," the Federals were driven rearward. Ford's men then entered the city limits of Brownsville, while fighting raged through the outskirts.[47]

Skirmishing between blue and gray continued into the end of July. Ford continued to threaten Brownsville until the Yankees finally gave up and evacuated the city. Then, the Federals fled eastward for the safety of Brazos Santiago and the Union Navy in the Gulf.

With the bluecoats on the run, Ford dispatched Capt. William N. Robinson with a section of Lieutenant Colonel Giddings's command in pursuit of the fleeing Yankees. Ford's aggressiveness resulted in additional rearguard fighting east of Brownsville along the flatlands of the coastal plain. With pride, Captain Robinson reported to Colonel Ford that all the Yankees were withdrawing eastward in haste. The captain later reported that the Federals had concentrated just off the Texas mainland at Brazos Santiago.

At last, Colonel Ford and his Rio Grande Expeditionary Force had succeeded in driving the Yankees from the Lower Rio Grande Valley and off the Texas mainland. The Federals were forced to endure a humiliating exile on that tiny barrier island. Colonel Ford raised the Confederate flag over Brownsville for the second time in barely three years.[48]

Ford accomplished more than simply keeping an eye on the Yankees bottled up on Brazos Santiago with his victory. First and foremost, he continued to simultaneously maintain good relations with the Juaristas, the French, the Indians, and the Mexicans, while keeping his distance from the constant cross fire between these various warring parties in the most politically chaotic sector on the border. As the result of negotiations and communications with the Imperial French Expeditionary Force, Ford in particular came to believe that the

French had recognized the Confederacy—the South's long-sought diplomatic and political objective—which was now too little, too late.

New strategic developments now came into play: the Confederates were occupying Brownsville, Cortina and his Juarista brigade of an estimated 1,500 troops were holding Matamoros, and the French had garrisoned Bagdad. Cortina advanced with a large force to drive the French at Bagdad from the mouth of the Rio Grande on the Mexican side. Repulsed in their attack on the French garrison at Bagdad, Cortina's forces then swung north across the Rio Grande to escape French retaliation in the relative safety of Texas. Now, north of the border, Cortina targeted Brownsville for capture and planned to keep the Rebels from uniting with French Imperial forces.

Situated behind the White Ranch's outpost, the Palmito Ranch position was the secondmost advanced Confederate position anchoring the eastern end of the Rio Grande line. Skirmishing began when the Rebels of the Arizona cavalry regiment stationed at Palmito Ranch clashed with Cortina's troops and a Union task force from Brazos Santiago. Under Cortina's artillery fire, the Arizona Confederates were driven back from Palmito Ranch on September 6.[49]

Accepting the challenge, Colonel Ford took action. In Ford's words, "I have sent a strong party under command of Captain [William H. D.] Carrington to ascertain the position and strength of the enemy [and] I intend attacking him before he has concentrated his force."

Colonel Ford ordered his main force under Colonel Giddings from Brownsville to strike immediately in a gamble to regain the initative. With handpicked troopers, Giddings, now a full colonel with his battalion increased to nearly regimental strength, moved forward to turn the tide. Colonel Giddings, his 370 Texas Rebels, and the Arizona cavalrymen recaptured the San Martin and Palmito Ranch positions on September 9. Striking in his customary hard-hitting manner throughout the day, Colonel Giddings pushed the Juristas and a superior number of Federals eastward toward the Gulf of Mexico and their island sanctuary.

Along the way, both the retreating Yankees and Mexicans left behind "dozens" of wounded soldiers and prisoners of war. The hot running fight continued for more than six miles toward the blue waters of the Gulf. Colonel Giddings then realigned his troops to finish the fight with a flank attack. He hurled his left flank forward through the clumps of mesquite and chaparral to strike the vulnerable right rear of the retreating Yankees.

With the Yankees on the run Colonel Giddings kept up the pressure for two more hours. Only the setting sun and the lack of ammunition allowed the Federals to escape the Rebel advance. More skirmishing followed the next day but the Yankees were eventually driven back to Brazos Santiago. After winning the first battle of Palmito Ranch, Colonel Giddings proudly reported to Colonel Ford how the Rio Grande River "is now free and open to trade as far as the Yankees are concerned." Not once but twice, Colonel Ford was successful in winning the Lower Rio Grande Valley for the Confederacy and eliminating the possibility of future threats.

While losing only a handful of men, Colonel Giddings inflicted heavy losses on the enemy. Union soldiers missing in action during the running fight fled across the Rio Grande to Mexico to escape the Texas Rebels. To evade both the war and Colonel Ford, these Yankees became deserters, remaining in Mexico. Other prisoners included Mexican troops who had sided with the Union.

The day after Colonel Giddings's victory at Palmito Ranch, Colonel Ford still held firm in Brownsville, while surrounded by large numbers of Cortina's Mexicans. Only a last-minute French counterattack saved the pinned-up Texas Rebels who were trapped inside Fort Brown, facing Cortina's no-quarter policy. The French advance drove the encircling Mexicans from Brownsville.

Both Colonels Ford and Giddings looked with pride on their recent successful operations and battlefield victories across the Rio Grande Valley. Ford had cleared the entire Lower Rio Grande of Yankees, except for the tiny island enclave of Brazos Santiago, while the Ford-Giddings team had repulsed the Federal attempt to recapture Brownsville and the Lower Rio Grande Valley.

Now less than one thousand exiled Federals held the island known simply as "the Brazos," maintaining a symbolic Union presence on this remote barrier island. The island exile represented a dismal end to a grand dream of Federal conquest. Newspapers across Texas heaped lavish praise on Colonel Ford and his Texas cavalrymen, publishing such triumphant headlines as "Bully for the Expeditionary Forces." Thanks in large part to Colonel Ford's tactical skill, not a single Yankee soldier remained on the mainland of Texas by the end of September 1864.[50]

After another victory and with the fighting at an end, Ford once again lost both his command and his position as the ranking Confederate officer in the Lower Rio Grande Valley. Affairs became so quiet in this remote sector as a result of Colonel Ford's string of successes that General Slaughter took command of the Brownsville area in the fall of 1864.

Colonel Ford's "Cavalry of the West" dispersed until only six companies of Colonel Giddings's battalion and a scattering of other cavalry commands remained on duty in the Brownsville area and the Lower Rio Grande. Meanwhile, Colonel Ford still relished the fact that if the Federals advanced, then once again "our job [would be] to drive them into the sea, while at the same time watching for a possible counterattack."[51]

CHAPTER 3

The Men Destined to Fight
at Palmito Ranch

AFRICAN AMERICANS IN BLUE

During the last years of the Civil War, a quiet revolution took place behind the scenes to help the Union win a decisive victory in what had become a lengthy war of attrition. This revolution came as a result of the North's belated realization of the value of using African American soldiers.

African Americans, who had previously been denied the "privilege" of serving in the war, were now fighting and dying for the Union. This sudden change of policy by Northern leadership came partly as a result of war weariness, unprecedented casualty lists, and a long series of bloody defeats, such as Fredericksburg in Virginia, that had greatly diminished enthusiasm for enlistment in Union armies by the end of 1862. The Northern people were tiring of the struggle. This historic weakness of a democracy when engaged in a long, costly war began to sabotage the Union war effort by late 1862. The North was simply growing weary of the slaughter and seemingly endless series of battles, which brought neither decisive victory nor any hope of an end to the conflict.

Consequently, the Union decided to utilize a vast untapped manpower resource in this war of attrition. Enlisting tens of thousands of black soldiers would bring new energy and vitality to the Union war effort, while denying the South its own use of African Americans. These former slaves had played an essential role in bolstering both the Southern economy and war effort by performing the rear-echelon duties that allowed the bulk of the Southern male population to serve in the military.

Ignoring the lessons of its own historical past and the history of African Americans in the United States, the North was not easily convinced that freed slaves would fight and die with the same sense of duty as white soldiers. Deep-rooted racism led to doubts among the vast majority of Americans—in both North and South—that blacks could match the whites' prowess on the battlefield.

The role of blacks in America's early history told a far different story. From beginning to end, black patriots served with distinction during the American Revolution. During the darkest days of the fight for independence, hundreds of African American soldiers served as a vital component of George Washington's Continental regiments, especially from colonies like Maryland and Rhode Island. Just a few decades later hundreds of African Americans of the San Domingue Free Black Battalions helped to win Gen. Andrew Jackson's lopsided victory at New Orleans during the War of 1812.

But the distinguished military legacy of African Americans was forgotten when Northern blacks first demanded the right to fight after the outbreak of civil war. Blacks in Cleveland, Ohio, drew upon a long list of valid historical precedents to plead their case to Northern officials not long after the firing on Fort Sumter: "[A]s in the times of '76, and the days of 1812, we are ready to go forth and do battle in the common cause of the country."[1]

More than 180,000 African Americans served in the ranks of Union armies before the war's end, representing 12 percent of Union armed forces. In the process, these black soldiers altered the character and composition of "Mr. Lincoln's" armies to a degree unimaginable in 1861. But most important, tens of thousands of former slaves and free blacks in Union blue also transformed the ideology of the struggle to save the Union.

Pres. Abraham Lincoln's Emancipation Proclamation of September 1862 rejuvenated the war effort of the North by embracing the moral high ground and turning the fight into one for human freedom. Just when the South was seemingly drawing closer to a negotiated peace settlement because of the military stalemate, this theoretical shift stripped away the Confederacy's own moral claim of a righteous struggle for self-determination in the tradition of 1776, as this brothers' war was shown to be a political and ideological conflict most of all. By the war's midway point, the goal of human freedom had come to bolster the political, moral, and psychological foundations of the Union war effort.

The importance of African American manpower by early 1865 was partly evident in the makeup of Union forces stationed along the Gulf coast, especially in the District of Key West and Tortugas. The majority of northern troops in this district were African Americans. And at this time, the bulk of the garrison of the South's largest city, New Orleans, consisted of two black brigades under Gen. John P. Hawkins. Off the coast of Texas the diminutive garrison of Brazos Santiago included black units such as the 62nd and the 87th U.S. Colored Troops (USCT). Only the 34th Indiana Volunteer Infantry, which arrived in December 1864, represented white soldiery at Brazos Santiago by early 1865.[2]

The 62nd USCT had only recently been stationed on Brazos Santiago, replacing the hardened veterans who had joined the offensive to capture Mobile, Alabama, a force that included a USCT division led by General Hawkins.

The history of the 62nd was short compared with most white regiments. During the first half of December 1863, the men of the regiment had enlisted for three years. Representing a victory by the Radical Republican leadership in the slave state of Missouri, the black unit was originally organized as the 1st Missouri Volunteers of African Descent or the 1st Regiment Missouri Colored Infantry.

The soldiers, consisting of both free blacks and former slaves, first learned the art of war at Benton Barracks on the north side of St. Louis and while attached to the District of St. Louis, Department of Missouri. Many of these men were taught to read and write by their white officers. Additionally, some also received educational instruction at Christian Commission schools established to teach recently freed slaves how to read and write. Those needing instruction were mostly ex-farmhands who had labored for years in Missouri fields as slaves. Other blacks of the regiment, such as David Clark of the Washington Adams family, who were house servants, generally needed relatively less educational instruction.

The regimental designation of the unit was changed during the spring of 1864. The 1st Missouri Colored Infantry became the 62nd U.S. Colored Infantry at Baton Rouge, Louisiana. From here, the black unit from Missouri was stationed with other troops along the Mississippi River from March to June 1864. Like many African American troops in the Union armies at this time, the soldiers of the 62nd were primarily assigned to menial tasks, principally erecting fortifications—a source of discontent for both white officers and black soldiers in the 62nd's ranks.

Then, the regiment served at Morganiza, Louisiana, southwest of New Orleans, from June to September 1864. Here, the black troops participated in their first action during an otherwise uneventful bayou expedition. But the real enemy for the black soldiers in Louisiana was the brutal ravages of disease. The regiment lost a third of its strength to disease, including nearly 350 enlisted men who found shallow graves in the bayou country. Not surprisingly, the men of the 62nd rejoiced upon receiving orders to transfer to Brazos

Santiago in September 1864. To these hard-luck soldiers, the order seemed like a godsend, taking them from the lethal swamps of Louisiana. Most of all, the new orders brought elation because the assignment enhanced the probability of these African Americans finally gaining the opportunity to demonstrate their worth on the battlefield.

By 1865, the men of the 62nd USCT were armed with .577 caliber Enfield rifles imported from England. This ran contrary to the misconception that African American soldiers were armed mostly with inferior weaponry because of discrimination. The Enfield was also the favorite weapon of the Confederacy's elite soldiers.[3]

The soldiers of the 62nd were good and reliable, despite their relative inexperience. Enthusiasm, adherence to discipline, and high morale helped to make up for the lack of knowledge. Gen. Daniel Ullmann, a brigade commander who had been one of the first to urge President Lincoln to enlist black troops, pronounced the well-trained soldiers of the 62nd the "best under my command" in Louisiana.[4]

In addition, Brig. Gen. William A. Pile, a former Methodist minister and onetime chaplain of the 1st Missouri Artillery, and ex-commander of the 33rd Missouri Volunteer Infantry with plenty of combat experience, was greatly impressed by the men of the 62nd USCT. He described the 62nd as a "well drilled and disciplined regiment and well fitted for field service."[5]

In fact, General Pile, who had been in command at "the Brazos" before departing for the Mobile offensive, was so taken by the 62nd that he attempted to have the regiment transferred to his division. The black troops played a key offensive role in the capture of Fort Blakeley, Alabama, on the day that General Lee surrendered at Appomattox.[6]

Most of the African American soldiers of the 62nd USCT hailed from Missouri, the northernmost slave state west of the Mississippi. Here, slavery had thrived since the state's formation in 1821. By 1860, the vast majority of Missouri slaves came from the Missouri and Mississippi River counties, respectively west and north of St. Louis.

Missouri's "black belt" spanned mid-Missouri's agriculturally rich river counties, called "Little Dixie," along the Missouri River. During the antebellum period, slaves worked in the fields of tobacco, hemp, corn, and wheat of both large planters and small yeoman farmers. Cotton was not a cash crop or staple on the Western frontier of the state. Nevertheless, some of these slaves labored in cotton patches of small middle-class farmers in the Missouri and Mississippi River country.[7]

Unlike the famous 54th Massachusetts Volunteer Infantry in which white officers, in relative terms, could more easily harmonize with African American soldiers, the 62nd USCT experienced some problems in race relations. Unlike the soldiers of the 54th, many of whom were educated free blacks, the Missouri blacks were almost all former slaves, uneducated and illiterate. Seemingly verifying stereotypes, this situation raised the level of racism among some lower-ranking white officers of the 62nd, while the top leadership of the regiment remained more fair and open-minded.

By the time the regiment was stationed at Brazos Santiago, some white officers of the 62nd USCT were guilty of kicking and striking black enlisted men for various infractions. This mistreatment escalated until Col. Theodore Harvey Barrett warned his white subordinates "that an officer who could not control his temper was unfit for command." The colonel's threat halted the abuse at the lower officer levels in the regiment. Thereafter, the black enlisted men and white officers worked together in greater harmony, thanks to Colonel Barrett's efforts. An enlightened man in regard to slavery, Barrett had been appointed colonel in December 1863, when the regiment was organized at Benton Barracks, Missouri.[8]

Just as the soldiers of Col. Robert G. Shaw, the 54th Massachusetts's young colonel who was killed at Fort Wagner, South Carolina, could count on their leader, the African Americans of the 62nd USCT could count on an ally in Colonel Barrett. A political appointee in his twenties, the colonel possessed limited combat experience before taking command of the 1st Missouri Colored Infantry.

Like his Palmito Ranch counterpart, Colonel Ford, Barrett's service had already cost him his health. He suffered from bouts of typhoid fever. A journalist of the *New York Herald* reported in May 1865 how Colonel Barrett was, "a very young man, a New Yorker by birth, but [he] has lived in the West the greater part of his life."[9]

By keeping his less enlightened white officers in check by ending their abusive behavior, Colonel Barrett demonstrated a protective paternalism toward the newly freed slaves from Missouri. He advised some of them to purchase land by amassing their monthly pay rather than squandering those dollars on things of little or no value. He wisely cautioned the black soldiers that "it is a great deal better for you to live upon your land, than to hire land from another, or to work for another."[10]

Despite experiencing racial problems, the black soldiers of the 62nd USCT remained enthusiastic and eager to meet the enemy. One Union officer described the psychology and ideology of the typical African American soldiery in this war: "[T]hey had more to fight for than the whites. Besides the flag and the Union, they had home and wife and child. They fought with ropes round their necks [and] with us, at least, there was to be no play-soldier

[and] in case of ultimate defeat, the Northern troops, black or white, would go home, while [blacks from the slave states] must fight it out or be re-enslaved," by the victorious Rebels.[11]

By this time, the motivation among the African Americans of the 62nd at Brazos Santiago continued to remain high. And this motivation among the black troops was not at all diminished by the approach of the war's end. Most of all, these young African Americans from Missouri were fighting for their own future and that of millions of other African Americans. Additionally, the troops were eager to demonstrate their equality to white soldiers on the battlefield in the hope of winning greater equality for all blacks in American society—a war on two fronts.

Most of all, the African Americans of the 62nd fought for the opportunity to strike a blow against the hated institution of slavery. The idealism of the African American soldiers was seen in the words of one black Yankee who wrote with pride in a letter: "[W]e hope to meet the enemy again, fight, conquer him, end the rebellion, and then come home to our Northern people, to freemen who look South with joyous hearts, and behold not a single Slave State—but only free territory, from Maryland to Texas . . . our armies will defeat the rebels, and hang slavery."[12]

Inspired by the belief that this was a holy war and crusade against wrong, another African American in blue penned in a letter of the righteous nature of this struggle: "God [has] worked wonders through the agency of this rebellion. He has struck the chains of bondage . . . and given new strength and vigor to the doctrine of Universal Freedom and Equal Rights."[13]

The determined soldiers of the 62nd were sure to fight most tenaciously against the Texas Rebels because of their belief that this was a "no-quarter" war for them. Black soldiers captured on the battlefield were often executed by their Rebel captors. For instance, wrote one North Carolina Rebel in a letter, the Confederate soldiers were, "perfected [sic] exasperated at the idea of negroes opposed to them & rushed at them like so many devils," to take revenge on the unfortunate blacks.[14]

The most infamous example of the horrors faced by African American soldiers on the battlefield was the massacre at Fort Pillow. Here, in southwest Tennessee on the Mississippi River above Memphis, on April 12, 1864, the veteran forces of Gen. Nathan B. Forrest, a former slave trader from Memphis, stormed the earthworks to overrun Fort Pillow. After a stout defense, a good many of the inexperienced black soldiers were slaughtered by the victors, including wounded African Americans and men who had already surrendered. At Fort Pillow, more than 40 percent of the black garrison was killed as a result of the Rebels' vengeful wrath.

By 1865, however, the "Fort Pillow Massacre" only added a new war cry for African Americans in uniform, including the soldiers of the 62nd USCT. One black soldier described in a letter that when African Americans charged into battle "with the shout of 'Remember Fort Pillow!' . . . you would have thought that nothing human could have withstood their impetuosity [as] we know no defeat."[15]

In contrast with the North's wholesale enlistment of both free blacks and slaves, the Confederacy only belatedly discussed the possibility of black enlistment despite losing the war of attrition. African American soldiers in gray uniforms offered only a partial solution to the manpower crisis that doomed the Confederacy. Open-minded Southern leaders with insight, like Irish-born Maj. Gen. Patrick Cleburne, knew as much, but suffered for their beliefs.

Texans were especially adamant about refusing to consider the novel idea of black soldiers in gray uniforms. When the Richmond government contemplated the formation of African American units, an angry editor of the Galveston *Weekly News* responded in indignation: "[W]e think it is a matter of regret that any suggestion should ever have been made in high official quarters, that any emergency can arise to compel the South to an abandonment of the foundation principle upon which the institution of slavery rests."

In February 1865 at Goliad, Texas, the scene of the most infamous massacre of the Texas Revolution, the citizens, forgetting that blacks played an active role in the Revolution, including the 1835 capture of Goliad, concluded that "the discussion of the question, whether it is expedient or politic to abolish southern slavery, is premature, unwise and unnecessary, and impresses the Northern mind with the belief that we feel unable to sustain the institution [which is] not to be wrestled from us by any power on earth." Clearly, many Texans preferred total defeat rather than accepting the concept of blacks fighting on their own side, an attitude apparently shared by those in areas of Texas that had sided with the Union. In total, less than 50 African Americans from the 36,000 blacks of military age in Texas served in the Union army. Symbolically, hundreds of ex-slaves from Missouri were now stationed on Brazos Santiago as if to fight on behalf of Texas slaves.[16]

By 1865, the commander of the 62nd USCT was Lt. Col. David Branson, succeeding after Colonel Barrett took overall command of the Brazos Santiago garrison, following the departure of troops for the Mobile campaign. A former coal merchant and dealer from Pennsylvania, Branson was fated to soon encounter one of the most knowledgeable frontier tacticians in Texas, "Old Rip" Ford. Like his immediate commander at Brazos Santiago, Colonel Barrett, Lieutenant Colonel Branson, not yet age twenty-five, possessed little combat experience. In fact, he began the war as a humble private in the 28th Illinois

Volunteer Infantry, before earning the rank of sergeant and sergeant major, and then acting adjutant. He had often commanded the 62nd with ability when Colonel Barrett was absent due to illness, gaining some experience.[17]

Young Branson was living in Mississippi when the Rebel cannon opened fire on Fort Sumter. Here, like few Yankee officers, he had seen the horrors of Southern slavery firsthand. This experience helped to make him a compassionate officer to the men of the 62nd.[18]

Branson's long-awaited opportunity for advancement came with the organization of the 1st Missouri Colored Infantry, when he became the regiment's lieutenant colonel. By all accounts, the Barrett-Branson pairing was an effective one. The younger Branson harbored no envy of the colonel or his authority, fostering a team spirit at the regiment's highest levels. Lieutenant Colonel Branson was a fine young officer, and he took his role seriously. The handsome Branson was described by one observer as "possessing a face indicating remarkable courage and activity, and a physique that denotes endurance and a long life."[19]

In the spirit of Colonel Barrett, Lieutenant Colonel Branson stood up for his black soldiers whenever possible and at every opportunity. For instance, in Colonel Barrett's absence, in the sweltering bayou country of Louisiana, an angry Branson complained to authorities about the unfair treatment received by his black troops, denouncing the fact that his men "have been worked [since the regiment's arrival] eight to ten hours daily on the fortifications [while] no white troops have been worked on these fortifications during said period except those held as prisoners and undergoing punishment."[20]

Like Colonel Shaw of the 54th, Lieutenant Colonel Branson's sense of duty to his men and concern for their welfare made him a friend of the ex-slaves and free blacks of the 62nd. Unfortunately, his concern for the soldiers' welfare and the close leadership team forged with Colonel Barrett might have led to the resentment of lower ranking white officers who took out their frustrations on the black troops. Regardless of these isolated examples of mistreatment, however, Colonel Barrett and Lieutenant Colonel Branson emphasized drill and discipline to forge a fine regiment of African Americans who were eager for action by early 1865.[21]

Lieutenant Colonel Branson was also an idealist. He viewed his role as helping to morally uplift the ex-slaves he commanded. He was once driven to anger when he discovered his men engaged in gambling. With an odd mixture of paternalism and discipline, Lieutenant Colonel Branson laid down the law: "Hereafter when any soldier of this command is found to be or have been playing cards he will be placed standing in some prominent position in the camp with book in hand and required then and there to learn a considerable lesson in reading and spelling and if unwilling to learn, he will be compelled by hunger to do so . . . no freed slave who cannot read well has a right to waste the time and opportunity there given him to fit himself for the position of a free citizen."[22]

By the beginning of 1865, Colonel Ford was well aware of the presence of black troops on Texas soil, which always brought the fear of potential slave revolt to the people of Texas. Not surprisingly, when he had appealed for volunteers to drive the Yankee invaders into the Gulf of Mexico, Ford had included among the, "ruthless enemies" of Texas not only "Abolitionists" but also "negroes."[23]

Since the beginning of the Civil War, Texans across the state were horrified by the prospect of an invasion largely because of the fear of the North's use of black troops. The *Houston Telegraph* caused panic when speculating that the black soldiers were dispatched to Texas "with a view eventually of colonizing American citizens of African descent—free Negroes—in this State." Hence, it was feared by the people of Texas that a social revolution would be initiated by the Yankees in a conquered Texas during Reconstruction.[24]

Throughout the spring of 1865, the African American soldiers on Brazos Santiago felt the boredom of their island exile and the lack of battlefield action. Unlike the first black regiments of the war, such as Col. Thomas Wentworth Higginson's and James Montgomery's 1st and 2nd South Carolina Colored Infantry, that conducted liberation raids into the remote countryside of Florida, Georgia, and South Carolina, Colonel Branson's soldiers did not engage in such activities on the Texas mainland. Instead, the black troops of the 62nd drilled under the scorching sun, fighting no Rebels and, worst of all, doing nothing to break the shackles of slavery.

On Brazos Santiago, the African Americans remained idle, and the only fighting was against the seemingly endless swarms of sand fleas and intense heat. This assignment gave these men so far from home plenty of time to worry about the fate of family members still in bondage. With a gift for understatement, one disgruntled African American soldier wrote in a letter: "[W]e found Brazos [Santiago] a most undesirable place, there were plenty of flies and mosquitos and sand burrs. We had our [regimental] headquarters at this place which was knee deep in [salt] water." Consequently, the soldiers of the 62nd remained especially eager to see some action before the war's end.[25]

Like some black units, perhaps the men of the 62nd USCT on Brazos Santiago swore an oath of vengeance for the massacre at Fort Pillow. The importance of the moral, spiritual, and psychological motivation of "Remember Fort Pillow" for these young African American soldiers of the 62nd would become evident in the upcoming battle of Palmito Ranch.[26]

HOOSIER YANKEES

By the beginning of 1865, the only white regiment stationed at Brazos Santiago was the 34th Indiana Volunteer Infantry. This veteran Hoosier regiment, also known as the Morton Rifles, had not seen defeat in service on either side of the Mississippi. In the war's early days, the Indiana unit was initially called the "Mountain Guards." And, in the words of one soldier, this was a "[proud] name[, which] was [only] reluctantly exchanged for Veteran Volunteers." Col. Robert G. Morrison, age twenty-five and a former merchant, now commanded the Indiana soldiers who were garrisoned on the steamy barrier island in the Gulf. Establishing the only demographic link between the two units at Brazos Santiago, these veteran Hoosiers were Westerners like the African Americans from Missouri.

Serving as a captain at the beginning of the war, the Vermont-born Morrison earned his lieutenant colonel's rank in December 1863. By 1864, Morrison was a capable, experienced fighter and a fine leader. His loyalty to the unit ran so deep that he avoided court-martial duty in New Orleans simply because it meant departing the regiment and missing the opportunity to fight beside his Indiana boys. The young officer pleaded to the authorities in a letter: "I have the honor to apply to be relieved from siting [sic] on Genl. Court Martial . . . by reason of my regiment being ordered to Brazos, Texas, and I desire to be present with the regiment." Morrison got his wish, rejoining his Hoosier troops at Brazos Santiago on January 15, 1865.[27]

Organized at Anderson, Indiana, in mid-September 1861, the 34th Indiana had seen more service and action than any other Union regiment now stationed on Brazos Santiago. The 34th first served in Kentucky and fought at Island Number Ten near New Madrid, Missouri, in March 1862. Then, it played a role in the capture of Fort Pillow, Tennessee, where African Americans would be slaughtered by General Forrest's cavalrymen in April 1864. The 34th also served in Arkansas, fighting at Grand Prairie, before joining General Grant's forces to face the challenges of the Vicksburg campaign.

After crossing the Mississippi River—from eastern Louisiana to western Mississippi, just below Vicksburg—with General Grant's army during the largest amphibious landing of the war, the Hoosiers fought with distinction at the battle of Port Gibson, Mississippi, on May 1, 1863. Here, in the smoke-wreathed forests of Claiborne County, the 34th launched a bayonet attack against a Rebel position, regaining the initiative in this hard-fought sector. Despite suffering heavy losses, the Hoosiers captured two artillery pieces of a Virginia battery and almost fifty prisoners. The Indiana attackers earned the distinction of being the first Yankees to reach the guns of the Old Dominion battery, where hand-to-hand fighting erupted in the snarled woodlands around Magnolia Church.[28]

Then, barely two weeks later, the 34th Indiana, serving in Gen. Alvin P. Hovey's western division of Indiana, Wisconsin, Iowa, and Ohio troops, again fought well during the most decisive battle of the Vicksburg Campaign, Champion Hill, Mississippi. On May 16, 1863, the 34th Indiana attacked the 46th Alabama Infantry, despite having been decimated by massed artillery fire. In hand-to-hand fighting, the Hoosier soldiers captured the Alabama battle flag and more than 125 prisoners. After Champion Hill, the hard-fighting infantrymen of the 34th endured the dangers and rigors of the forty-seven-day siege of Vicksburg.[29]

After General Grant's decisive victory at Vicksburg, the Hoosier regiment saw service in the swampy bayou country of Louisiana, embarking on expeditions deep into enemy country. Like the black troops of the 62nd, the 34th Indiana was stationed in New Orleans for nearly a year until orders came to report for duty at Brazos Santiago in December 1864. The nearness of the war's end combined with the routine garrison duty in Louisiana and New Orleans caused this veteran regiment to lose some of its fighting edge by May 1865. The 34th Indiana, nevertheless, was destined to lose more soldiers in the battle of Palmito Ranch on May 13 than any other previous engagement.[30]

By this time, the 34th Indiana and the 62nd USCT were two very different commands quite apart from the factors of race and demographics. The Indiana soldiers were now hardened veterans who had already seen enough killing to last them a lifetime. Past heroics on battlefields guaranteed that the infantrymen of the 34th would pitch in the next fray with enthusiasm despite the lateness of the battle. But by early 1865, the novelty of playing the game of "spit and polish" soldiers had long worn off for these tried veterans, especially on the bleak barrier island of Brazos Santiago.

In contrast, the inexperienced African Americans of the 62nd were all business in regard to the fundamentals of soldiering, partly because of a mixture of excessive enthusiasm, naïveté, and idealism. They were also most eager to prove themselves in battle to their commander and country, much like the Indiana soldiers had been during the war's early days.

Maj. Joseph K. Hudson, third in command of the 62nd and the officer who had led the regiment's only expedition into enemy territory in Louisiana, together with a number of his fellow officers, was aware of the friction and differences between the rookie blacks and the veterans of the 34th Indiana. A healthy rivalry had developed between the two regiments, which was heightened by some racial tensions and the veterans' usual disrespect for inexperienced soldiers. In consequence, the black soldiers and their white officers became increasingly anti-Hoosier, while the Indiana soldiers became increasingly anti-black.

After surviving the nightmarish fighting at Port Gibson and Champion Hill, the Indiana soldiers were motivated by the desire of not becoming the war's last casualty. For these veteran Hoosiers, the war's glory days had faded away with the deaths of so many comrades in the body-strewn woodlands of Champion Hill and the trenches of Vicksburg.

Partly as a result of this attitude, Major Hudson was shocked to discover that the Indiana soldiers, including officers, "were very lax in discipline [and] the guard duty was done loosely, and while on duty, the soldiers' bearing as a general state, was unsoldierly." Like other officers of the 62nd, Major Hudson was worried that the slack discipline of the 34th Indiana would have a negative influence on his black troops. But Capt. William C. Durkee of the 62nd and the inspector general at Brazos Santiago, was not fooled by the nonchalance of these Indiana veterans whose knowledge and combat experience "was better understood by the men than performed" by them. Despite their casual appearances and demeanor, the men of the 34th Indiana were dependable soldiers. By this time, the Indiana Yankees only took the business of soldiering seriously on the battlefield.[31]

Durkee, nevertheless, was shocked by the Hoosiers' lack of discipline. But what upset the meticulous inspector general most of all was the fact that he "had seen [Indiana] men on dress parade doing what they should not, turning their heads and spitting [and] talking in the ranks."

What could not be denied, however, was the fact that these Indiana soldiers were tough. And it no longer mattered to them if officers of the 62nd USCT condemned them because of their "lax" discipline. The hardened Western soldiers of the 34th Indiana were among the famed conquerors of Vicksburg and the Mississippi River, and had fought under another no-nonsense Westerner who also lacked "spit and polish" ways and proper protocol, General U. S. Grant.[32]

Captain Durkee, nevertheless, incorrectly believed that the Hoosier soldiers "were badly demoralized on arrival at Brazos, and it increased all the time that they were there." Part of the problem was that there was little to do on the remote island. This inactivity only fueled the animosity and resentment between the 34th Indiana and the 62nd USCT. Like everything else on the island, the overall discipline of the garrison languished and deteriorated. One disgruntled Indiana lieutenant complained that the sandy isle was consumed by a "salt atmosphere . . . [that] will rust all kinds of metals, such as iron, brass and steel."

The recent garrison duty in Louisiana and in lively New Orleans played a part in developing this nonchalant attitude among the Indiana soldiers. Bustling and cosmopolitan New Orleans could easily erode the best discipline even among elite troops, especially with the war rapidly drawing to a close.

Fancy saloons, brightly dressed working Creole, French, black, and Anglo girls on the streets and corners, gambling dens and high-class brothels along Royal and St. Charles Streets, renowned French restaurants, and even darker corners of the city, where a young Indiana farm boy could get into serious trouble, made New Orleans the favorite Southern city of the 34th Indiana.

The lures of New Orleans were too much for many Hoosiers who were unfamiliar with the hard realities of city life. With some truth, consequently, Captain Durkee believed that the laxness of Hoosiers' discipline had developed "prior to coming to Brazos; they had been scattered in different places [in Louisiana], in and about New Orleans [and] the cause of its increase on the Brazos was owing to the leniency of the officers."[33]

Despite its generally relaxed disposition at Brazos Santiago, the 34th Indiana yet basked in its well-deserved reputation as a crack regiment. Lt. John E. Markle, regimental quartermaster, thus described the Indiana soldiers, who "always had a good reputation [and] they received frequent flattering notices." In fact the regiment had been highly complimented by its divisional commander at Port Gibson and Champion Hill, General Hovey, and later by Gen. Napoleon Jackson T. Dana. General Dana bestowed his compliment on the 34th when it was stationed in Louisiana where Colonel Morrison commanded the regiment. The general declared that the 34th Indiana was "as fine a drill and as disciplined a regiment as he had seen in the Regular Army." According to Lieutenant Markle, General Hovey announced on the battlefield of Port Gibson that the 34th was "one of my best regiments" of his hard-fighting division, which General Grant credited with winning the day at Champion Hill.[34]

One of the young Hoosier soldiers who made the 34th Indiana a fine regiment was Pvt. John Jefferson Williams of Company B. Handsome with dark hair and eyes, Private Williams was born in Indiana in the small community of Redkey, Jay County, before migrating to Westchester, Indiana.

By the outbreak of the Civil War, he was a hardworking blacksmith, who had married as a teenager and carved out a life for himself in Portland, Indiana. Unlike his more seasoned comrades of the 34th, Private Williams was relatively new to the business of war. He enlisted in late March 1864. By 1865, nevertheless, he had become "a good soldier, loved by all." Reliable common soldiers in the ranks like Private Williams made the 34th Indiana an excellent regiment, which could be depended upon during a battlefield crisis.[35]

All in all, wrote Capt. John P. Conklyn, of the 117th USCT, high respect was due the Indiana regiment because these men had served with distinction "in Arkansas, in Louisiana, at the siege of Vicksburg, at P[ort Gibson], Champion Hill, and other places, where Major-General Dana told them they were equal to the best troops in the Regular Army, and other officers ranked them among their best troops, that the condition of the [34th Indiana Volunteer Infantry] at the Brazos was as it had been in other places, with the exception of personal appearance . . . discipline was strict and that it was steadily improving under the command of" the capable Lieutenant Colonel Morrison.[36]

As more time passed on Brazos Santiago, Colonel Barrett and his inexperienced officers increasingly resented the 34th Indiana. This was partly due to the fact that the veteran Indiana officers had the kind of extensive combat background that the 62nd's officers envied. Unlike the present commander of Brazos Santiago, Colonel Barrett, the military expertise gained by the Indiana officers came from hard-earned experience. By this time the officers of the 34th Indiana knew better than to commit the folly of sending an inadequate force onto the Texas mainland, too far from the safety of Brazos Santiago, in the futile pursuit of glory and fame. Barrett's favoritism toward his own African American regiment at the 34th Indiana's expense would play a role in influencing his leadership and tactical decisions during the coming battle at Palmito Ranch.[37]

TEXAS YANKEES

Among the Federal garrison of Brazos Santiago by early 1865 were the soldiers who the Texas Rebels denounced as "renegades," the Texas Yankees. What has generally been forgotten about the Civil War in Texas was that this bitter conflict experienced the epitome of the "brothers' war." Here, Texans often battled against Texans with a ferocity seldom seen during the four years of conflict. From the war's beginning, the number of Texas Unionists was high, thanks in part to the region's large German population and its distinctive history and culture. The Unionists included Sam Houston, the legendary hero of San Jacinto and governor who refused to become a secessionist despite the popular sentiment of his own state.

To Colonel Ford and his Western frontier soldiers, the Texans in blue were the ultimate enemy. These Yankees were viewed by the Texas Rebels as the "vile and despicable traitors, worthy of nothing more pleasant than a military firing squad." Not surprisingly, an editor of the *Houston Tri-Weekly Telegraph* prayed to God for the worst of all fates to be visited upon the Texas Yankees: "[G]rant that their carcasses may all enrich the soil their lives have cursed!" Hated by their fellow Texans and viewed as untrustworthy by

Northerners because of their Southern roots, these Texas Federals felt the wrath from both friend and foe, making their sacrifices in fighting for the Union high.[38]

Colonel Ford's counterpart during the struggle for possession of the Lower Rio Grande Valley had been Col. Edmund Jackson Davis. Tall and thin, Davis was a refugee Texan with old scores to settle after having been forced to flee his homeland. Davis's wife and family were likewise exiled, fleeing across the border to Matamoros. Unlike Ford who had come to the Lone Star State at the end of the Revolution, Davis migrated to Texas a decade later, two years after the Mexican-American War. Destined to become the only Texas Union general of the Civil War, the Florida-born Davis possessed solid West Point training: a rare qualification on the Texas frontier and in the remote Lower Rio Grande Valley.

Before the war, Davis had been a respected lawyer, city councilman, and district judge at Laredo, Corpus Christi, and Brownsville. He had lost the Cameron County election for delegate to the secession convention to "Old Rip" Ford. Like Colonel Ford, Davis understood the importance of making allies of the Tejanos. To fight his former neighbors and fellow Texans in gray, Colonel Davis began organizing the 1st Texas Union Cavalry in New Orleans, Louisiana, during the fall of 1862.

These Texas Yankee cavalrymen of the 1st Texas were assigned to duty in the swamps and bayous of Louisiana in 1863. Then, they were reassigned to the Rio Grande Valley by the autumn of that year. When the Federals reclaimed the valley, these blue-clad horsemen played a role in impeding the flow of Confederate trade across the Rio Grande, after pushing upriver to Ringgold Barracks and then eventually as far as Roma to the northwest. The Texas horse soldiers helped to win control of the main waterway of the borderlands from the Tejano Rebels under Col. Santos Benavides, taking possession of a lengthy stretch of the Rio Grande.

After the Union gained possession of the Lower Valley in 1863, Colonel Davis recruited large numbers of Tejanos from the Rio Grande river towns, and Mexicans from border communities in northern Mexico, such as Matamoros where he was captured and later released. So many Hispanic recruits came forward to serve the Union that a new regiment was eventually organized, the 2nd Texas Union Cavalry.[39]

To complement the 1st Texas Union Cavalry, the 2nd Texas was formed in December 1863. Virginia-born Col. John L. Haynes, who accomplished more than anyone to create this cavalry unit, was placed in command. A Mexican-American War veteran and former Regular officer who closely identified with the Hispanics in blue, Haynes was an early and longtime defender of Tejano rights in Starr County, Texas, and as a result, was unpopular to many less enlightened Texans.

The ethnic composition of the 2nd Texas Cavalry was almost entirely Hispanic, consisting of many Tejanos from the Rio Grande Valley. However, three-fourths of the troopers were actually born in Mexico, hailing primarily from such Mexican border towns as Mier, Matamoros, Camargo, and Guerrero. These Tejanos rode to war wearing wide sombreros instead of the standard blue kepi, reflecting their ethnic heritage and culture.

The regiment also had a strong immigrant component. Like numbers of Colonel Ford's Rebels, some cavalrymen of the 2nd Texas Union Cavalry were Germans from the picturesque, rugged hill country of Edwards Plateau northwest of San Antonio. In the war's beginning, these pro-Union "foreigners" were persecuted by the Confederacy. Colonel Haynes, who was also persecuted, was appalled by the cruel treatment of Texas Unionists because it seemed as if "the traitors [would] hang us all as tories and traitors." In addition, many other immigrants besides Germans rode in the column of the 2nd Texas, including troopers from Scotland, France, Cuba, Ireland, Italy, Prussia, Spain, Canada, and Nicaragua.

The 2nd Texas Cavalry was a natural focus for leading Rio Grande Valley Federal leaders and Hispanics. More than a thousand Texas troopers in blue now represented the Rio Grande area, a fact that especially infuriated Colonel Ford and his Texas Rebels.

Colonel Haynes, a transplanted Southerner from Mississippi and prosperous merchant of Rio Grande City, became a special target of the Texas Confederates. He possessed a diplomatic and political background, having served in the Texas Legislature from 1857–59, while representing the people of Starr County. Like Colonel Davis, Haynes was highly motivated, especially after having been forced to flee to Mexico at the war's beginning. In the process, he had lost all that he had acquired before the war, and now had old scores to settle with the Texas Rebels.

Both of these leading refugee Texas leaders, Colonels Davis and Haynes, had met President Lincoln at the White House to inform him of the sad plight of Texas Yankees in the seceded state. They requested urgent assistance and proposed a plan for the landing of Union troops at the Rio Grande's mouth for an invasion of the state. The resourceful Colonel Davis was Colonel Ford's adversary during the struggle for possession of the Rio Grande Valley, commanding all the Union cavalry in this border region of the lower valley.[40]

The Texas Rebels' special hatred for the troopers of the 1st and 2nd Texas Union Cavalry went far beyond simple anti-Union sentiment. The detested "renegade" status of these Texas Yankees was compounded by the fact that many "foreigners" served in these two regiments. Such demographics and compositions played a role in fueling an ugly ethnic war on the Rio Grande border.

Colonel Ford had initially called for volunteers to resist the Hispanics in blue, or, as he explained, the "plundering Mexicans." Proud of his own command, Colonel Davis described how his Texan cavalrymen consisted of "443 Mexicans and 500 Americans (including in this designation Germans, Irish, &c), the whole (including the part brought from New Orleans) being recruited [in Brownsville]." As fate would have it, the Tejanos along the Rio Grande were now engaged in their own civil war within a larger civil war. Tejano Rebels faced off against Tejano Yankees in an ethnic brothers' war on the border.

The ancient hatreds stemming from fighting Mexicans during both the Texas Revolution and the Mexican-American War, and countless border fights, was a motivating factor for these Texas Rebels who had fought for decades in a struggle for survival. Many of Colonel Ford's men had family members and relatives who had been killed by the Mexicans during the 1830s, 1840s, and 1850s and vice versa. A number of 2nd Texas Cavalry Tejanos, including several Salazar brothers, hailed from Goliad, the scene of the most brutal massacre of the Texas Revolution.

By early 1865, ancient hostilities and hatreds were still powerful, motivating forces to Colonel Ford's Rebels. These rugged individuals had survived a savage existence on the untamed frontier only by fighting harder and more ruthlessly than their old enemies, their historic foes, Indians and Mexicans.[41]

Among the first assignments of the 2nd Texas Cavalry had been to patrol the Texas Gulf coast, watching the mouth of the Rio Grande and Brazos Santiago. Desertions, however, became a problem because of the lack of promised supplies—including clothing and pay—Anglo prejudice, and the nearness of home, which beckoned these men to return across the nearby border. Colonel Haynes saw the only solution to this problem as transferring the regiment to another theater of operations.

The Texas horsemen were ordered to be transported by steamer to Louisiana during the early summer of 1864. Not departing with the brigade were Companies A and C, 1st Texas Cavalry, which Colonel Ford defeated in the hot fight at Las Rucias Ranch. The reception of the initial orders to report to Louisiana had resulted in a near riot among the Tejanos and Mexican troopers. These Hispanic soldiers had not expected to be dispatched to some faraway region of the vast "gringo" country to the north. No soldier, especially a Tejano or Mexican in Yankee blue, wanted the dubious distinction of dying far from home in a conflict raging hundreds of miles north of the Rio Grande.[42]

While still angry about having to depart their native Rio Grande Valley, these Texans fought Trans-Mississippi Rebels at places like Vermillion Bayou and Carrion Crow Bayou in the steamy swamps and cypress forests of Louisiana. They also fought on the other side of the "Father of Waters" in Mississippi.

By November 1864, the two Texas cavalry regiments in Louisiana were consolidated to officially become the 1st Texas Volunteer Cavalry with Colonel Haynes in command, though by March of the following year the 2nd Texas had been reactivated. Meanwhile, two newly formed Texas horse companies under Maj. Edward J. Noyes remained among the garrison of Brazos Santiago, after the Federals evacuated Brownsville during the summer of 1864.[43]

During the campaigning in the bayou country of Louisiana, Davis won a general's rank, and led mostly black troops. This was a rank that "Old Rip" Ford deserved but would never receive from an unappreciative Confederacy.

By March 1865 and the time of General Wallace's arrival for the Point Isabel conference, General Davis had returned to Brazos Santiago for a brief period. Unfamiliar with the fratricidal nature and ethnic composition of the conflict in the Rio Grande Valley, General Wallace had initially believed that General Davis might prove helpful in convincing General Slaughter and Colonel Ford to accept his peace proposals. On the contrary, Davis was in truth a spark that probably would have inflamed passions to sabotage any hope of future good relations, a cease-fire, and perhaps even the proposed future joint Union-Confederate expedition into northern Mexico.[44]

Also in early March 1865, a 2nd Texas Cavalry lieutenant named James Hancock returned to Brazos Santiago on a special assignment. Lieutenant Hancock's mission was to recruit men among the Unionist refugees who had fled the Texas mainland via Mexico to reach the island sanctuary. Here, on "the Brazos," a new cavalry company was formed, half of which consisted of Tejanos. By May 1865, this company was preparing to join the other units of the newly activated 2nd Texas Union Cavalry on duty in Louisiana.[45]

By the last year of the war, this intensely personal conflict among the diehard Texans in both blue and gray had become especially brutal. When Colonel Ford's troopers had smashed into Companies A and C, 1st Texas Cavalry, at Las Rucias Ranch the previous year, the Texans in blue fought desperately. With justification, the Union Texans were convinced that the Texas Confederates "would treat them as traitors."

On that day, Colonel Ford's Rebels won a lopsided victory. In this fight "all was lost" for the Federals. Colonel Ford's frontier warriors virtually wiped out two Texas Federal companies while losing barely half a dozen men. Of the more than one hundred Texas Yankees who resisted Colonel Ford's attack at Las Rucias, only eight soldiers escaped to the safety of Brownsville to tell the tale.

According to one account, the treatment of the Texas Yankee captives by the Texas Rebels was conducted in the most "inhuman manner." But the situation could have been much worse for the Texas Federals if not for Ford's timely intervention. The captured Texas Yankees "would have been murdered on the ground since they were Texas Renegades had it not been for Colonel Ford." Tragically, almost a dozen of those lucky Texas Federals spared at Las Rucias were fated to die in a Texas prison within only four hours of their arrival. Evidently, either the escort troops or the prison guards accomplished either by neglect or outright murder what Colonel Ford's troopers failed to do at Las Rucias.

The mutual feeling of hatred between Texans on opposing sides had surfaced at an early date and worsened as the war lengthened. Tapping into this hostility, Colonel Ford had called volunteers to fight the detested "perfidious renegades," the Texas Yankees. And at such places as Las Rucias Ranch, the full fury of the Texas Rebels' wrath had been unleashed.[46]

By May 1865, the awful potential for an explosive encounter between the combined Union force of Texans, including Confederate deserters and African Americans, and Colonel Ford's Texans on the battlefield was about to be realized. As fate would have it, these intense passions were about to be given full rein at an obscure place called Palmito Ranch weeks after General Lee surrendered at Appomattox.

CHAPTER 4

The Last Stage Is Set

By the spring of 1865, Colonel Ford's rough-hewn troopers of his "Expeditionary Force" were described by one shocked observer as a "motley force of spirited irregulars." But in reality under Colonel Ford's able leadership, these men were some of the best horse soldiers of the Western frontier. They may have been "motley" crew in looks and coarse in speech and manners but when led by Colonel Ford and other able lieutenants, such veterans could not be underestimated on the battlefield.

A false rumor, nevertheless, circulated among the Union high command at Brazos Santiago that Colonel Ford's cavalry consisted largely of unreliable deserters from other Rebel units. Some foundation existed for this rumor. Confederate deserters in Texas often employed the convenient excuse that they were joining up with "Old Rip" Ford when in fact they were deserting to cross the Rio Grande to wait out the war with other deserters in Mexico.

At this time, Ford still held no official rank in the Confederate army, after twice refusing candidacy as the 2nd Texas Cavalry's colonel. In addition, he had turned down an appointment to major. Even though Ford never received a commission from the Confederate government, he continued to be treated, paid, and addressed as "Colonel" by both superiors and subordinates.

For Colonel Ford, matters of rank were relatively unimportant. "We have proclaimed to the world that we are struggling for liberty, against violations of the constitution, and against usurpations of power," explained Ford in 1863. He, consequently, continued to lead the rugged individuals of the Western frontier by example and hard-won respect rather than by virtue of rank.[1]

The first days of May 1865 descended upon the isolated Lower Valley of the Rio Grande like a thick warm shroud. Summer-like weather had already come to the parched lands along the border. In fact, the weather along the Rio Grande Valley was warmer in May than even in the heart of the Deep South. The Lower Rio Grande Valley was itself a unique land in many respects. The region offered the warmest, driest, and mildest climate in the Southern nation. Along the flat coastal lands of the Valley, tropical breezes from the Gulf and the distant Caribbean blew warm in winter and cool in summer.

With each passing day, the short life of the Confederacy continued to ebb away. During the first days of May 1865, the Rebels along the Rio Grande were about to be shocked by unbelievable news from the Eastern Theater, which finally reached the Lower Rio Grande Valley.

A steamer from Boca Del Rio on its way to Brownsville, pushed up the turbid river. Laboring through the placid waters, the riverboat steamed past one of the few sections of high ground between the coast and Brownsville. To the locals in the area, this elevation along the Rio Grande, owned by the Orive family, was known as Palmito Hill. This high ground dominated Palmito Ranch and overlooked the river and the Mexico shore to the south.

The isolated hill was located just southeast of the main dwelling and buildings of Palmito Ranch, which were situated next to the Rio Grande, or on the west bank with the river immediately to the east, as it flowed northward in a wide bend, before turning east again toward the Gulf of Mexico. Part hill and part bluff and essentially the windswept remains of an ancient sand dune, Palmito Hill stood at the highest point in the area—only thirty-six feet above sea level. Nevertheless, it was a well-known elevation in this flat region of the coastal plain.

Here, at Palmito Hill, some of Colonel Giddings's Texas cavalrymen were stationed in support of Palmito Ranch, which served as Colonel Ford's advanced outpost nearest the Gulf and the Yankee garrison on Brazos Santiago. As the steamboat passed the ragged Texas Confederates along the shore, a deckhand tossed copies of the *New Orleans Times* onto the north bank of the river. Eager for news at what was now the most isolated southernmost outpost in the Confederacy, some pickets, in dusty gray and butternut, grabbed the New Orleans newspapers to learn of the war's recent developments.

In this way, Capt. William N. Robinson's Rebels, of Colonel Giddings's battalion, were the first in the Rio Grande Valley to read the mind-numbing news of the collapse of resistance across the Confederacy. Even the news of President Lincoln's death brought shock to these boys in gray and no doubt some rejoicing. To these Texas Confederates who had fought for years, the worst of all fates had befallen their Southern nation in the faraway Eastern Theater.

Soon the news of what had happened in the East spread to Brownsville. Capt. William H. D. Carrington, a promising officer who held Ford's trust, never forgot his dismay upon reading the headlines of the *New Orleans Times,* which told only too well of the dismal truth. The New Orleans papers stated that General Lee had surrendered at Appomattox Court House in distant Virginia. These Texans were now some of the last Rebels to receive the disheartening news. For instance, Gen. Kirby Smith knew as early as April 19 of General Lee's surrender at Appomattox Court House.[2]

With the news of Confederate surrenders, scores of Texas Rebels along the Rio Grande saddled up and rode out of camp without speaking a word. By this time, little needed to be said. Knowing that the end had come at last, these Western frontiersmen headed for their towns, ranches, and families across Texas. The 500 Rebels who were on duty in the first days of May in the Lower Rio Grande Valley soon dwindled to only 300.

Almost as quickly as it began, the epidemic of desertion finally subsided. The exodus ended after the first ten days of May. Despite the fact that General Lee's Army of Northern Virginia had surrendered more than a month before, the remaining die-hard Confederates of the Lower Rio Grande Valley continued their duties as before. More out of loyalty to comrades than anything else, these soldiers remained beside their units and friends whom they would not abandon regardless of the circumstances.

At Brazos Santiago, meanwhile, the Yankees knew not only about General Lee's surrender at Appomattox Court House, but also of General Johnston's surrender at the Bennett House in North Carolina. Unlike many of Colonel Ford's soldiers, these Yankees were duty-bound by their dependence on government transportation home from their island exile.

Clearly, garrison service on the island was no easy duty for young soldiers, especially with the war almost at an end. To these young Federals far from home and family, Brazos Santiago was a hot, sand-swept hellhole without the cantinas, senoritas, or tequila that made Brownsville and Matamoros infamous. Even Colonel Ford, the conqueror of this remote island in 1861, lamented that "the Brazos" was located in the middle of nowhere. What is more, he continued, the island was unsuitable for human habitation: "[T]here is no water on Brazos Island, save beach water of an unhealthy character— there are no rations—it is isolated."[3]

For good reason, the Federal garrison held much contempt for remote Brazos Santiago, despising their bleak existence. One Union officer, stationed on the island after his journey by steamboat across the Gulf of Mexico in

1865, scribbled in a letter to his wife that "I am finally on land once more, if the low, sandy beach, destitute of trees, shrubs or grass, can be called land." At least in theory, Brazos Santiago needed to be garrisoned to watch the mouth of the Rio Grande, to maintain a symbolic Union presence on Texas soil, and to blockade the Rio Grande and Brownsville.

For these young Hoosier soldiers and the black infantrymen from Missouri, this parched, unforgiving land seemed almost an alien landscape. Despite the Gulf waters stretching eastward as far as the eye could see, the greatest complaint among the Union garrison was the lack of fresh water. One Federal officer, complained that "if you dig down you obtain water, but it is as salt[y] as the sea." Such deplorable conditions caused numerous deaths from disease among the Brazos Santiago garrison during the last year of the war. On January 2, 1865, Pvt. Urbano Hinojosa, 2nd Texas Union Cavalry, was one such unfortunate victim, dying of chronic dysentery.[4]

But the ravages of disease were considerably less than that suffered by the 62nd USCT when it was stationed in the hellish swamps and bayou country of Louisiana. Unlike their Texas Rebel counterparts who went home after learning of General Lee's surrender, the African Americans garrisoning Brazos Santiago could not ride off into the sunset. With the Trans-Mississippi Theater yet to officially surrender, the news of Appomattox brought no hope of an immediate return home.

In fact, the African Americans of the 62nd were the least likely among the garrison to walk away from Brazos Santiago. For these men, their war would not close until slavery was destroyed. The risks were greater for the black soldiers of "the Brazos." Venturing from Brazos Santiago and onto Texas soil might yet result in capture and then a quick reintroduction into slavery.

On the mainland, never had Colonel Ford's domain along the Rio Grande remained so quiet. With the war all but over, the colonel became less vigilant. Ford's unwariness was justified for several reasons. Both the March 1865 truce with General Wallace and the surrender of Rebel armies brought a calm to the Lower Valley not seen since 1861. It was clear that the bloodiest war in American history was now fading away like the elusive dream of Southern independence. By this time, the news of Confederate surrenders in Virginia and North Carolina only reconfirmed the wisdom of the Point Isabel truce.

Since the initial establishment of the agreement, Colonel Ford had issued a large number of furloughs. Without a present threat, he had also dispersed his troopers over a wide area so that they and their horses could subsist in a drought-ravished, arid countryside. The sprawling bottomlands along the Rio Grande were green and luxuriant, with plenty of waterfowl and wildlife.

Combined with the fact that more than 200 Confederate desertions had culled the Southern ranks and that the Point Isabel truce had ended the fighting, Colonel Ford now commanded fewer than 300 Texas cavalrymen to protect the hundreds of miles of Confederate territory by the second week of May 1865.[5]

But despite their small numbers, the remaining Texas Rebels stood solidly beside Colonel Ford largely out of personal loyalty to him. These tough cavalrymen would only lay down their rifles if the colonel himself stopped fighting. If Ford chose to once again ride into Mexico to wage war south of the border against either the Mexicans or the French, or east to Brazos Santiago to tangle with the Yankees, then these Rio Grande country Rebels would follow him. This war would only end for them when Colonel Ford said that it was finally over.

Without exaggeration, Captain Carrington, a company commander of Colonel Giddings's Battalion, summarized that at this time Colonel Ford was

> idolized by his men [and] many of them had served under him in his Indian campaigns . . . they knew his bravery and his unsleeping vigilance [and] they knew his great prudence and his unyielding perseverance in accomplishing his purposes. He had fought more than a score of battles and never failed to achieve a decided victory. On a more extended sphere of action he would have been the [Marshal Joachim] Murat [Napoléon's most dashing and effective cavalry commander] of the Confederacy. His tactics were peculiar [unorthodox and innovative in the manner of General Forrest]. He knew nearly every man in his command; he studied the character and the ability of every officer [and] he believed that his cavalry in a fierce charge was invincible. Hence, whenever the right time arrived, he hurled squadron after squadron of his troopers upon the foe with irresistible force.[6]

Even after the news came of General Lee's surrender at Appomattox, Colonel Ford's Rebels remained eager to pay back the Texas Yankees. In this sense, the war in the Lower Rio Grande Valley was far from over. These old animosities continued to exist, if not thrive, regardless of what happened far to the east at Appomattox Court House or anywhere else for that matter. On Brazos Santiago, the Union forces continued to represent the most hated aspects of enemy soldiery to the thinking of Colonel Ford's Texans: African Americans and "renegade" Texans.

Worst of all to Colonel Ford's men, some Texas bluecoats were in fact deserters from Confederate ranks. These men were the epitome of turncoats and traitors to the Texas Rebels. Colonel Ford had issued his call in December 1863 to form "the Cavalry of the West" with a rallying cry to destroy this "unholy" alliance. He wrote that "the people of the West [will] turn out [to oppose that] mongrel force of Abolitionists, negroes, plundering Mexicans, and perfidious renegades."[7]

Such concerns of the Texas Confederates were not completely unwarranted, especially if these troops served as occupation forces during the forthcoming Reconstruction. To the Texas Rebels, black soldiers on Texas soil yet fueled their greatest fear, the possible nightmare of slave insurrection unleashed upon the land. As throughout the antebellum period, the fear of slave revolt was a constant obsession of the Southern people—from Texas to Virginia—with a large population of slaves in their midst. And in regard to the rumor that free blacks were to be colonized in Texas, the Southerners' obsessive fear of free African Americans also seemed to be well founded. Free blacks often sparked slave uprisings. Denmark Vesey, a free black, led an aborted slave revolt of an estimated 9,000 slaves in Charleston, South Carolina, in 1822. That lesson, along with the 1831 Nat Turner revolt in Virginia, and other smaller slave insurrections were reminders to Southerners of an ever-present threat.

Such lessons were not forgotten by the Texans and other Southerners, with four million potential black rebels in their midst. But, what the Texans of the Civil War generation had seemingly forgotten was that, from the earliest days of Texas's colonization, blacks were an ally. During the 1820s, Stephen Austin had emphasized to the Mexican government that the presence of slavery—and its accompanying black manpower—in the northern Mexican province of Texas was absolutely necessary for the "defense" of the colony's isolated frontier against Indian raiders. And during the Texan attack that captured Goliad in October 1835, a free black by the name of Samuel McCulloch, fell wounded while charging beside white Texans in the struggle for Texas independence.[8]

Despite these deep-seated fears and hatred, the Point Isabel truce managed to keep the Texans at Brownsville and the advanced outpost at Palmito Ranch, and the Yankees at Brazos Santiago separated, despite coexisting within easy striking distance of each other. In this sense, the war's end meant little in regard to what fueled this localized ethnic and regional conflict, which often transcended even the sectional issues of the Civil War itself.

Perhaps it was appropriate that the last battle of the Civil War was about to be fought on the banks of the Rio Grande. From the beginning of the conflict, the Civil War in south and west Texas often revolved around that river and the trade that crossed it. In truth, what both sides had been fighting for in Texas for years was the symbolic heart and soul of not only the Lower Valley but also of south and west Texas: the Rio Grande River.

This sluggish watercourse winding through the Texas borderlands was the lifeblood to this arid region. What is more, the river had also served as the cultural, social, agricultural, economic, and commercial artery for four peoples—the native Americans, the Spanish, the Mexicans, and the latecomers, the Anglos—during more than ten centuries of strife. Despite the fact that the Rio Grande would have been classified by Easterners as merely a stream instead of a river, this historic waterway was nevertheless "great" in terms of the importance of its impact on the history of the people of four cultures who had depended on the river for their survival.

The Rio Grande descended from a northern region to flow more than 2,000 miles southward before emptying into the Gulf of Mexico. The meandering passage of the river was in many ways symbolic of life's journey itself, while easing leisurely through this untamed land of the Southwest frontier: a promising birth amid the bounty of the southern Colorado mountains, before churning for hundreds of miles through the broad expanses of rolling hills, mesas, plateaus, basins, and wide valleys and deserts, until reaching the coastal sand plains bordering the Gulf of Mexico.

Here, at long last, the Rio Grande's passage now became easier across the flatlands of the coastal plain just before meeting the blue expanse of the Gulf: the end of the journey for the second longest river system in the United States, after the Mississippi and Missouri Rivers. General Grant described that the Rio Grande, "like the Mississippi, flows through a rich alluvial valley in the most meandering manner, running towards all points of the compass at times within a few miles."[9]

For hundreds of miles, the Rio Grande, sometimes blue-green but more often dark and murky, rolled relentlessly onward like the push westward of the American nation. While the American republic had expanded westward and then southward to the Rio Grande, the Rio Grande, as from time immemorial, had continued southeastward to meet the march of destiny during the 1820s, when colonizing settlers from the United States first settled in Texas.[10]

But by May 1865, what was now at stake in this struggle was more than simply possession of the Rio Grande. Perhaps the battle of Palmito Ranch was the result primarily of simple greed and ambition long after the Civil War's idealism and romanticism had vanished forever. Indeed, the upcoming clash in Cameron County might have been all about gaining possession of the thousands of bales of cotton in storage at Brownsville.

Quite possibly, Colonel Barrett might have been motivated to order an advance from Brazos Santiago in an effort to capture Brownsville and its riches, with the backing of Union authorities and cotton speculators. By this time, these "victors" were eager to reap the spoils of war by becoming wealthy in the name of saving the Union before the war ended. Even Colonel Ford possessed a stake in this vast cotton fortune. He maintained longtime connections with the commercial and cotton interests of the firm of Stillman, King, and Kenedy.

Young Colonel Barrett, like some other Union commanders in Confederate territory, perhaps now viewed an opportunity in capturing thousands of bales of cotton at Brownsville, representing more than a million dollars. Clearly, Confederate cotton was a tempting target for an ambitious colonel who made only a few Yankee greenbacks per month. It is not known but perhaps Colonel Barrett, who was foremost a political officer, viewed the capture of the cotton surplus as an economic means to support his lofty political aspirations after the war.

Throughout the conflict along the border, the thousands of bales of cotton flowing across the Rio Grande year after year were white gold. For Confederate troops fighting against the odds in the Trans-Mississippi, this invaluable resource was the most important means for securing the bountiful supplies, horses, medicines, war matériel, and weaponry that kept them struggling against Union armies for years.

In the war along the border, Colonel Ford had long supplied his men by this means. He sold cotton to provide what the Confederate government could not distribute to his troops in the remote Rio Grande Valley. The selling of bales of cotton had served as the lifeblood of the agricultural Southern nation, supporting its war effort. Cotton brought the South tons of invaluable foodstuffs, Enfield rifles from Britain and even weapons from Northern firms, ammunition, medicines, and textiles to fuel the Confederate war machine on both sides of the Mississippi.

Bales of cotton transported south across the Rio Grande into Mexico bypassed the Federal naval blockade to partly negate the Mississippi River's loss in economic terms. Transported by ships from neutral Mexican ports such as Bagdad or Matamoros, the cotton eventually made its way across the Atlantic to eager European buyers. During this struggle along the Rio Grande, therefore, cotton often became a primary bone of contention because the Southern war effort in the isolated Trans-Mississippi was dependent upon the vital commodity.

To Colonel Ford, the piles of 500-pound bales of cotton at Brownsville represented much more than money. He saw this cotton reserve as the hope for a brighter future. By this time, Ford's ambition was to embark upon the joint Union-Confederate expedition to northern Mexico—a forgotten explanation as to why the upcoming clash at Palmito Ranch was destined to erupt more than a month after General Lee's surrender at Appomattox Court House.

In this sense, the upcoming battle along the Rio Grande was more important for the South than other battles late in the war. By rekindling the dream of Manifest Destiny, both Texas and the dying Confederacy could perhaps wipe away some of the bitterness of the past four years with a joint U.S.-Mexican expedition against the monarchist French in Mexico. And, as Colonel Ford believed, such a united effort would have led to a healing process rather than the harshness of Reconstruction. Striking into northern Mexico meant the South's and Texas's redemption.

In this respect, Colonel Ford and his troopers were prepared to fight for a brighter future for both themselves and the United States. It now seemed to many people in both the North and the South that "a cure [was now] waiting [for the splintered American nation] at the Rio Grande."

Gen. Phil Sheridan shortly declared that "six months of campaigning by Virginians and Mississippians and Texans, shoulder to shoulder with New Englanders and Westerners . . . might be wonderfully reconstructive in its effect and reunite our fractured young national bones faster than any other treatment could possibly do." Clearly, "Old Rip" Ford agreed with the Union general's views.

Consequently, this unique strategic situation along the border and possible Union-Confederate effort in northern Mexico now made the Rio Grande the most important river in the Confederacy. The Rio Grande also made the Brazos Santiago Pass, the vital gateway to the Gulf of Mexico, important for the same reasons.

Already, the large volume of trade that passed through this "backdoor of the Confederacy" had transformed Brownsville and its sister city across the Rio Grande, Matamoros—the only neutral port open to the Confederacy— into thriving boom towns. In reality, Matamoros, Mexico, was now a key Confederate port. By this time, Matamoros was, "to the rebellion west of the Mississippi [what] New York [City was] to the United States."[11]

After the commander of Brazos Santiago and the 34th Indiana, Col. Robert B. Jones, resigned in early April 1865, the second week of May 1865 presented Colonel Barrett, who succeeded Colonel Jones, with his last chance to achieve glory. He had arrived on Brazos Santiago on February 24, 1865, eager to make a name for himself before the war's end. And glory could not be won by adhering to a two-month-old unofficial truce that was not of Colonel Barrett's making.

In February 1865, Barrett had reported that no Rebel threat existed to his Brazos Santiago garrison. He consequently requested permission from department headquarters to advance upon Brownsville and capture the city. But his request had been "emphatically refused" by his superiors who knew that they must keep this overly ambitious but inexperienced commander in check. Colonel Barrett, however, was not deterred by the decisions of his more sensible superiors.

At this time, the capture of Brownsville seemed like an easy undertaking to Colonel Barrett. Already a mistaken report had filtered into Colonel Barrett's headquarters that the Confederates were preparing to evacuate Brownsville and retire northward to the vicinity of Corpus Christi. Brownsville, therefore, seemed ripe for the picking. Brownsville's capture would be the highlight of this eager young colonel's career, and he lusted for the chance to win glory.

Taking advantage of independent command and with his superiors far away, Colonel Barrett now saw the strategic and tactical situation along the Rio Grande as a golden opportunity to be exploited by aggressive leadership. This young commander imagined that all the North would soon learn about his military ability.

This was an aggressive decision by Colonel Barrett. An ambitious commander exiled in the most remote corner of the Confederacy, who had been previously unable to make a name for himself, he realized that he had to take action now before it was too late. The capture of Brownsville, especially if it was about to be evacuated by the Rebels as reports seemed to indicate, and finally stopping Confederate trade from Mexico might open the doors for future military advancement or the springboard to a political career.

Hence, the young man jumped at his last chance for national recognition before the war abruptly ended. In the words of an officer of the 34th Indiana, Colonel Barrett was eager "to establish for himself some notoriety before the war closed." If Brownsville was about to be evacuated, then perhaps only a slight show of force would be enough to capture the city. With around a thousand well-armed and trained Federals on Brazos Santiago, glory seemingly lay waiting.

The latest reports to Colonel Barrett's headquarters seemed an accurate assessment of the military situation in Brownsville and along the Lower Rio Grande. Many Texas Rebels garrisoning Brownsville and the vicinity had already deserted. Colonel Barrett knew as much from the numerous reports that continued to filter into his headquarters. The reports indicated the deteriorating condition among the Confederate garrisons of Brownsville and the Western Subdistrict of Texas. For all practical purposes, the conflict along the Rio Grande had concluded months before with the Slaughter-Wallace truce of March 1865.

In many respects, these reports were quite accurate. With a relative handful of Yankees bottled up on Brazos Santiago, the Texas Confederates suffered from the loss of substantial manpower by desertion and dispersal. The rumors of Confederate organizational disarray were nothing new. The first reliable intelligence of the full extent of the collapse in Rebel vigilance, preparedness, and military capabilities reached Brazos Santiago in early 1865. Col. Robert B. Jones, at the time commanding Brazos Santiago, became aware of the Confederates' deteriorating situation.

Colonel Barrett was encouraged by other factors that made him optimistic about capturing Brownsville. General Slaughter hardly posed either a threat or deterrent to Brownsville's capture. Slaughter possessed little combat experience or ability. He was a perfect Rebel commander for such a sleepy, backwater assignment as garrisoning the quiet Rio Grande Valley. In short, General Slaughter was not a fighter.[12]

To the Rebels of the Rio Grande Valley, Colonel Ford was their leader. In the words of one Texas Rebel, "[General] Slaughter was called commander but John S. Ford in reality led and ordered our force."[13]

Unlike the energetic Colonel Ford, General Slaughter, a fossilized Mexican War veteran whose only competence had been demonstrated as Gen. Braxton Bragg's inspector general in 1862, was not the type of officer to take the initiative, even if he possessed overwhelming numbers. As one observer noted, Slaughter's "military capacity seems to have been limited to writing critical reports about his subordinates." And that was exactly why this rusty old Virginia cavalier was the ideal doorman for the job of guarding this "back door of the Confederacy," a position calling for little leadership ability or initiative.

General Slaughter's ineffective leadership was obvious to experienced men of action. As early as February 1865, Colonel Jones had learned from various reports, in his words, that General Slaughter's command in Brownsville was "in a demoralized state." The ever-worsening condition among the Confederates was not hard for Union commanders to understand considering General Slaughter's leadership failings combined with the fact that the war was nearly over.

During the same period before the news arrived of the surrender at Appomattox, General Slaughter reported that "fully one-fourth" of his force was ready to forsake the cause and go home. Then, the news of the surrenders of Generals Lee, Johnston, and Taylor created widespread "apathy and indifference [and] the Army of the Trans-Mississippi was in spirit crushed." And what little remained of General Slaughter's Western Subdistrict of Texas was assured to shortly crumble.

It was no exaggeration when Colonel Jones, whom Lt. Col. Robert Morrison replaced as the Indiana regiment's commander, concluded that his forces then garrisoned on Brazos Santiago "could occupy [Brownsville] any day." Colonel Jones requested permission to advance on Brownsville from headquarters but received a negative response. Quite likely, it seemed like what little was left of the Rebel "rabble" would probably just give up without a fight.

Only a mere handful of ragged Texas Rebels now stood between Colonel Barrett and the fulfillment of his visions of glory. In addition, he knew that the Confederates at Brownsville had already learned of General Lee's surrender. The Rebel defenders, therefore, would probably flee westward up the Rio Grande instead of fighting.

By the second week of May, Colonel Barrett was not about to let this opportunity slip through his hands. Now that Colonel Jones had resigned and he commanded Brazos Santiago, he was determined "to do great things" and this now meant Brownsville's capture.

Seemingly all that Colonel Barrett now had to do was to push forward to scatter the remaining handful of Texas Rebels between him and Brownsville, before raising "Old Glory" above the largest city on the Rio Grande. This seemed like a good plan, and made sense except for one seemingly insignificant detail that the young colonel failed to factor into his ambitious scheme of achieving glory: the determination of a grizzled frontier warrior who was old enough to be his father, "Old Rip" Ford.[14]

This realization would have made little difference to the young colonel, however. Most of all, Barrett "was obsessed by a desire to gain some recognition before leaving the army." From 1861–64, he had not been presented with any opportunity to prove his abilities or win glory. A successful civil engineer before the war, the New York–born Theodore Harvey Barrett began the war as a lieutenant of the 10th Minnesota and then as captain in the 9th Minnesota. During the crushing of the bloody Sioux uprising that erupted in Minnesota during the summer of 1862, Barrett engaged in his first combat in September. But he discovered that there was no glory in fighting the rampaging bands of Sioux. Thanks to political connections rather than military performance or tactical ability, he served on the Northwest frontier until winning command of his 62nd USCT in December 1863. He then traveled to St. Louis, Missouri, to take charge of the black soldiers.

The boring and unrewarding occupation duty in the mud, rain, and cypress swamps of Louisiana also failed to present Barrett with an opportunity for either advancement or glory. While he treated his men with equality, he nevertheless utilized the services of an African American servant, a private, which was a common practice among many high-ranking Union officers. Barrett briefly commanded a black brigade of the Corps d'Afrique at Port Hudson, Louisiana, in March 1864. Then, at age thirty and by virtue of a combination of political connections and seniority, Colonel Barrett officially assumed command of all the forces at Brazos Santiago on April 17, 1865.

Fresh-faced and unwrinkled, Barrett stood in striking contrast to his counterpart, the gray-bearded, weather-beaten, and illness-emaciated Colonel

Ford. Unlike Colonel Barrett, Ford was toughened from a hard life on the frontier. In addition, he possessed more than thirty years of fighting on both sides of the Rio Grande. Despite frequently being racked by a variety of diseases and sickness, which were the legacies of the Mexican War and his many years of arduous service on the Western border, "Old Rip" was as hard-nosed when sick as most men were when healthy.

Young Colonel Barrett was not to be spared from the unmerciful ravages of disease. The surgeon of the 62nd wrote from the swamps of Louisiana at the end of August 1864 that Barrett was stricken with typhoid fever and jaundice. Employing forceful language, the surgeon advised that "an *immediate* change of climate is *absolutely* necessary to save [his] life." Once he was away from the Louisiana swamps, Brazos Santiago restored Colonel Barrett's health. "The Brazos" had a comparable affect on the overall health of the entire 62nd.

In contrast with his wily old Rebel opponent, Colonel Barrett was vain and a dreamer: wet behind the ears as both a leader of men and a combat officer. But by May 1865, the Federal colonel felt he knew all he needed to know. But in terms of tactics, Colonel Barrett had much to learn: what Colonel Ford had been teaching his enemies for a quarter of a century. The confident Colonel Barrett, however, held nothing but contempt for Colonel Ford and his threadbare Texas boys, committing the ultimate folly of underestimating his opponent. This was the kind of psychological advantage that Ford would soon exploit to the fullest.

Despite the approach of a fast-moving storm blowing in from the Gulf, Colonel Barrett decided to fulfill his ambition of advancing upon Brownsville. Without seeking advice or counsel from his subordinates or orders from headquarters, the eager young colonel ordered Lieutenant Colonel Branson, the commander of the 62nd USCT, to take 250 troops from Brazos Santiago by steamboat to Point Isabel and the Texas mainland.

Even though the truce between blue and gray was still firmly in place, Colonel Barrett initiated the first steps of an unauthorized advance upon Brownsville more than a month after General Lee's capitulation at Appomattox. Selecting these African American troops for the assignment was an easy choice for Colonel Barrett. He early realized their worth and was intent on giving his "pet" regiment the opportunity to win laurels before the war ended. Such a demonstration by his black troops would reflect favorably upon his own leadership.

During the opening movements of the operation on the Texas mainland, Lieutenant Colonel Branson's mission was initially to conduct a probe toward Brownsville: the first phase of a larger plan of advancing westward to capture the city. But by launching his expedition, Colonel Barrett would break the long-standing truce, which had been respected by both sides for two months.

At first, Barrett remained cautious, taking into account his own lack of leadership experience at independent command. Hence, this initial advance from "the Brazos" was only a probe to test Confederate strength before he made the final decision to pursue his ultimate goal, Brownsville. Colonel Barrett later claimed that his intention of moving toward Brownsville was to secure, "forage for the command, and also to capture a herd of horses" grazing near Point Isabel for the unmounted men of the 2nd Texas Cavalry.

While Colonel Barrett felt that much could be accomplished, he also realized that defeat would bring disgrace instead of glory, especially after he violated the truce. Despite putting faith in an earlier intelligence report that a Union advance westward from Brazos Santiago and toward Brownsville "would [not] meet with any opposition," Colonel Barrett remained hesitant with his future now at stake.

As if an ill portent of developments to come for Union fortunes, a raging storm sweeping over the Gulf became more severe in the humid darkness of May 11. Things began to go badly from the beginning of this first stage of the Union advance.

The African American troops at the fort on the north end of Brazos Santiago, were roused early that morning by beating drums. In the pitch blackness, at 4:00 A.M., Lieutenant Colonel Branson assembled his soldiers of the 62nd USCT in neat ranks and then marched them to the landing on the island's north end almost directly across the Laguna Madre from Point Isabel. Each of Lieutenant Colonel Branson's 250 black soldiers carried 100 rounds in leather cartridge boxes and rations for an expedition of seven days. Already burdened by their heavier-than-normal loads, the African Americans stood in formation ready to finally push forward to the Texas mainland.

Contrary to his later statements, the amount of extensive preparations indicated that Colonel Barrett had already planned a lengthy expedition—a push all the way to Brownsville—by the 62nd. He was little concerned that these troops had yet to receive their baptismal fire.

The planned crossing of the wide Laguna Madre to Point Isabel would not be made as scheduled, however. The steamboat to be used to ferry the troops across Laguna Madre became inoperable at the last moment. With no way to cross and with no other alternative to the steamer, Colonel Barrett's optimistic plans for landing troops on the Texas mainland had to be canceled. With the storm growing more severe, Lieutenant Colonel Branson then ordered his men to return to their tented encampment with Colonel Barrett's initial approval. Clearly, this was a dismal start for the Federal advance toward Brownsville and the fulfillment of Colonel Barrett's ambitions.

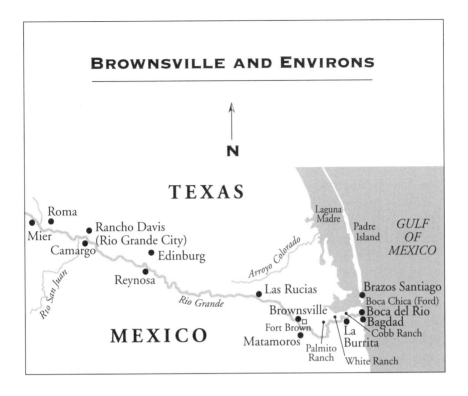

Barrett, however, changed his mind before the end of day. He gradually become more frustrated by the delay. The young colonel was determined to launch his expedition and would not be denied; he refused to forsake his plan for an advance. Rather than aborting the seemingly ill-timed expedition, he ordered the Union soldiers to immediately cross the Boca Chica Pass in small boats at the lower, or southern, end of the island instead of at Brazos Santiago's northern edge. Barrett's snap decision ran contrary to his later-stated purposes for launching the expedition: to obtain forage and horses for the command.

At long last Lieutenant Colonel Branson led the Federal column southward along the white sand beach on the eastern edge of Brazos Santiago to embark upon their mission just after sunset on May 11. The delay provided time for Colonel Barrett to strengthen the column with fifty men of the 2nd Texas Cavalry and a pair of six-mule teams to haul munitions and supplies. Reducing the heavy loads the men were forced to carry on their backs was a smart decision. In addition, Barrett ordered the number of rations carried to be reduced by nearly one-half to enough for only three days, further lightening the soldiers' loads. Since they would now be gaining the Texas mainland below Brazos Santiago, they had no need for the extra rations.

Amid the blinding rainstorm and darkness that continued to surge westward from the raging Gulf, the Yankees marched south several miles through the wet and clinging sand, while the surf roared in the darkness just to their left. After boarding skiffs, the Federals rowed south through the dark waters of the Boca Chica, a narrow inlet from the Gulf of Mexico separating the south end of Brazos Santiago from the Texas mainland below Point Isabel. The normally easy crossing was made more precarious by the storm's severity and took hours though, fortunately, no Union soldiers were lost.

With some understatement, Lieutenant Colonel Branson never forgot how "owing to a severe storm the crossing was with great difficulty effected." After paddling across the rough, windswept waters of Boca Chica, Lieutenant Colonel Branson and his soldiers landed several miles north of the mouth of the Rio Grande, southeast of Brownsville. By 9:30 P.M., Lieutenant Colonel Branson's task force was firmly emplaced on the Texas mainland just below the southern end of Brazos Santiago.[15]

The next morning, after a chilly night in the wetness, more than 300 Yankees pushed southwest, following the telegraph lines stretching from Boca Chica to the Brownsville Road. Leading the way was Capt. Fred E. Miller and his Company F of the 62nd. Commanding the skirmishers of Company F, Captain Miller was assisted by a trusty local guide who was familiar with the area.

Then, after pushing several miles southwestward across the coastal plain, the column turned west on the Brownsville Road to advance parallel to the Rio Grande and toward White's Ranch, after gaining the main road leading from the Gulf Coast to Brownsville. Finally, the skies cleared, and the dark clouds parted to reveal partial sunshine. A rising sun began to heat the flat coastal lands bordering the Gulf of Mexico. The marching troops in the blue ranks hoped that their wet uniforms would soon dry. Shortly the mid-May sun was blazing. The column eased through the prairie lands and sand flats of Cameron County, now refreshed by the storm.

Mounted at the head of the column, Lieutenant Colonel Branson led 250 men of the 62nd USCT and around fifty unmounted troopers of the 2nd Texas Cavalry, under 1st Lt. James W. Hancock, farther into the Texas mainland. Slogging onward with muskets on shoulders like infantrymen, these wet troopers from Texas resented their horseless condition. The mostly Hispanic cavalrymen, who had originally enlisted in the cavalry to avoid this kind of foot soldiering, were understandably disgruntled over their unexpected conversion to infantry status.

Lieutenant Colonel Branson had come a long way in this war since first enlisting as a private in the Enrolled Missouri Militia (EMM), Company I,

28th Regiment, in Linn County, Missouri, during late August 1862. The EMM's role was to pacify war-torn Missouri, a state that had been embroiled for years in savage guerrilla warfare on a scale unseen anywhere else in the nation. At that time, Private Branson served without either distinction or promotion in Capt. Adam Miller's Osage County, Missouri, provisional company of local EMM troops, seeing no serious action in his home state.

Like Colonel Barrett, Lieutenant Colonel Branson possessed little leadership or combat experience before becoming a ranking officer of the 62nd USCT at Benton Barracks on December 27, 1863. He won promotion to the rank of lieutenant colonel only on March 13, 1865. The sudden Union advance upon Brownsville was Branson's first real leadership challenge during an active operation. Never before had Branson commanded as many troops in the field as now.

For the first time as commander of an independent force, he was leading a large number of troops into hostile country. Even worse, young Lieutenant Colonel Branson was now on his own, distancing himself farther from immediate support. As if unconcerned, meanwhile, Colonel Barrett remained safely behind in his Brazos Santiago headquarters, allowing his twenty-three-year-old rookie lieutenant colonel to conduct the initial phase of the expedition with untested troops.

As directed by Colonel Barrett, Lieutenant Colonel Branson's first objective was to reach White's Ranch, southwest of Boca Chica and northeast of Palmito Ranch. Recent intelligence had indicated that only sixty-five Rebels held this easternmost advanced Rebel position guarding Brownsville's right flank. The White's Ranch outpost was the closest Confederate position to Brazos Santiago.

Despite his inexperience, Lieutenant Colonel Branson demonstrated a fair degree of tactical ability. After landing on the mainland, he advanced in a "long circuitous" route toward White's Ranch to surprise the Rebels. When finally near the ranch, Branson divided his command for the final approach. Captain Miller's Company F first swung north three-quarters of a mile, then doubled back west of the ranch, and then turned east to slip below the Rebel position to establish a blocking position on the south. Lieutenant Colonel Branson, meanwhile, closed in from the north, east, and west to complete the encirclement.

After a stealthy approach under cover of the dense stands of chaparral to surround the Confederate outpost, the Federals neared their objective. With the target within easy range and the Rebel outpost surrounded on every side, the Yankees charged upon the main buildings of White's Ranch during the early morning hours of May 12. When Colonel Branson's men searched the small cluster of buildings seven miles southwest of the southern end of Brazos

Santiago near the Brownsville Road, they discovered that the Texans of Colonel Giddings's cavalry battalion "had been gone a day or two," wrote a disappointed, but perhaps also relieved, Lieutenant Colonel Branson.

The recent intelligence report proved false. But where were the Rebels now? Had they retired all the way to Brownsville? For that matter, was Brownsville itself evacuated? Had these ragamuffins deserted and gone home after learning of General Lee's surrender at Appomattox? As Colonel Barrett envisioned, perhaps Lieutenant Colonel Branson and his bluecoat troops could march into Brownsville unopposed to raise the Stars and Stripes over the city.

Meanwhile, while the Yankees demonstrated an unexpected aggressiveness in overrunning White's Ranch, Capt. William N. Robinson and his Rebel soldiers at nearby Palmito Ranch, southwest of White's Ranch and just below, or south of, the Brownsville Road, were anything but ready for action. These Texans continued to believe that the long-standing Wallace-Slaughter truce was still in effect. With Colonel Giddings on leave, Captain Robinson was now in charge of these troopers of the veteran battalion. Like other Confederate leaders, including Colonel Ford, Captain Robinson was about to be surprised by the Yankees' advance from Brazos Santiago.[16]

Initially the commander of Company A, Colonel Giddings's Battalion, Captain Robinson came from good Texas stock. He was a proud son of the Texas Revolution. His father, James W. Robinson, had served as the acting Texas governor during the struggle against Mexico. Like his son, Robinson senior was an outspoken critic of Sam Houston's Fabian tactics of defensive maneuvering before he took the offensive to turn the tide at San Jacinto. In much the same way, the younger Robinson denounced Governor Houston's Unionism during the present revolutionary struggle. James Robinson had served as the first lieutenant governor of Texas from 1835–36. And now his son, wearing an officer's uniform of Confederate gray, continued the family tradition of repelling the invaders of Texas soil.[17]

After overrunning White's Ranch, meanwhile, Lieutenant Colonel Branson began to cipher out the tactical situation. From the information gained from his scouts or the civilian guide, Branson learned that Captain Robinson's Rebels were now stationed at Palmito Ranch. The lieutenant colonel now realized "that the enemy had moved camp further up the [Rio Grande] to Palmetto [sic] Ranch, and now it was too late to get there before daylight." Both Branson and his men felt the frustration with the missed opportunity.[18]

Just beyond White's Ranch, located roughly halfway between the Gulf Coast and Palmito Ranch, Lieutenant Colonel Branson canceled his plans to push onward to strike Palmito Ranch—established as a Confederate position in February 1864 and formerly known as Camp Slaughter. With no threat or Rebel soldier in sight, he decided that it was now time to rest his weary men before advancing upon Palmito Ranch, and perhaps even Brownsville, at first daylight. By doing so, he took a wise precaution. Not taking any chances on the Texas mainland, Branson now ordered Capt. Harrison Dubois with Companies G and H, of the 62nd, to picket the front in a long skirmish line, while his weary men slept in peace.[19]

As Lieutenant Colonel Branson explained his plan: "[O]wing to the exhausted condition of the men I could not reach Palmetto [*sic*] Ranch before daylight to surprise it, and therefore hid my command [around 3:00 A.M.] in a thicket and among weeds on the banks of the Rio Grande one mile and a half [below and southwest of] White [*sic*] Ranch, where we remained undiscovered until [around 5:30 A.M.], when persons on the Mexican shore [across the river to the south] seeing us started to give the alarm to the rebels [upriver at Palmito Ranch]. At the same time soldiers of the Imperial [French] Army were marching up that bank of the river."[20]

Lieutenant Colonel Branson's task force was discovered by French Imperial troops, who controlled Matamoros. Finely uniformed and well trained, the Frenchmen were marching along the Rio Grande. But Lieutenant Colonel Branson was now confronting a more pressing problem than the French: Captain Robinson and his band of Rebels.

By this time, Branson was determined to catch the Rebels at Palmito Ranch by surprise at daybreak. He hoped to hit the usually vigilant Confederates before they received the warning. Captain Robinson and his cavalrymen might well be in their beds when the Federals struck.

After a restless night in the cool thickets along the Rio Grande, the Yankees were up early on the morning of May 12 and were soon on the move toward Captain Robinson's outpost, with Captain Miller's reliable skirmishers of Company F leading the way. Without hesitation so as not to lose the element of surprise, Lieutenant Colonel Branson hurried his troops westward along the Brownsville Road. Less than an hour after beginning the march, Captain Miller reported the presence of Rebel scouts along the main road. Lieutenant Colonel Branson, consequently, also ordered Company H out as skirmishers to protect the advance and reinforce Company F.

Then, swinging left off the main road leading to Brownsville, the Federals turned southwest at the head of the river's wide bend, which curved southward and toward the main house and outbuildings of Palmito Ranch. Just southeast of the Brownsville Road, these buildings stood about halfway between the head and the narrow neck of the bend. Lieutenant Colonel Branson led his troops rapidly toward the still unalerted Confederate position. Eager

PALMITO RANCH
MAY 11–12, 1865

```
0          1          2
```
SCALE OF MILES

```
0    5    10
```
SCALE OF MILES

TEXAS

Padre
Island

Brownsville
Palmito
Matamoras Ranch Point Isabel
White's
Ranch

Brazos
Santiago

Boca
Chica

Rio Grande

MEXICO Bagdad

N

May 11 (A.M.):
Branson & 62nd USCT (200 strong)
attempt to cross to Point Isabel

Brazos
Santiago

May 11 (P.M.):
Branson/62nd USCT/2nd TX
(250 strong) cross to Boca Chica

Boca
Chica

May 12 (2 A.M.):
Branson/62nd USCT/2nd TX
surround White's Ranch

White's Ranch

Rio Grande

May 12 (3 A.M.):
Branson/62nd USCT/2nd TX
hide in thickets

MEXICO N Bagdad

for action and armed with new .577 caliber Enfield rifles, the black skirmishers of Companies F and H now led the way toward their first meeting with the Texas Rebels.

Within an hour after Lieutenant Colonel Branson's soldiers first pushed forward, the forces of blue and gray were finally about to clash on the Texas mainland. Thanks to the warning from the Rebel scouts on the road, a handful of Texas pickets in position below White's Ranch was waiting for the Federal advance, which seemed to suddenly appear out of nowhere. These advanced Rebels opened the first fire upon an aggressive enemy that they recently believed was still on the island of Brazos Santiago.

Meanwhile, at the buildings of Palmito Ranch, the sleepy but now alerted garrison of around sixty-five Texas Rebels quickly snatched rifles and shotguns from stacks around smoldering campfires, hurriedly rallying to the call to arms. Breakfast was left uneaten as the Rebels strapped on gear and rushed to grab their frightened horses in the cool of early morning. Despite being startled by the realization that a good many Federals were already upon them, and no doubt angered by the truce violation, Captain Robinson quickly formed his band of cavalrymen.

Like a good guerrilla leader, to avoid detection and mask his small numbers, Robinson led his troopers westward off the road and onto the open prairie of the coastal plain. He then ordered his men into the cover of the thick clusters of chaparral just west of Palmito Ranch and below the San Martin Ranch. Employing the element of surprise, the Texas captain decided to strike first once the Federals marched within close range. Like Colonel Ford, Captain Robinson understood that the best defense was to immediately take the offensive in order to regain the initiative, especially when caught by surprise. Consequently, he encouraged his horse soldiers forward toward a vastly superior force of invading Yankees before the buildings of Palmito Ranch. Despite their small numbers, the yelling Texas cavalrymen advanced northeastward from the thick chaparral like Comanches bent on revenge.

Slowly but stubbornly, the Texans methodically gained ground, battling with a spirit that masked the diminutive size of their force. Robinson sought to gain the initiative by fighting Indian-style from the brush. Robinson's Rebels put up a bold front before overwhelming numbers, loading and firing while steadily advancing toward White's Ranch. The fury of the resistance shocked the bluecoats. Lieutenant Colonel Branson turned cautious, especially now that he only commanded infantry while facing an unknown number of mounted Rebels. To the Yankees, this Rebel force fighting from behind cover seemed too aggressive for its reported size. In fact, Lieutenant Colonel Branson now believed that he was confronted by a greater number of Confederates because of their aggressive tactics.

The Federals' advance toward Palmito Ranch slowed to a crawl, with the Yankees battling their determined opponents on the level prairie. Lieutenant Colonel Branson described that he was engaged in "skirmishing most of the way [south toward Palmito Ranch] with the enemy's cavalry." Against the odds, the Rebels continued to fight from behind good cover, holding their ground as long as possible. But there were simply too many Yankees for Captain Robinson's cavalrymen to handle. They, nevertheless, proved that plenty of fighting spunk remained in this band of Texas Rebels, despite the Confederacy's collapse.

After hot skirmishing for several miles across the flat and bushy prairie lands of Cameron County during five hours of combat, Captain Robinson ordered his cavalrymen to mount up. He decided to abandon Palmito Ranch and withdraw west toward Brownsville. After skirmishing with the Texas Rebels most of the way from White's Ranch to Palmito Ranch, the Yankees finally took possession of Palmito Ranch around noon. Immediately, the Federals began to round up captured Rebel supplies, two horses and four cattle, and three Confederate prisoners—two of whom were too sick to retreat to Brownsville.

Fortunately for Lieutenant Colonel Branson's tactical plan, the "persons" who had first sighted the blue column from south of the Rio Grande had failed to warn Captain Robinson of the Yankee advance in time. The main body of Rebels at Palmito Ranch, consequently, were left unaware of the Federals' advance. Therefore, none of the supply of ten days' rations for almost 200 Rebels could be destroyed by Captain Robinson's men before being forced to retire. Here, in the calm that now surrounded the burning of a crude barracks and other buildings of Palmito Ranch the worn-out Union troops rested. Other soldiers gobbled down both Federal and Rebel rations, and watered and fed their horses from captured forage. Victory for the invaders meant disaster for the owners of Palmito Ranch. Young Atenogenes Orive and other family members watched in horror as their home was consumed in flames.

All the while, the victorious bluecoats basked in the glow of their first success on the Texas mainland. To the rookies of the 62nd USCT, whipping the ragged Texas Rebel cavalry now seemed easy. Surely more Union victories lay on the horizon for them and their commander. No doubt Lieutenant Colonel Branson and his men now expected a triumphant march into Brownsville, after Captain Robinson and his men had vanished into the Texas underbrush.

After destroying the Rebel outpost of Palmito Ranch and burning down the buildings and capturing supplies, Branson ordered his men to shoulder muskets once again. He now continued his advance southward toward the Rio

Grande and the high ground of a combined bluff and hill known collectively as Palmito Hill. Near the riverbank, formed by an old bend in the river, this high point was the most commanding ground in the area, dominating the level plain of the river and overlooking the muddy waters of the Rio Grande.[21]

By continuing to advance, Lieutenant Colonel Branson's inexperience in independent command now became apparent. Emboldened by his incomplete "success" at Palmito Ranch, he ignored his own vulnerability. Indeed, the Union force had already penetrated more than ten miles into Confederate territory and far from "the Brazos" and possible reinforcement. In addition, the men of the 62nd had yet to engage in combat. An inexperienced young officer was leading troops who were as green as himself deeper into Confederate territory. Not only were the Rebels now alerted to Lieutenant Colonel Branson's advance, but the Mexicans and the French also were aware of the Federals' presence. The danger continued to grow for Lieutenant Colonel Branson's command. A task force, isolated and without support, of less than 300 soldiers was simply too small to venture deep into Confederate territory on its own.[22]

Meanwhile, the billowing clouds of black smoke swirling up from the destroyed Confederate outpost at Palmito Ranch only infuriated Captain Robinson. From the cover of the chaparral, he could now only watch the result of Yankee "treachery" in violating the long-standing truce. Robinson now devised a tactical plan based upon the current situation.

From his new position below the San Martin Ranch just west of Palmito Ranch, Captain Robinson prepared to lead his band of cavalrymen back into action. Employing Indian-style tactics of ambush, Captain Robinson signaled for his hidden Texas Rebels to strike, to challenge the Yankees' further advance toward Brownsville.

Lieutenant Colonel Branson and his Yankees were amazed that Captain Robinson had not withdrawn back to Brownsville in panic as expected, after having been overwhelmed by superior numbers. Instead the Rebel captain had maintained a forward position and now led his troopers into action once again. Despite the odds, Captain Robinson continued to skirmish aggressively with the Federal pickets below Palmito Ranch in the early afternoon heat of May 12. The Yankees from Brazos Santiago were now learning that these tough Texas Rebels could not be scared off. Even more, the bluecoats now realized that this war was far from over. It was clear that Captain Robinson and his cavalrymen refused to concede the loss of Palmito Ranch.

Robinson was only beginning to fight on this day. So far, the Texas captain's decisions had been aggressive, and Robinson now continued this bold style of frontier fighting. Without waiting for reinforcements from Brownsville or requesting specific orders from Colonel Ford, Robinson had acted on his own. He had recalled other Rebels from his picket outposts, which stretched westward along the river from White's Ranch to Brownsville, to increase his strength from 65 men to around 190, before returning to engage the Federals and resume the fight. But the captain wanted to do more than simply halt the advance of the Yankee invaders. He wanted to hurl them back to their island exile in the Gulf of Mexico.

After more hard fighting, the initiative was regained by the Rebels. A determined Captain Robinson now threatened to reclaim the lost Palmito Ranch position. Commanding the remaining cavalrymen of the six small companies of Colonel Giddings's battalion, Captain Robinson was proving more than a match for Lieutenant Colonel Branson and his task force. Despite facing a superior and better-equipped adversary, Robinson continued to act with initiative and tactical skill.

By this time, Robinson was determined to recapture his outpost, which he reasoned had been lost to superior numbers, a truce violation, and a surprise attack. This was a personal fight for the young Texas captain. He felt that he had lost his outpost as a result of deception and not tactical brilliance or fair play. As if to emphasize that point of the unethical nature of another clever Yankee ruse, Captain Robinson was intent on reclaiming Palmito Ranch for his own.

With the Texas cavalry swarming around him, Lieutenant Colonel Branson suddenly lost his nerve. Demonstrating his skill as a hard-hitting cavalry commander, Captain Robinson's aggressiveness did the trick. With the Rebels becoming more threatening, Branson suddenly ordered a retreat.

Fearing the worst, the lieutenant colonel dispatched Captain Miller and Company F as skirmishers to protect the withdrawal. As the day continued to heat up along with the intensity of the skirmishing, at around 3:00 P.M. the Yankees began to slowly retrace their steps rearward, or northward. The initial Union success and elation in capturing both White's Ranch and Palmito Ranch were no more. So successful was Captain Robinson's counterattack that the Yankees by this time believed that the Texans had been reinforced by large numbers of Confederates from Brownsville. Lieutenant Colonel Branson now believed that Captain Robinson's band of Rebels represented "a considerable force of the enemy."

In following on the heels of the retreating Federals, Captain Robinson's plucky cavalrymen harassed the rear of the withdrawing blue column in guerrilla fashion. With the Texas cavalrymen buzzing around them like angry bees, the Yankees retreated across the sand flats toward White's Ranch. This rearguard position was now held by the skirmish company [Company H] of the 62nd USCT and a small detail of dismounted horsemen from the 2nd Texas Cavalry.

Hot skirmishing continued across the coastal plain under the blazing sun, with the gunfire escalating along the Rio Grande. In attempting to catch the Rebels by surprise and capturing their advanced outposts, Lieutenant Colonel Branson had only stirred up a hornets' nest of Texans intent on revenge. Captain Miller, commanding the Federal skirmishers, was amazed by the Rebels' continued aggressiveness. He described that "the rebel cavalry [was] following closely and skirmishing continually" with his hard-pressed men of Company F.

To the Texas Rebels' delight, at least one Texan in blue fell seriously wounded in the exchanges of gunfire sweeping through the thickets of underbrush and chaparral. In addition, Captain Robinson's Rebels, who suffered no casualties, captured at least one prisoner, a soldier of the 62nd. The captured Yankee must have been an object of some curiosity. This was the first time that these Texas Confederates, who now confronted their worst fear, had an up close view of an African American soldier in a blue uniform.

It was now clear to the Yankees that Colonel Barrett's initial bid to capture Brownsville had been thwarted by the unexpected agressiveness of an enemy they believed to be badly demoralized. Only the encroaching darkness finally ended the skirmishing, thwarting Captain Robinson's bid to drive the Federals all the way back to the coast.

The chastised white Texas and black Missouri bluecoats now took up defensive positions at the former Confederate outpost at White's Ranch. Here, the Yankees hurriedly dug in for protection against the Rebels, making their stand on the Texas mainland. After hunting for a weakness to exploit, however, Captain Robinson reasoned that the position was simply too strong to attack. Reluctantly, he was forced to end his offensive actions for the day. Shortly thereafter, the weary Texas Rebels, pleased with their accomplishments on this busy day, bivouacked in the thickets above Palmito Ranch, after pickets were assigned to cover the front. Here, after a long day, the Texans basked in their success against the odds, after winning back the initiative and forcing the Federals to retreat.

To keep Colonel Barrett apprised of the new tactical situation, Lieutenant Colonel Branson dispatched a courier from White's Ranch to Colonel Barrett on Brazos Santiago. Barrett was not pleased with the news of the setback, which came as a nasty surprise. The former commander of the 62nd was angry over what had inexplicably happened to his task force. Lieutenant Colonel Branson's retreat sabotaged his visions of victory and a triumphant entry into Brownsville.

Instead of effortlessly capturing the city as planned, Colonel Barrett now had not only violated the truce but also lost the initiative. He perhaps could have justified the breaking of the truce to headquarters and the unauthorized advance with a victory and Brownsville's capture. But now Barrett had nothing to show for his unauthorized advance deep into enemy territory and truce violation, except for three sullen Rebel prisoners, four cows, and two horses—far from the kind of glory envisioned by the ambitious young colonel. This was hardly the type of military achievement that conformed with Colonel Barrett's lofty image of himself as a promising military commander.

THE YANKEES UP THE ANTE

Without hesitation, Colonel Barrett decided to enlarge the scale of operations to salvage victory from defeat. He upped the ante, escalating the scope of his offensive operations on the Texas mainland to a new level that he felt would guarantee success. This inexperienced political officer could not fathom how a handful of threadbare Texas Rebels, who lacked the common sense to know when they were beaten, could have thwarted his bid to take Brownsville. But Barrett was beginning to learn that he was no longer up against the disorganized bands of renegade Sioux in Minnesota.

Colonel Barrett issued new orders upon receiving Branson's report. Around 10:00 P.M., Barrett ordered a full battalion of the 34th Indiana Volunteer Infantry to prepare to move out "in light marching order with one day's rations [and] in one hour" to reinforce Lieutenant Colonel Branson that night. The men of the 34th Indiana would get no sleep tonight, a fact that did nothing to deter Colonel Barrett from ordering a lengthy nighttime advance deep into enemy territory to revitalize this vision of winning glory. Meanwhile, the other Indiana companies, remained on garrison duty.

With the blast of a bugle, the Hoosiers hurriedly assembled on the parade ground of the main Federal encampment at the north end of Brazos Santiago. As could be expected, these hardened veterans were ready for a new challenge on short notice.

After waiting an hour in the darkness, 200 soldiers of the assembled Indiana battalion finally received orders to march south at a brisk pace. The rapid march along the sandy beach in the night was exhausting, even for the Indiana veterans. After embarking on wooden skiffs, the Hoosiers crossed the Boca Chica in the darkness around 1:00 A.M. on the morning of May 13. After passing across the Boca Chica, the Yankee soldiers, with Springfield rifles at sides and in neat ranks, formed in battalion lines.

Here, the bluecoats waited in the darkness for Colonel Barrett's arrival. He was determined to lead his expedition to the kind of success that he had so clearly imagined from his headquarters desk. Despite his eagerness, the colonel for whatever reason kept the assembled Hoosier troops waiting in line during the night "for sometime," wrote a disgruntled Lt. Charles A. Jones.

The lengthy delay did nothing to add to the haughty colonel's popularity among the rank and file.

At last, the colonel from Minnesota made his grand appearance after finally crossing the Boca Chica. Before his assembled troops, Barrett began barking orders to the Hoosiers, as if they were rookies who knew nothing of war. They wondered exactly what the colonel planned to accomplish or demonstrate with the war now all but over. Capt. I. L. Fussell, of Company D, wrote that Colonel Barrett "either without any definite purpose or for some purpose that has never been made clear, ordered a reconnaissance on the mainland toward Brownsville."

Finally, the column under Lieutenant Colonel Morrison moved out into the night, aiming to rendezvous with Lieutenant Colonel Branson's force. On the windy and cool night along the Gulf, the Indiana soldiers marched southwest at a rapid pace across the level coastal plain toward White's Ranch.

All that night, an anxious Colonel Barrett drove the sleepless Indiana soldiers hard, demonstrating little concern for their exhausted condition, keeping them moving briskly without a break. The worn Indiana infantrymen finally reached White's Ranch and Lieutenant Colonel Branson's position around daylight. Unlike his troops, Colonel Barrett, desiring to punish the Texas Rebels, was eager for action. Despite the clear indications and tactical realities that advised against it, an impatient Colonel Barrett now ordered an immediate "advance to be again made in the direction of Palmetto [*sic*] Ranch." After marching most of the night and without either rest or sleep, the Hoosier soldiers continued onward in what was becoming their most ill-fated expedition to date.

THE CONFEDERATES UP THE ANTE

Around 10:00 P.M. as Colonel Barrett was preparing to up the ante, the Confederates were making decisions of their own to turn a minor skirmish into a higher-stakes contest. After battling the Yankees to a standstill and recapturing Palmito Ranch, Captain Robinson was now encamped with around 190 of his Texas cavalrymen on Mios Ranch. This position was an abandoned stagecoach stop on the Brownsville Road about a mile northeast of Palmito Ranch. Situated on the flatlands north of Palmito Ranch, the Mios Ranch was located immediately north of the head of a bend in the Rio Grande, which jutted out in a wide loop as the river extended to its farthest point northward.

Only after he had pushed the Federals all the way back to White's Ranch had Captain Robinson dispatched a courier to General Slaughter at Brownsville to inform headquarters of the unexpected fighting around Palmito Ranch. Most important, the captain finally requested reinforcements.

After driving the Yankees from the field, Robinson believed that the Federals "will return to the island tonight," after having been beaten on May 12.

Captain Robinson's 7:30 P.M. letter to headquarters at Brownsville on May 12, from "near Palmito Ranch" wrote of the day's fighting against a superior opponent without embellishment: "Skirmishing has continued all day. We are presently camped near Mios Ranch. From a captured soldier of the 62nd Colored Infantry, we have learned that there are 300 soldiers in the enemy force, with more expected in the morning. My command numbers 190 men. We have no casualties yet, but need reinforcements if we are to stay in the field much longer."[23]

With pride, Captain Robinson summarized the details of the recent fighting in another report. "I moved to the road at twelve and found the enemy, numbering 300 [men] occupying Palmito Ranch [and] we commenced a skirmish with them and compelled them to fall back [and] I followed them to White Ranch," achieving success against a superior opponent and an unexpected victory.

At the quiet Brownsville headquarters of General Slaughter, meanwhile, Captain Robinson's messenger finally arrived late in the evening of May 12 to deliver the news of the Federals' unexpected advance. The dust-covered courier reported to "Old Rip" that "the Yankees had advanced [from Brazos Santiago], and [Captain Robinson] was engaged with them just below San Martin Ranch," which was located immediately west of Palmito Ranch. Colonel Ford was infuriated by the news of the truce violation that now endangered his troops and threatened Brownsville. He ordered the courier to return and reassure Robinson that he promised to "come to his aid as soon as men could be collected" at Fort Brown. Most important, he advised Captain Robinson to maintain contact with the invaders, keeping the Federals occupied to buy time for the arrival of Confederate reinforcements.

By this time, Colonel Ford had more on his mind than simply thwarting a Yankee probe on the Texas mainland. The old Indian fighter sensed that an opportunity existed for a greater success. He had emphasized to Captain Robinson "to hold his ground, if possible." Ford directed his subordinate "to begrudge the enemy every inch of ground." Clearly, Ford wanted to keep the Yankees occupied and as far away from their Brazos Santiago sanctuary and its reinforcements for as long as possible. Most of all, he realized the importance of ensuring that these interlopers of the Texas mainland would remain isolated and vulnerable to a counterattack.

Colonel Ford flew into action. He ordered couriers out into the night to recall as many troopers from the immediate area as possible. Ford faced a challenge in attempting to rally troops from their widely scattered positions. By this time, only about 300 Rebels remained stationed in the Brownsville area. Most of the 1,000 Confederates of General Slaughter's subdistrict were scattered throughout the Rio Grande area not only to protect the border but also to secure badly needed forage and water for horses and foodstuffs for soldiers.

Such a wide dispersal of Rebel forces in the Lower Rio Grande was necessary for Confederate troops to merely subsist in a drought-plagued land ravished by years of warfare. Rebel artillery horses, for instance, had to be sent twenty miles up the Rio Grande for forage. As Colonel Ford rationalized: "[T]he Confederate mounted forces [had been] sent to wherever they could find wood, grass and water [and] in this manner the Confederate forces were scattered between the Rio Grande and Arroya Colorado [as] there was no fighting and none expected."

During the first two months of 1865, the manpower of Colonel Ford's isolated Southern Division of the Western Subdistrict of Texas fell from 1,419 to 937 men. And by this time, the Arizona regiment of Confederate horsemen had been "ordered to another point in Texas," lamented Colonel Ford. Meanwhile, most of the Hispanic troopers of Colonel Bienavides's regiment had been posted higher up the Rio Grande, guarding the river and border.

At the end of January 1865 General Slaughter explained both his strategic dilemma and the lack of available manpower to meet any determined Federal advance from Brazos Santiago:

> [T]his command [is] composed entirely of wild bands of men, scattered from San Antonio to [Brownsville and] my force is about 1,500 effective men; 170 are in Northern Division [and] a portion stationed at Camp Verde guarding [the] country against depredations of Indians, daily occurring; another portion stationed at Eagle Pass, guarding trade [across the Rio Grande from Mexico] in that direction, as also protecting the country against Indians [and] on the Rio Grande from Eagle Pass to Edinburg, a distance of 280 miles, I have a force of 200 men. This force is also engaged in protecting trade and watching bands of banditti in Mexico.

Worst of all, however, "the cessation of active hostilities on the lower Rio Grande had allowed many officers and men to visit their homes on furlough." The liberal granting of furloughs to both men and officers because of the truce now meant that the Rebel soldiers needed to hurl back the Union advance upon the Texas mainland were scattered and well beyond reach. Times were rough on both soldiers and the folks back home, with farms deteriorating along with the Confederacy. Inflation was spiraling and the economy was in shambles. Many Rebels in the Trans-Mississippi had not been paid by the Richmond government in months. But even this no longer mattered because Confederate money was now worthless. More soldiers simply walked away from the war and went home. Hence, only a skeleton command of Confederates remained in the Brownsville area with most Rebel troops being scattered at outposts along the Rio Grande.[24]

Commanding in the Brownsville area, Colonel Ford had to overcome the initial reservations of District Commander General Slaughter. He was not keen on Ford's idea of hurrying reinforcements to Captain Robinson's aid and upping the ante in the fight east of Brownsville. At Brownsville that evening, Ford dined with General Slaughter. The relationship between the two Confederate leaders was far from cordial. From the beginning, the unpopular General Slaughter was jealous of Ford's combat record, reputation, and popularity. In addition, General Slaughter, a stuffy old school Virginian, never fully understood the frontier ways of Colonel Ford and his independently minded Texas Rebels.

Eager to assist Captain Robinson at Palmito Ranch, "Old Rip" impatiently asked, "General, what do you intend to do?"

Colonel Ford was shocked when he received the one-word reply: General Slaughter said, "Retreat!" An unnerved General Slaughter was ready to evacuate Brownsville by this time. Instantly, Colonel Ford unleashed an explosive outburst, demonstrating little respect for his cavalier superior: "You can retreat and go to hell if you wish! These are my men, and I am going to fight!"

A heated argument ensued between General Slaughter and Ford, but this was nothing new. Detesting his incompetent commander, Colonel Ford declared angrily that "I have held this place against heavy odds [and] if you lose it without a fight the people of the Confederacy will hold you accountable for a base neglect of duty."

This was no small amount of insubordination. But "Old Rip" could not have cared less, when Captain Robinson and his boys were fighting on their own and without support. Despite the hot exchange of words, Slaughter finally agreed with "Old Rip" to increase the scale of the operation. While Colonel Ford prepared to march his forces east to join Captain Robinson and Colonel Giddings's battalion with the first light of May 13, General Slaughter concentrated his troops around Brownsville to face a newly revealed Juarista threat from Cortina who hoped to recapture Matamoros from the French just across the river.

In fact, General Slaughter no longer planned to join Colonel Ford on Fort Brown's parade ground at daybreak, as promised, for a combined push to meet the Yankees—perhaps he never did. General Slaughter and his troops would stay behind in the safety of Brownsville instead of rushing to Captain Robinson's aid—a fact not yet realized by Ford. Slaughter was determined to remain out of action because, in his own words, "I had heard of General Lee's surrender and did not want to fight." As usual, Colonel Ford would have to do all the fighting.[25]

Meanwhile, the final showdown in Cameron County began to unfold at daylight on May 13. The stage was set for the last dramatic act of the Civil War. As so often in the past, Colonel Ford was at a serious disadvantage. The last-minute gathering of his scattered forces during the night left his soldiers without sleep or breakfast, in poor condition for a contest with the invader. In addition, "Old Rip" realized that his recall orders "found some of the detachments badly prepared to move [; and] the artillery horses had to travel most of the night of the 12th to reach Fort Brown [and] so had many of the men," lamented the colonel.[26]

At daybreak on May 13, the sun rose slowly over the Gulf of Mexico, lifting like a giant red ball over the sparkling blue waters. With the dawning of a new day, Colonel Barrett was eager to regain the initiative to exploit the tactical advantage that he had initially won by capturing Palmito Ranch. While both sides mustered strength for a final showdown east of Brownsville, thirty-four days had passed since General Lee's surrender at Appomattox Court House.

With visions of glory burning brightly, Colonel Barrett led his reinforcements of some 200 soldiers of the 34th Indiana toward White's Ranch on the double to link with Lieutenant Colonel Branson. Then, after uniting the two forces, Barrett reasoned that the combined might of more than 500 Federals would be sufficient to push aside Captain Robinson's force and capture Brownsville. Ignoring the wise counsel of both his former commander, Colonel Jones, and his superiors, who had earlier cautioned that the Brazos Santiago garrison was insufficient to overwhelm Brownsville, a confident Colonel Barrett was determined to fulfill his ambitions at any cost.

Colonel Barrett ordered his column forward. He decided to venture deeper into hostile, unfamiliar country with an infantry force handicapped without the support of either mounted cavalry or artillery. One experienced Yankee noted with surprise that Barrett now advanced with "no [mounted] cavalry or artillery, nothing but infantry" to once again meet Captain Robinson's Rebel horsemen. By this time, Colonel Barrett had already made a number of serious tactical miscalculations and mistakes long before even meeting the Texas Rebels.[27]

But Colonel Barrett's gravest error at this point was his unfounded overconfidence and underestimation of his opponent. He completely ignored all of the recent indications of Rebel fighting spirit and determination to hold Brownsville at all costs. Such unfounded optimism had led to Colonel Barrett's breaking of the Wallace-Slaughter truce in the first place. It is not surprising that the blue-clad veterans in Colonel Barrett's ranks now seemed to instinctively realize that they were headed for certain trouble.

One Yankee officer earlier wrote how Brazos Santiago was "commanded by the Colonel of a colored regiment, [who most of all was] wishing to establish for himself some notoriety before the war closed [and therefore he had] started a colored regiment [the 62nd U.S. Colored Infantry] to Brownsville, on the Rio Grande, in direct violation of orders from headquarters." A young officer's blind ambition was taking hundreds of Yankee troops on a risky mission deep in enemy territory and a rendezvous with the most capable Confederate leader in the Rio Grande Valley, "Old Rip" Ford. Colonel Ford now prepared to fight again in earnest at a time when "every [other Confederate] command but his had surrendered [and when he had] no government."[28]

Lt. Col. Robert G. Morrison,
34th Indiana

The men of Company C, 34th Indiana Volunteer Infantry

Lt. Col. Nimrod Headington,
34th Indiana

*A sketch of 1st Sgt. Patricio Perez,
2nd Texas Cavalry, U.S.A.,
from a photograph*

Capt. Theodore Harvey Barrett
MINNESOTA HISTORICAL SOCIETY

Col. Theodore Harvey Barrett
MINNESOTA HISTORICAL SOCIETY

Lt. John B. Harris, 34th Indiana
BILL DOAN COLLECTION

Capt. William Wilmington,
34th Indiana
BILL DOAN COLLECTION

*A sketch of Col. John Salmon
"Rip" Ford, as he looked in 1865,
from a photograph*

"Rip" Ford in old age

Cpl. Benjamin Franklin Harter,
34th Indiana

Capt. Abraham M. Templer,
34th Indiana

Sgt. Levi Simon, 34th Indiana

Pvt. John Jefferson Williams, 34th Indiana, the last Union soldier killed in battle during the Civil War

Lt. Arvil A. Butcher, 34th Indiana

The only marker commemorating the Battle of Palmito Ranch, located off the battlefield

BATTLE OF PALMITO RANCH

THE LAST LAND ENGAGEMENT OF THE CIVIL WAR WAS FOUGHT NEAR THIS SITE ON MAY 12-13, 1865, THIRTY-FOUR DAYS AFTER ROBERT E. LEE SURRENDERED AT APPOMATTOX.

COL. THEODORE H. BARRETT COMMANDED FEDERAL TROOPS ON BRAZOS ISLAND 12 MILES TO THE EAST. THE CONFEDERATES OCCUPIED FORT BROWN 12 MILES TO THE WEST, COMMANDED BY GEN. JAMES E. SLAUGHTER AND COL. JOHN S. (RIP) FORD, WHOSE TROOPS HAD CAPTURED FORT BROWN FROM THE FEDERALS IN 1864.

ORDERED TO RECAPTURE THE FORT, LT. COL. DAVID BRANSON AND 300 MEN ADVANCED FROM BRAZOS ISLAND. THEY WON A SKIRMISH WITH CONFEDERATE PICKETS ON MAY 12. BARRETT REINFORCED BRANSON'S TROOPS WITH 200 MEN ON MAY 13 AND RENEWED THE MARCH TO FORT BROWN. CONFEDERATE CAVALRY HELD THE FEDERALS IN CHECK UNTIL FORD ARRIVED WITH REINFORCEMENTS THAT AFTERNOON. FORD'S ARTILLERY ADVANCED AND FIRED ON THE NORTHERN END OF THE FEDERAL LINE WHILE THE CAVALRY CHARGED. THE CONFEDERATE RIGHT CHARGED THE SOUTHERN END OF THE FEDERAL LINE AND CAPTURED PART OF THE UNION INFANTRY. BARRETT ORDERED A RETREAT TOWARD THE U.S. POSITION ON BRAZOS ISLAND.

WHILE THE CONFEDERATES REPORTED NO FATALITIES IN THE BATTLE OF PALMITO RANCH, THE UNION FORCES REPORTED FOUR OFFICERS AND 111 MEN KILLED, WOUNDED, OR MISSING.

CHAPTER 5

The Final Fury,
the Last Battle of the Civil War

THE EARLY MORNING SUN ROSE HIGHER OVER THE FLAT COASTAL PLAIN OF THE
Texas mainland, as the sun's rays illuminated the borderlands along the Rio
Grande on May 13. Colonel Barrett and his reinforcing battalion of Indiana
soldiers advanced rapidly down the Brownsville Road toward White's Ranch
in the half-light and early morning cool of a new day.

At White's Ranch, Lieutenant Colonel Branson was once again encoun-
tering stiff Rebel opposition. As could be expected, Captain Robinson and
his cavalrymen kept up the pressure. Clearly, Robinson understood the importance of harassing his adversary as long as possible, wearing him down
through exhaustion and buying precious time for Colonel Ford's arrival.

In the early morning light, Captain Robinson's troops seemed to be
swarming everywhere, blasting away at the Yankees. This deteriorating situation was no way for Lieutenant Colonel Branson to celebrate the two-month
anniversary of his promotion to his present rank. To parry the Texans' threat,
Branson dispatched a lengthy skirmish line of five companies of the 62nd
USCT, about 125 men, to protect his front.

Even before daylight, some black soldiers had begun skirmishing with
Captain Robinson's Texans: aggressive Rebel tactics that ensured Federal
weariness for the final showdown on May 13. To counter the fast-moving
Texans, Lieutenant Colonel Branson spread out his African American skirmishers over a wide area to cover his front and flank. Indeed, a full half of
Lieutenant Colonel Branson's entire command now served as skirmishers to
keep the Rebels at bay.

Meanwhile, the other half of the 62nd continued to rest in arms behind skirmish lines in cover along the riverbank. No doubt, many of these black rookies felt anxious about facing a mounted force of Texas Rebels on the open prairie, and with good reason after the massacre at Fort Pillow. As the sun slowly rose, the skirmishing heated up, escalating in intensity.[1]

At last, Colonel Barrett and his Indiana soldiers neared White's Ranch and Lieutenant Colonel Branson's command. All the while, the sound of skirmishing echoed louder across the eastern edge of the Palo Alto prairie, creating a noisy racket in the early morning. In the words of Lt. Charles A. Jones, "[A]t daybreak we arrived [at White's Ranch], and found a detachment of the Sixty-second United States Colored Troops at that place under the command of Lieutenant-Colonel Branson [and now] we halted at that place and took breakfast."[2]

Finally reaching the burned-down Confederate outpost of White's Ranch, most of Lieutenant Colonel Morrison's weary Hoosiers stacked muskets. The Indiana soldiers finally gained some relief and the opportunity to rest. Here, the men of the Hoosier 34th began to cook breakfast and boil coffee after their seven-mile march to White's Ranch. Then, an uneasy Colonel Barrett finally began to respond to the increasing Rebel threat. He ordered Lieutenant Colonel Morrison to dispatch a line of men "to skirmish a small clump of wood, with a view to ascertaining whether it contained any Rebel forces or not, as it had been reported to me that it did," explained Barrett later.[3]

Meanwhile, the weary Indiana soldiers not selected for skirmish duty now gained some much-needed rest after the rapid night march. Wearing the heavy wool uniforms now soaked from the previous night's storm, the soldiers of the 34th Indiana were chilled to the bone by this time. The lingering cool night air blowing westward from the Gulf only increased the Hoosiers' discomfort.[4]

These Indiana Yankees were in relatively poor shape for a lengthy fight. Lt. William T. Bryson described that "some of the regiment had been on the expedition [an earlier mission to Padre Island] and they had, when they returned, sore feet—a great many of them had." Indeed, 150 of these Indiana soldiers "had just returned from an expedition up Padre Island, eighty miles."[5] This ill-fated foray had failed to achieve its goal of rustling any cattle for the garrison.

Unlike an over-eager Colonel Barrett, Lieutenant Colonel Morrison, a veteran commander with good sense, would not have driven his men so hard, especially at night and with the promise of more fighting early the following morning. Morrison was a fine leader who knew how to take care of his boys. Lt. John E. Markle, quartermaster of the 34th Indiana, explained that his commander, Lieutenant Colonel Morrison, possessed the steadfast qualities of an excellent combat commander: "I have known him to be engaged in a fight, and never knew him to falter."[6]

Knowing surprisingly little about the art of war or his men's limitations, especially following their recent arduous duty on Padre Island, Colonel Barrett had pushed the Indiana soldiers much too hard down the Brownsville Road throughout the long night. From the beginning, the veteran Hoosiers disliked this arrogant officer. Worst of all, these veterans now sensed their own vulnerability with an inexperienced commander leading this seemingly ill-fated expedition.[7]

Colonel Barrett wasted no time after his arrival at White's Ranch. He was emboldened by the fact that the Texas Rebels withdrew from the thickets and into the open prairie, after catching sight of the sudden arrival of hundreds of Yankee reinforcements.[8]

Clearly, Captain Robinson's withdrawal gave the inexperienced colonel a false sense of success, which only increased his overconfidence: a potentially fatal development for the isolated expedition of infantrymen far from Brazos Santiago.[9]

While some Indiana soldiers rested around White's Ranch and the other Hoosiers served as skirmishers, Colonel Barrett ordered the remainder of the 62nd, five companies at White's Ranch, and the detachment of the 2nd Texas Cavalry to push southwest toward Palmito Ranch "to support the skirmish line" of Captain Miller's Company F.[10] Colonel Barrett now planned to complete the job of clearing the way for a general advance upon Brownsville that Lieutenant Colonel Branson had started the previous day. He believed that this time would be different, however. Barrett now planned to hit the Rebels with a knockout blow from a combined force of more than 500 Yankees.[11]

After the Africans Americans advanced nearly a mile in about half an hour, Lt. Martin Robinson, one of Colonel Barrett's staff officers, rode back to the remaining Indiana soldiers who were resting at White's Ranch. He ordered the Hoosiers to move up immediately. This would be a staggered advance, however. Because of the late start, these Indiana soldiers would keep the existing distance between themselves and the black troops who continued leading the attack toward Palmito Ranch.[12]

With a clattering of gear, the Indiana soldiers fell into line as ordered. But these veterans dreaded the prospect of more hard duty on the Texas mainland under Colonel Barrett who, they worried, would get them in serious trouble. In addition, the Hoosiers remained in much worse condition for arduous campaigning than the relatively fresh African Americans.[13] The Indiana soldiers had endured the recent downpours, marched all night, and performed strenuous duty, such as unloading steamboats and gathering wood. Before this expedition they had recently scoured Brazos Santiago for miles. After the Brazos had been cleared of driftwood, the Hoosiers performed the same strenuous duty on Padre Island.[14]

Consequently, at least half of the Indiana soldiers now "had sore feet" from their march up Padre Island only two or three days before.[15] And this had been no small assignment, especially immediately before the expedition to the Texas mainland. In one soldier's words, "[A] considerable number of the Thirty-fourth [had] only a few days previous, marched 190 miles on Padre Island . . . and returned to the Brazos with sore feet."[16] And Sgt. Maj. Joseph L. Myers, 34th Indiana, complained that his men's feet "were in bad condition [because] they had been in damp dirt four days [as] they were marching eleven days previously [to May 13]."[17]

But orders were orders, and Colonel Barrett was hardly concerned about the Hoosiers' welfare at this point because he was thinking about his future. He remained obsessed with glory and Brownsville's capture. One exhausted Indiana blue-clad in the bivouac at White's Ranch lamented: "[W]e had scarcely got our coffee water warm when we were ordered to fall in, and at once took up our line of march [west] on the Brownsville Road."[18]

Not long after receiving the order to move out, the Indiana soldiers pushed forward, marching west. With the 62nd USCT advancing in front and closing in on Palmito Ranch, Captain Robinson's men suddenly returned to continue contesting the Yankees' advance. The Texas Rebels fired from the bushes, yucca plants, and chaparral throughout the morning, skirmishing with the black troops.[19]

Meanwhile, the 62nd continued inching ahead and the 34th Indiana, following behind, steadily advanced up the bank of the Rio Grande and westward toward Palmito Ranch. Along the way, the black soldiers of Company F led the advance, skirmishing in front. Captain Miller was proud of his African American skirmishers who displayed courage before a heavy fire and "drove the enemy steadily before them."[20]

To cover the advancing column's rear and to guard the cache of captured supplies and prisoners, Lieutenant Colonel Branson left behind a detail of fifteen to twenty trusty Indiana soldiers at White's Ranch. Here, one badly wounded Yankee was treated by a surgeon.[21]

Suddenly, after advancing about three miles westward from White's Ranch and across a flat expanse of arid land, the 34th Indiana halted to rest. Meanwhile, after turning off the Brownsville Road, the African American soldiers of the 62nd, with Captain Miller's skirmishers leading the way, continued on, turned left, or southward, and "passed around the bend of the [Rio Grande] whose banks were covered with chaparral at that place, and were out of sight," wrote Lieutenant Jones, of the Indiana regiment.[22]

Here, the Hoosiers rested for a couple of hours, but were soon ordered to resume the advance toward Palmito Ranch. Lieutenant Colonel Morrison's exhausted men snatched their rifles and scrambled into line. The Indiana soldiers prepared to push forward once more.[23]

As the firing of the skirmish line echoed across the sand flats and prairies along the Rio Grande, the main body of Yankees continued to advance after turning southward along the main road to follow the river. Protecting the front, the black skirmishers pushed the Rebels rearward during the advance. All the while, Captain Robinson's Rebels were drawing the Federals farther south and ever deeper into Confederate territory.[24]

At last, the first bluecoat skirmishers neared Palmito Ranch, and Captain Robinson was finally forced to release his tenuous hold on the position. He wisely ordered a withdrawal of his main body while keeping a line of skirmishers who continued to contest the Yankees' advance. After retiring westward across the prairie, the main body of Rebels stood their ground at the San Martin Ranch about a mile west of Palmito Ranch.[25]

Ahead of Palmito Ranch, however, the fighting was not yet over. More skirmishing flared along with the ever-intensifying heat of day. The black troops of the 62nd and the detachment of the 2nd Texas Cavalry finally reached the buildings of Palmito Ranch around 9:00 A.M., after driving off the last of Captain Robinson's stubborn Rebels. As usual, the Texans melted away into the thickets and the chaparral. For the second time in two days, Captain Robinson lost his outpost at Palmito Ranch to the Yankee invader. These tactical setbacks were considered only temporary by Robinson, however. Once again he had managed to buy precious time for the arrival of "Old Rip" and his reinforcements from Brownsville.[26]

As if in retaliation for the Texans' constant harassment that had tormented them both day and night, the Yankees now continued their work of destruction at Palmito Ranch, which had been left uncompleted the previous day. Lieutenant Colonel Branson described: "[A] halt was made at Palmetto [*sic*] Ranch and the remaining supplies of the enemy that had escaped the flames the day before were now burned."[27]

While the flames crackled behind them and dark clouds of smoke rose higher in the humid air, the African Americans stacked their Enfield rifles, rested, and ate breakfast. Meanwhile, the 34th Indiana soldiers had halted to the rear of the 62nd USCT. Demonstrating a measure of caution, Colonel Barrett was concerned about the vulnerability of his advanced position at Palmito Ranch and ordered the Indiana regiment to continue to linger behind the 62nd to protect the rear.[28]

Two hours passed while the Yankees rested under the hot sun, and Captain Robinson and his soldiers anxiously awaited Colonel Ford's arrival. Here, near the cluster of the Orive family buildings on Palmito Ranch, the Rio Grande flowed a short distance to the east because of the curvature of the river's wide bend. This bend looped northward before the river continued flowing eastward to the Gulf. Originally part of the expansive Espiritu Santo Ranch, which dated back to an old Spanish land grant, Palmito Ranch was one of the oldest ranches in the area, first settled by the Orive family in 1827, nearly ten years before Texas won its independence from Mexico.[29]

Despite this lull, the fighting did not stop. The skirmish companies of the 62nd and the dismounted men of the 2nd Texas Cavalry continued to exchange fire with the Texas Rebels. The constant gunfire ensured that the idle men at Palmito Ranch could not rest with a possible engagement brewing just beyond their sight.[30]

Throwing all caution to the wind, meanwhile, Colonel Barrett decided to continue the push farther beyond Palmito Ranch and toward the alluring prize of Brownsville. His overaggressiveness would only make his task force more vulnerable with each passing mile that distanced him from Brazos Santiago.[31]

In addition, Barrett now found himself in an alien and unfamiliar landscape, which did nothing to dissuade him. The area around Palmito Ranch was later described by a journalist of the *New York Herald* as a "vast sandy plain, interspersed here and there with green prairie and Mexican chaparral [and] in many places intersected by bayous [resacas, or former bends of the Rio Grande] and lagoons, so that sudden movements [of troops] would in all likelihood result in [the gaining of the element of] surprise."[32]

Captain Robinson, a veteran combat commander, realized as much. He therefore sought to take immediate advantage of the situation. Immediately southeast of the San Martin Ranch, the Rebel captain skillfully remained just out of striking distance to draw the Yankees deeper into a trap.

Indeed, Captain Robinson's graycoats were gradually luring the Yankees farther away from their base camp and reinforcements at Brazos Santiago, while drawing them ever closer to Brownsville. On the field of Palmito Ranch, Robinson and his men successfully employed delaying tactics, standing firm to deliver punishment, and then quickly slipping away through the thickets to take a new defensive position. The combination of Captain Robinson's tactics and the lure of Palmito Ranch, located about halfway between Brazos Santiago and Brownsville, was the bait that was creating a trap for the Federal Expeditionary Force. The capture of Palmito Ranch now meant that Colonel Barrett's command was a full dozen miles away from the nearest reinforcements at Brazos Santiago, while only a dozen miles east of Brownsville. Even now, a good many Confederate reinforcements under Colonel Ford were preparing to come to Captain Robinson's aid.[33]

Continuing his earlier folly, Colonel Barrett planned to advance farther without either mounted cavalry or artillery. The colonel decided to advance toward Brownsville despite having received word that the Rebels possessed at least one battery. Making yet another tactical mistake during the march from White's Ranch, Colonel Barrett had allowed his least experienced troops to lead the advance while his veterans, the Indiana soldiers, remained in the rear.[34]

Additionally, unlike the black troops with five days' rations, Colonel Barrett had failed to order his Indiana soldiers to bring a sufficient supply of rations for the push all the way to Brownsville. The worn Hoosiers, therefore, now carried only enough rations for one meal. These Indiana men were now in far greater need of both rest and rations than were the African American Yankees.[35]

Consequently, the rookie colonel attempted to compensate for his logistical error. He therefore ordered the men of the 62nd to issue part of their rations to the Indiana soldiers, providing the Indiana troops, who had been ordered to rejoin the main column at Palmito Ranch, with enough food to last them until the evening of the following day. In addition, Barrett also "ordered all the disabled men, and those not able to make a heavy march, to be sent back with the wounded men, horses and cattle to Brazos Santiago."[36] Clearly, these were some of the first signs that this expedition was overly ambitious and that Brownsville was Colonel Barrett's real objective. The colonel planned to continue his advance along the Brownsville Road with the 62nd and the 2nd Texas, while the 34th Indiana was to follow the course of the river.[37]

Colonel Barrett also failed to fully understand the importance of time during the advance toward Brownsville. Despite the fact that the colonel knew that Confederate reinforcements from Brownsville might be coming down the main road, the overly confident Colonel Barrett nevertheless continued to delay his advance from Palmito Ranch, as if time had no meaning.

Thanks partly to Captain Robinson's skillful efforts, Colonel Barrett had been forced to conduct his advance at a leisurely pace from White's Ranch. He had even ordered halts for his men to rest before reaching his first objective, Palmito Ranch. He foolishly divided his command while deep in enemy country, keeping his two regiments so far separated that they were often out of sight of each other and beyond mutual supporting distance. In fact, during the advance, the Indiana unit had occasionally lingered so far behind the 62nd that the Hoosiers were sometimes unable to even hear the sounds of skirmish fire between the African Americans and Texans. All in all, the Federal advance thus far was characterized by careless tactical decisions made by a novice commander, without the benefit of artillery or cavalry, while pushing deep into the exclusive domain of "Old Rip." Clearly, in tactical terms, a deeper penetration into Confederate territory embodied a considerable amount of risk, if not folly.[38]

At last, after wasting two precious hours at Palmito Ranch, a confident Colonel Barrett made final preparations around 9:30 A.M. to resume the offensive on Brownsville. He planned to advance two skirmish companies of the 34th Indiana southward from Palmito Ranch to lead the way for the Hoosier regiment. Thankfully, Captain Miller and the exhausted African Americans of his skirmish company (Company F) now gained some much needed rest.[39]

Colonel Barrett ordered Lieutenant Colonel Morrison to lead the advance farther down the river and toward Palmito Hill, near the Rio Grande two-thirds of a mile south of the buildings on Palmito Ranch. Colonel Barrett was preparing to take his Indiana regiment farther away from the Brownsville Road by ordering Colonel Morrison to advance southward from the buildings of Palmito Ranch toward Palmito Hill.[40]

South of the Brownsville Road and directly below, or south, of the buildings of Palmito Ranch, Palmito Hill stood at the southern end of the river's wide bend that swung northward to nearly touch the Brownsville Road to the north, before straightening and continuing to flow eastward once again. The river first turned from flowing east to north near Palmito Hill, which overlooked the river. The high ground of Palmito Hill paralleled the course of the river southward and then westward toward Brownsville for a short distance. Here, where the Rio Grande ran west-east before swinging northward along the river's bend, Palmito Hill become a woody brush-covered bluff bordering the Rio Grande before it turned northward in the wide bend to pass by the cluster of buildings on Palmito Ranch. Both Palmito Hill and the bluff extended in a crescent shape, with the bluff the southern and western extension of the hill.

To lead the advance southward toward Palmito Hill, Lieutenant Colonel Morrison selected his two companies on the regiment's left to act as skirmishers, Lieutenant Jones's Company K and Captain Montgomery's Company I. With clanging accoutrements, and weary feet and tired legs, the soldiers of these two Hoosier companies double-quicked to the column's head. Here, Colonel Barrett immediately ordered Company K forward as the foremost skirmishers.[41]

But Lieutenant Jones, a veteran, balked at the seemingly unreasonable directive, reflecting some animosity toward the egotistical young colonel and skepticism about the wisdom of continuing the advance. As Lieutenant Jones described the confusing situation that resulted: "I did not move at that time and told him that Captain Montgomery outranked me [and that] both [Indiana] companies at that time [were] to be deployed as skirmishers by direction of Colonel Barrett [and] upon that intimation Captain Montgomery moved his company forward in advance of my company."[42]

Here was one of the first indications during the expedition that some friction and tension existed between Colonel Barrett, the former commander of the 62nd USCT, and the men of the 34th Indiana. By this time, the Indiana soldiers had good reason to feel hostility. The Hoosiers were fully aware of the favoritism that Colonel Barrett almost always demonstrated toward his former black regiment. Such partiality always came at the 34th's expense. This, of course, caused resentment among the Hoosiers. And the Indiana boys disliked the white officers of the 62nd, who complained too often about "infractions."

In addition, the majority of the Indiana soldiers were weary from the recent Padre Island expedition, unlike the African Americans who were relatively fresh. Despite the fact that the Indiana troops had been force-marched rapidly to the field on a grueling night trek, two Hoosier companies were now ordered out as skirmishers and to continue the advance without rest. Meanwhile, the black soldiers had gained much-needed rest at Palmito Ranch.[43]

Captain Montgomery's Indiana men took an advanced position as skirmishers, while Lieutenant Jones's company was held in reserve. Colonel Barrett then ordered Lieutenant Jones to the left of Captain Montgomery, extending the skirmish line to cover a wider area. Montgomery was now the senior officer among the skirmish company commanders. He possessed a good deal of combat experience like Lieutenant Jones. Once the two Hoosier skirmish companies had extended in a lengthy line, Colonel Barrett ordered his Indiana Yankees forward. Following the course of the river southward, these bluecoats finally moved out as the day was heating up around 10:00 A.M.[44]

The exact mission and specific objectives of the two skirmishing companies remained unclear to the Indiana soldiers, however. For whatever reason, Colonel Barrett kept his plans from his men. Later, Barrett would claim that he directed Lieutenant Jones's company "to push on up the river, with a view of ascertaining the strength of the enemy, and if possible obtaining a road branching toward the right, going towards Port Isabel."[45]

Colonel Barrett's leadership decisions continued to be questioned and scrutinized by the veteran Indiana officers, who were confused by his orders and uncertain of exactly what the colonel expected of them. Such lack of communication and misunderstanding among the expedition's leading officers was sure to lead to far more serious problems for Colonel Barrett and his task force. These veteran Indiana officers knew a real leader when they saw one, and Colonel Barrett in their view did not fit the bill.

Lieutenant Jones, perplexed by the lack of specific instructions, complained that he had received no detailed orders from Colonel Barrett. With some surprise, if not shock, the veteran officer described: "[N]o point was designated for me to reach, neither to bring on an engagement or not to bring on an engagement, neither to halt."[46]

Meanwhile as the Hoosiers pushed southward from Palmito Ranch, along the Rio Grande and toward Palmito Hill, Captain Robinson and his Rebels once again suddenly appeared like magic and began blasting away with Colt revolvers, shotguns, and rifles.

In delaying the Federal advance and buying more time, Captain Robinson and his horse soldiers held firm against the odds, skirmishing with the Yankees for what would become a total of twelve hours. By this time, Robinson's challenge had grown considerably compared with the previous day, after the arrival of sizable Union reinforcements under Colonel Barrett. Robinson's 190 Texas cavalrymen, nevertheless, somehow continued to thwart the advance of more than 500 Yankees during this mismatch along the Rio Grande.[47]

Palmito Hill was now the Federals' immediate objective because it was the dominant high ground in the area. Even though Colonel Barrett had finally taken possession of the Rebel outpost at Palmito Ranch, he felt that he now needed to secure Palmito Hill, which was a wise decision.

The two skirmish companies of the 34th Indiana continued to ease southward and parallel to the river, while suffering under scattered Rebel fire in an effort to take possession of the hill. Safely out of harm's way, Colonel Barrett and his 62nd USCT remained in position northward, or to the right, of the Indiana regiment, in the open prairie. Meanwhile, the 2nd Texas Cavalry plugged the gap between the 62nd and the 34th Indiana, which continued to advance south of the main road toward Palmito Hill. While the black troops moved southwestward just above the Brownsville Road, the dismounted troopers of the 2nd Texas advanced along the road in a parallel movement.[48]

Wary of Rebel tricks and frontier tactics, Colonel Barrett had realized that he had to make sure that no Confederate force lay hidden in the maze of chaparral along the hill and river bottoms to the south. Most of all, he refused to relinquish the initiative. The two Indiana skirmish companies, therefore, moved south and closer to the Rio Grande to flush out any Texas Rebels hidden in the brush. With bayonets sparkling in the sunlight, the veteran Hoosiers pushed across the flat river bottoms choked with mesquite, chaparral, and cactus. In business-like fashion, the Indiana skirmishers surged toward the high ground along the river.[49]

This was no easy assignment for Lieutenant Jones, even though he was one of the most experienced officers of the 34th Indiana. Indeed, at this time, Captain Robinson's hard-fighting Rebels were in good defensive positions amid the snarled tangles of mesquite and chaparral along the river, blasting away at every Yankee in sight. In addition, the Indiana soldiers also encountered heavier clumps of underbrush, cactus, and chaparral along the steamy bottoms, impeding their advance as they neared the river.[50]

Lieutenant Jones explained the difficulty of moving his Hoosier troops over this more brush-tangled and rougher terrain south of Palmito Ranch: "I advanced [my company] to the river, which was [on] the left of Palmetto [*sic*] Bluff, driving the enemy from the banks of the river to the left of Palmetto [*sic*] Bluff [and] I could not go further. Captain Montgomery's company I had lost sight of [and now] it did not cover my right. They were coming up to the [top of Palmito Hill], chaparral being so thick between us that I lost sight of them. I moved my company by the right flank and gained the top of the [hill]." Palmito Hill, of which the river bluff—below the hill along the river to the southwest—was part, was now captured for the Union. A U.S. banner now fluttered over the commanding hilltop position overlooking the slow-moving, brown waters of the Rio Grande.[51]

Here, once atop Palmito Hill, which overlooked the flat wetlands of Mexico to the south, Lieutenant Jones and his sweat-stained Indiana skirmishers rested under the searing sun. Captain Durkee, 62nd USCT, and an acting staff officer for Colonel Barrett, now rode up to the worn Indiana men of Company K. Without having received specific instructions from Colonel Barrett, Lieutenant Jones explained to Captain Durkee that he "used my [own] judgment in getting around this bend of the river, and I asked him, he being mounted, if he had any orders for me. No, he said, he had not." Instead of bringing detailed orders to clarify the tactical situation, Captain Durkee soon wandered off until he gained "the top of [Palmito] hill [from where he prepared] to take a shot at the Johnnies."[52]

Relishing active campaigning after escaping garrison duty on Brazos Santiago. Captain Durkee squeezed out two quick shots from a .54 caliber Burnside breech-loading carbine from the crest of Palmito Hill. Then, an eager Lieutenant Jones, whose revolver had only limited range, asked the captain to hand the Burnside carbine to him for a shot. As if shooting squirrels back home in the Indiana forests, Lieutenant Jones blasted away at the Texas Rebels on the open prairie northwest of Palmito Hill. After enjoying himself, the lieutenant then returned the rifle to Captain Durkee. Clearly, many Federals viewed this expedition as little more than an adventurous waltz into Brownsville.[53]

As tactical developments would soon demonstrate, this expedition was anything but a lark. Colonel Barrett failed to maintain proper discipline among his troops or, more importantly, to act decisively. Instead, he allowed more precious time to slip away while his forces became increasingly more vulnerable during their advance southwestward.[54]

98   THE FINAL FURY

In reality, time was of the essence. Around 11:00 A.M., Colonel Ford and around one hundred Rebel cavalrymen, fifty artillery men, and six cannons, galloped out of Brownsville in a swirl of dust. Colonel Ford led his men to the rescue of Captain Robinson, racing east down the Brownsville Road toward Palmito Ranch for a rendezvous with Colonel Barrett and his Union task force.[55]

This was yet another example of General Slaughter's soldiers considering Colonel Ford to be their real commander and not the haughty Virginian. Without Ford's example and influence, the Brownsville Rebels might well have remained in town with General Slaughter, leaving Captain Robinson and his boys to their fate.[56]

Sweating and covered with dirt and grime, the Indiana Yankees of Company K, meanwhile, prepared to push across the brush-covered crest of Palmito Hill to continue advancing southwestward along the high ground of the bluff that followed the river. After realigning ranks along the sun-drenched hill, the Federals under Lieutenant Jones turned to advance southwestward along the river and then eventually directly west as the Rio Grande straightened out toward Brownsville.[57]

As Lieutenant Jones described the resumption of the Federal advance, he pushed forward "with my skirmishers to a small ridge at the bottom of [Palmito Hill]."[58] Here, about a dozen yards below the top of Palmito Hill, the fighting suddenly escalated. Clearly, the hard-fighting Captain Robinson was determined to contest every inch of ground. The Texas captain understood the importance of buying more time for Colonel Ford's arrival. Rebel resistance, consequently, stiffened once more. Such a torrent of Confederate bullets poured from the underbrush and mesquite that Lieutenant Jones ordered his Company K soldiers to lie down and seek cover from the leaden storm.[59]

With Captain Robinson's cavalrymen firing rapidly and causing more mischief among the Federals, Lieutenant Jones became concerned about the strength of the overly aggressive force of Texas Confederates before him. Indeed, he now commanded only twenty-seven men of his diminutive company. Therefore, partly because he had earlier lost contact with Captain Montgomery's skirmishers of Company I and had yet to link with them, the Indiana lieutenant now became "somewhat excited to know if I was going to have any support" during this increasingly hot fight, which was rapidly getting out of control. It was becoming clear that this would be no cakewalk into Brownsville after all.[60]

By this time, Lieutenant Jones had good reason to be concerned about the tactical situation. By the ever-growing amount of the resistance before him, he now believed that his Company K "was contenting [sic] . . . with three different squads of Rebel cavalry [with] at least thirty in each squad."

Worst of all, these swarming Rebels, presenting to the Federals nothing more than elusive targets slipping through the underbrush and chaparral, now "had almost a crossfire on me." This scorching fire succeeded in pinning down the hard-hit soldiers of Company K.[61]

Caught in a bad spot, the Company K skirmishers were now on their own hook in an advanced position, while fighting an unknown number of Rebels. Meanwhile, Captain Montgomery's Company I was somewhere to the rear but nowhere within sight. Even worse, Lieutenant Jones had raced to the top of Palmito Hill in a futile attempt to ascertain the exact location of his missing Indiana comrades of Company I amid the sea of chaparral. From this high point overlooking the Rio Grande and the sprawling river bottoms to the south and the prairie to the west, he was alarmed by a startling sight. Lieutenant Jones wrote of the confusing tactical situation that was now revealed to him: "I saw the two regiments or detachments of each of the [two Union] regiments, at least a half mile to my rear [and] they were marching toward the bluff [and] the regiments from that direction that I could see [now] were marching by a flank."[62]

Lieutenant Jones was horrified by the sight of the disjointed advance. He now realized that he and his Indiana skirmishers were without immediate support, while the Texas Rebels were closing in with each passing minute. By this time, Colonel Barrett's advance upon Brownsville was becoming increasingly careless, with the uncoordinated movements of his units made in a piecemeal, haphazard, and staggered fashion. Clearly, Barrett was losing his grasp of the increasingly confused tactical situation, while remaining to the north, or rearward, with his 62nd regiment. All the while, the disorganized Federal advance continued to make a superior force increasingly vulnerable.[63]

While Captain Robinson skillfully maximized the effectiveness of his small numbers with guerrilla and hit-and-run tactics, Colonel Barrett did the opposite. The Union commander minimized his numbers by applying tactics that diminished his strength, sapping the advance's momentum. Forced to make a sound decision on his own, therefore, Lieutenant Jones decided that "I did not deem it proper that I should advance any further with the [small] number of men that I had." Meanwhile, to the rear, the bulk of the 34th Indiana advanced to occupy the high ground of Palmito Hill, after the Hoosier skirmishers had departed the hill to advance southwestward along the bluff to skirmish with the Rebels before them.[64]

After battling Captain Robinson's Texas cavalrymen for around fifteen minutes, the hard-pressed skirmishers of Company K were finally rescued by the timely arrival of Captain Montgomery's long-missing Company I. In Lieutenant Jones's thankful words: "Captain Montgomery's company came out from the right of [Palmito Hill] and drove the squad of Rebel cavalry from my right, leaving me one squad [of Texas Confederates] directly in my front, and one on my left [and] the [one Rebel] squad that had been driven back had at this time deployed immediately across his and my front, being at a distance of about 1,000 yards between the two lines of skirmishers, my left resting on the river." Meanwhile, "two squads of Rebel cavalry [shifted] to a high point on my left [the bluff of Palmito Hill that stood above the river] and under cover of a small hill [a part of the high ground of the bluff]."[65]

Using sound tactical judgment, Lieutenant Jones realized that he needed additional support before he could resume his advance. The fact that the brisk skirmishing in front had finally slowed indicated to Lieutenant Jones that some Rebels had withdrawn. Now that the hail of bullets finally ceased pouring from the chaparral, the lieutenant dispatched a sergeant to Colonel Barrett with an urgent request for reinforcements.[66]

Fighting on his own initiative, Lieutenant Jones also sent the sergeant to report to the colonel because he desired specific orders from Barrett. He still "had no orders to bring on an engagement." Soon the Hoosier sergeant returned but with only ten soldiers of Company A, 34th Indiana, to reinforce Lieutenant Jones's small Company K.

Not surprisingly, Jones was angered by the insufficient support. With only a handful of reinforcements to increase his skirmish force to nearly forty men, and after he deployed and "doubled the [reinforcing] men on the left of my company," Jones, nevertheless, prepared to make his next move, after finally receiving specific orders from Colonel Barrett.[67]

With Colonel Barrett's orders to continue this tentative advance southwestward along the Rio Grande and toward Brownsville, Lieutenant Jones once again ordered his skirmishers forward through the thick stands of chaparral. The ill-conceived Federal advance once again lurched forward. The foremost bluecoats inched along the bluff of Palmito Hill and through the bottoms along the underbrush-clogged banks of the Rio Grande.[68]

Feeling fortunate and more confident with the arrival of reinforcements, Lieutenant Jones's Indiana boys struggled through the thicket-choked river bottom and along the slopes of the bluff. Elsewhere, skirmishing between the Hoosiers and the Texas gray-clads once more heated up with firing again rising to new levels. All the time, Captain Robinson and his Texas troopers continued to fight Indian-style. The Rebels blasted away at the advancing Yankees, then yielded ground only at the last minute and only when they wanted to relinquish it.[69]

Feeling no alarm at the intensifying skirmishing, Colonel Barrett described: "[N]early the entire forenoon was spent in skirmishing [with] the enemy taking advantage of every favorable position [and] early in the afternoon a sharp engagement took place . . . in the chaparral."[70]

Even the men of the 62nd, to the north above the Brownsville Road, were caught up in the exchange of fire of what Colonel Barrett now realized was more of an "engagement" than a skirmish. In the ranks of Company D, 62nd USCT private Henry Ellis fell when a bullet smashed into his right ankle. He described the moment when he was hit "by a shot from a Confederate soldier lying in the [prairie] grass, who was [himself] wounded, [and who] raised up and shot me." The first serious casualty of the 62nd in this war, Private Ellis was placed on a horse, and sent rearward for medical treatment.[71]

After proving to be a thorn, especially in the Hoosiers' sides, the Rebels quickly mounted and galloped farther west. Here, the Texans took up yet another new defensive position behind good cover and began reloading their weapons. Exploiting the advantage of rough terrain, the graycoats took advantage of every log, mesquite bush, and yucca tree, all the while continuing to pour a stream of lead from six-shot Colt and Navy revolvers and rifles. To Lieutenant Jones's soldiers from the farms and cornfields of Indiana, these fast-shooting Texans, dirty and long-haired, and looking like wild men, seemed more like Indians than soldiers.

Below the Brownsville Road, the 34th Indiana soldiers especially dreaded the thought of getting caught out in the open prairie by these roughriders. These veteran infantrymen had never seen an opponent who shot as fast, rode as swiftly, or acted so boldly in the face of overwhelming odds. During the Vicksburg campaign, the Indiana Yankees had fought veteran Western Rebels but never anything like these hellish cavalrymen from the Lone Star State. They fired on the run as effectively as from behind protective cover, before slipping away to fight again behind the next good position. The Texans' hit-and-run tactics caused considerable frustration among the Indiana infantrymen, who had never faced such an elusive adversary.

Most important, this ever-growing sense of frustration caused by the constant harassing fire and elusiveness of the Texans was playing a part in accomplishing Captain Robinson's primary tactical objective: making the advancing Yankees forget that, by continuing to press forward and farther away from their base and ever closer to Brownsville, they were becoming more vulnerable to counterattack.

Remaining fixated on striking a highly mobile enemy who was always just out of reach was drawing the Yankees deeper into a trap. Clearly, to Federal infantrymen, who were hampered by a disorganized advance, attempting to eliminate veteran Confederate horsemen on their own ground was not only futile but also risky. Meanwhile, more precious time and the best opportunity for the Federals to either withdraw or consolidate before the arrival of Colonel Ford's reinforcements from Brownsville continued to slip away.

Suddenly the firing ceased as the Rebels once again faded away into the dense underbrush and chaparral, after the Indiana skirmishers advanced another one hundred difficult yards along the river. In gaining additional ground and winning more parched terrain of no strategic value, Colonel Barrett described: "[O]ur forces encountered a considerable body of Rebels [and] a sharp skirmish ensued, lasting a few minutes, when they were driven out of sight, beyond the resting ground and under cover of chaparral and brush."

Lieutenant Jones was left less confident by the events unfolding around him. Most of all, he was concerned about the sudden quiet and feared a Rebel trap. "I could see nothing more of the enemy [and] I looked back and saw the 34th Indiana on the top of [Palmito] hill [and the] firing had entirely ceased," wrote Lieutenant Jones.[72]

Suddenly, after the firing finally died away and an eerie calm settled over the high ground along the Rio Grande, Colonel Barrett rode up to the worn Indiana skirmishers of Company K. He asked Lieutenant Jones, "Well, Lieutenant, how are you getting along?" Not volunteering any information, Lieutenant Jones, still angry at Barrett for failing to provide him specific instructions and reinforcements for so long, answered curtly, "Very well." Then, Colonel Barrett asked Jones what he thought was best to do in this situation. A veteran who knew he was dealing with an untried commander, Lieutenant Jones offered the undeniable tactical truth that had been demonstrated repeatedly that day at Palmito Ranch: "[I]t was not at all probable for infantry to catch cavalry." Colonel Barrett, however, ignored the wisdom and warning, discounting the sound advice from a junior officer.[73]

Instead, Colonel Barrett ordered Company K to push forward as before. He refused to take heed of Lieutenant Jones's hard-earned wisdom. Jones continued to be perplexed by the fact that the colonel refused to provide definite guidance in regard to the tactical situation or future plan of action. Amid an increasingly confused tactical situation and with no concise plan of operations, Colonel Barrett then asked Jones, "What do you think can be done?"[74]

Making the most of the opportunity, Lieutenant Jones responded that he "would like to try a little maneuver on the enemy" at this time, to take advantage of the lull.[75] Then, the lieutenant formulated a scheme to entrap his fast-moving opponent to negate the Rebels' superior mobility, firepower, and stealth. Incredibly, while being drawn farther away from Palmito Ranch and Brazos Santiago where the nearest reinforcements lingered about a dozen miles away, Colonel Barrett was not yet concerned about the escalating vulnerability of his task force deep in Confederate territory. He remained obsessed with the thought of glory from Brownsville's capture.[76]

If Confederate reinforcements suddenly arrived from Brownsville, then Colonel Barrett's task force could be cut off from the main road, which the

34th Indiana had departed in advancing southward upon Palmito Ranch. In fact, Barrett's command was divided by the road, with the 62nd to the north and the 34th to the south. A Confederate advance eastward up the Brownsville Road could split the Yankee force in two.

Understanding the need to regain the initiative, Lieutenant Jones was now intent on entrapping as much of the troublesome Texas cavalry as possible. In this context, he was stealing a page from the tactical handbook of Captain Robinson and Colonel Ford. Unfortunately, the proposed Federal tactical plan for entrapment would ultimately become more of a trap for the Yankees than their elusive adversary.

In part Lieutenant Jones's plan called for a detachment of fifty Indiana soldiers under his command "to move [west] along the banks of the river and through the chaparral," while another fifty-man Hoosier detachment took position amid the level, open prairie west of Palmito Hill, "on the extreme right in plain open view" of the Texans. This small force of Yankees, which was to be completely exposed in the open on the sand flats, would serve as the irresistible bait for the opportunistic Confederates who were sure to strike.

Lieutenant Jones explained his plan to Colonel Barrett: "[M]y maneuvering on the chaparral was to be concealed from the enemy, and I wanted the main body to fall back [while] skirmishers that were sent out on the right [were] to fall back also, covering the retreat [and then Jones's detachment] would try to get in the [enemy's] rear by moving forward, entirely concealed from the enemy in order to reach their rear, of which we had found the location." With no plan of his own, Colonel Barrett was receptive to the lieutenant's plan and informed Lieutenant Jones that "you may try it."[77]

In fact, Colonel Barrett was so keen about Jones's plan that he ordered Lieutenant Colonel Branson to bring up a detachment of the 62nd to support the Indiana soldiers. Unfortunately, however, Barrett failed to apprise either Lieutenant Jones or Lieutenant Colonel Branson of the broader tactical situation in which the two forces of Yankees were now involved.[78]

Leaving one-third, or the left side, of his Indiana skirmish line in position, with orders to later move into a designated position to serve as the decoy, Lieutenant Jones swung two-thirds of his Hoosier skirmish company by the left flank to set up his plan. To disguise these maneuvers, the Indiana lieutenant "deployed the remainder of my company at greater intervals" to maintain the same length along his front, so as not to betray his intentions.[79]

In addition, Lieutenant Jones also now had available about twenty soldiers of Company A, 34th Indiana. These men helped to extend the lieutenant's front. To assist Jones in laying his snare, Colonel Barrett dispatched the dismounted troopers of the 2nd Texas Cavalry southward to reinforce the advanced Indiana skirmishers. Soon the Texans in blue, formerly to the

Hoosiers' north and south of the 62nd, hustled into formation as Lieutenant Jones directed them to take position in advance of his line's left.[80]

At this time, Lieutenant Jones was surprised to discover that the leader of the 2nd Texas detachment, Lieutenant Hancock, wore "no badge or designation of rank for an officer." Perhaps Hancock wore no officer's rank so as not to risk becoming a target to Rebel sharpshooters or, if captured, possible retaliation. Lieutenant Jones, nevertheless, hurriedly explained the plan to the homespun lieutenant. Now a combined force of Company A, 34th Indiana, most of Lieutenant Jones's own Company K, and the fifty dismounted troopers of the 2nd Texas were to advance farther westward, into the area where the river straightened to flow west-east once again. Then, this strike force was to take a concealed position amid the chaparral along the river on the left and to the south. In total, Lieutenant Jones would then have two-thirds of his men in concealed positions along the river on the far left and south of Captain Robinson's Rebels.[81]

One-third of Company K, or about fifty soldiers, now began to swing northward and down the northern slope of the bluff into the open of the flat prairie as a decoy. When the Rebels leaped at the opportunity to attack the small and unsupported Yankee force in the open on the sand flats, two-thirds of Lieutenant Jones's task force would spring the ambush from its concealed position along the river. To deliver the coup de grâce, Lieutenant Jones's men would strike from the south, smashing into the Rebels' exposed right flank to crush the Texans once and for all.[82]

Meanwhile, after checking to make sure that his bait force was easing into the proper position as planned, Lieutenant Jones returned to the left. He then ordered the advance to continue westward along the riverbank. After the troops struggled through the thick bushes, briers, and snarled mesquite trees for about 100 yards, the Indiana lieutenant ordered a halt. By this time, he reasoned that his force had now advanced almost far enough west to be in position to advance northward to hit the right flank and rear of any Rebel force attempting to attack the Company K skirmishers in the open to the northeast.[83]

To ensure that this force was in a proper position to spring the ambush, Lieutenant Jones and Cpl. Joseph A. Keller scouted the terrain before them for about fifty yards. With the way clear and with the ambush now being set according to plan, Jones returned to his men with renewed confidence in his plan's success. He then again led his skirmishers forward, or west, a short distance.[84]

Just when everything seemed to be going smoothly, however, "I [suddenly] heard something on our right [and] I halted the different detachments [2nd Texas Cavalry and 34th Indiana]." Once again, Lieutenant Jones and Corporal Keller scouted northward off the high ground and into the prairie to investigate the source of the mysterious noise, fearing the Rebels' approach. With revolvers drawn, the two Yankees eased through the dense stands of chaparral, "crawling part of the way on our hands and knees, to see what we could see [and] after moving about twenty-five yards we saw troops, and found them to be—after getting a closer observation of them through the chaparral—the [62nd] United States Colored Infantry."[85]

Lieutenant Jones could scarcely believe what he now saw before him. After halting the advancing ranks of his black regiment, Lieutenant Colonel Branson stepped forward to meet a very surprised, if not angry, Jones. Jones saluted smartly, revealing his irritation and frustration. Then Branson informed the lieutenant that "I was ordered by Colonel Barrett to report to you with my command [but] I do not know what your movements are, or what you are doing." Barrett had failed to inform Lieutenant Jones that a detachment of the 62nd was coming to his support. With a great deal of understatement, Lieutenant Jones later stated that he was "somewhat surprised, and did not know those [black] troops were sent there for, and I told him it must be a mistake."[86]

But the Federals did not realize the cost of their tactical blunder. Thanks to the advance of the 62nd detachment to the Hoosiers' north, the lieutenant's plan of entrapment was already revealed to the astute, experienced Texas Rebels.[87]

In addition, the vigilant Confederates had already seen a sight that only fueled their determination to fight even harder and longer against the odds: African Americans in blue uniforms. In disbelief, Captain Carrington of Colonel Giddings's Battalion described how "a regiment of negro troops were also moving forward, perhaps to sustain skirmishers."

Once again, Colonel Barrett was failing to rise to the challenge as a field commander. This latest example was the worst yet. Indeed, he had informed neither Lieutenant Colonel Branson nor the 34th Indiana of either his tactical plan or objective. And no communication existed between the Indiana and the black regiment, resulting in more confusion and poor coordination of the overall offensive effort on this day. By this time, Colonel Barrett was relying upon the tactical plan of a young skirmish line lieutenant rather than any well-conceived plan of his own, relinquishing initiative to the tactical ability of a subordinate.

Lieutenant Jones, meanwhile, attempted to salvage his ambush plan as best he could. He "stepped out to the edge of the chaparral—about fifty yards [and] saw that the 34th [Indiana] was falling back and that the skirmishers on the right were falling back but the latter [the decoy force] having never been to the point designated." Jones then returned to Lieutenant Colonel Branson. For any chance of his plan succeeding, the Indiana lieutenant asked the colonel if he could shift his regiment into a reserve position behind, or north-east of, the decoy force himself, "or in other words, whether he would subject himself to be commanded by a [2nd] Lieutenant."

Increasingly aware of his own tactical inexperience by this time, Lieu-tenant Colonel Branson readily complied, after learning that Colonel Barrett had given permission for Lieutenant Jones to lay his trap. Lieutenant Jones then asked Lieutenant Colonel Branson "to move his men up to within a few yards of where I had my line."[88]

After returning to his troops, Lieutenant Jones continued to advance west through the brush along the river. This forward movement was now more risky, however, because he was much closer to the Rebel position. Greater risk resulted when the bluecoats, to their surprise, suddenly reached "a brush fence and a distance beyond that of about fifteen feet cleared out from the river to the prairie," wrote Lieutenant Jones of the obstacle.[89] The lieutenant now faced a dilemma. Indeed, he wondered "how I could cross the open space [spanning north] without being seen by the enemy, as their advance could be seen at that time."[90]

Fortunately for the Federals, at this time Captain Robinson was making adroit tactical adjustments of his own. He was busily shifting and redeploying his line a short distance to the rear. This retrograde movement by the Texas Rebels finally allowed Lieutenant Jones an opportunity to gain ground and overcome the obstacle. He therefore ordered his troops forward on the dou-ble. According to Jones: "[The Yankees crossed] over the brush fence without making a noise to be heard by the enemy, they being very near [and] I suc-ceeded in crossing my men across the space, and moved them by a right-wheel after I had deployed along the river bank in the chaparral."

After concealing his strike force in the tangled thickets and chaparral along the river southwest of the designated bait force's position in the open prairie, Lieutenant Jones once more returned to Lieutenant Colonel Branson and the 62nd USCT. It was no easy task to coordinate this complex tactical maneuver amid the scorching heat and high chaparral that reduced visibility to nearly zero; and especially because "we were so close on the enemy at the time that I moved my own men by whispering to the head of the column and letting the others follow," stated Lieutenant Jones of his stealthy movement westward along the river.

According to the revised plan, Lieutenant Colonel Branson now shifted his troops a short distance northward into a concealed position amid the chap-arral. Lieutenant Jones had informed Lieutenant Colonel Branson that "he would have to move his regiment to the left in order to cross under the banks of the river as much as possible to keep from being seen by the enemy[; and] after he got his command across, I told him that I wanted his regiment in close protecting distance of the skirmishers in line of battle."

Acting as a general reserve under cover, the concealed soldiers of the 62nd were then to advance westward out of the chaparral and open fire on the enemy before them as soon as Lieutenant Jones's strike force launched their attack from the south. Soon, Lieutenant Jones's trap was in place, despite the earlier confusion and wasting of additional time. The lieutenant had even dispatched Corporal Keller forward to scout a path through the maze of chaparral for his northward advance. Unlike Colonel Barrett, Lieutenant Jones maintained a clear understanding of the tactical situation. At long last, all seemed almost ready.[91]

Finally, Lieutenant Jones ordered his bait force of skirmishers northward and into the open prairie of the Palo Alto Plain. Simultaneously, he directed Lieutenant Colonel Branson "to move his regiment up, as I could see the enemy in front of us very distinctly at the time, being about 100 yards off [but] they had not discovered us yet." The Indiana lieutenant ordered Branson to advance to the 62nd, now concealed in the chaparral, "in order that when the enemy retreated they would run against his regiment."[92]

According to plan, once the bluecoat skirmishers opened fire from their exposed position in the open prairie, then the African Americans of the 62nd were to surge out of the chaparral to hit the Rebels from the east, while Lieutenant Jones struck from the south. At last, Lieutenant Jones's plan of ambush was working to order, or so it seemed.[93]

The carefully laid plans of the Indiana officer shortly self-destructed, however. Lieutenant Jones and his soldiers advanced too far north until they were adjacent to the 62nd to the east. One of Jones's over-anxious men on the right flank, unable to resist the temptation, fired a shot prematurely at the Rebels. This single shot set off a chain reaction that exposed the ambush to the Confederates, sabotaging Lieutenant Jones's plan after so much time and effort.[94]

The shot also unleashed Lieutenant Colonel Branson and his coiled-up African Americans. The over-eager rookies of the 62nd surged from their cover to fire a couple of volleys. Lieutenant Jones could only watch in frustration as "the [62nd] Regiment came out of the chaparral at a run in small squads, and not in line of battle, firing directly over our heads and through our ranks at the enemy."[95] The Yankees were proving a greater danger to themselves than the Rebels were at this point. Lieutenant Jones's detachment was now under fire from Union troops because of a plan of the lieutenant's own making.

To escape the blistering fire from their own comrades, Lieutenant Jones screamed for his Indiana soldiers to race for the cover of a shallow ravine.

Lieutenant Jones's ambush came closer to killing more Yankees than Rebels. Meanwhile, the alerted Confederates opened a blistering volley of their own, then continued shooting at anything that moved. In an unexpected reversal of fortune, the officer who had devised the ambush, Lieutenant Jones, now found himself caught between two fires, including volleys erupting from the men of the 62nd.[96]

Lieutenant Colonel Branson now attempted to gain control of the confused situation. He tried to form his soldiers in a battle line at the edge of the chaparral about twenty-five yards behind Lieutenant Jones's advanced skirmishers but met with little success. By this time another black soldier had fallen to the ground badly wounded. The victim was either Pvt. Wyette Rowlett or Pvt. Fleming Humes. The casualty only caused more difficulties for the increasingly frustrated Lieutenant Jones. Jones described that "there was a man wounded in the [62nd] Regiment [and] this circumstance caused great excitement in that regiment and delayed the movement which I wished them to make."[97]

Undeterred by the unraveling of his plan, Lieutenant Jones continued to lead his troops toward the elusive Rebels. With some surprise, the Indiana lieutenant described that "the enemy did not appear to give way" at this time, despite converging blue waves of both Indiana and African American troops advancing toward them.[98]

Captain Robinson, however, finally began to ascertain the risks of battling too many Yankees at too close a range in the dense chaparral. With the carefully laid ambush of the Yankees prematurely triggered, Captain Robinson and his troopers now realized the full extent of the danger they faced.

The Rebel cavalrymen swiftly galloped safely westward and out of harm's way. Then, as usual, Captain Robinson, who grew more determined to stand firm with the greater odds he faced, deployed his dismounted troopers in yet another good defensive position. He then awaited the Yankees' approach. In dismay, Lieutenant Jones described that "before I could get my men out of the chaparral, the enemy had got quite a distance from that place."[99]

With Lieutenant Jones's failed tactical plan, the Federals lost even more momentum during this ill-fated maneuver. The Yankees succeeded only in delaying their own advance and causing more confusion among their ranks. Lieutenant Jones reported the ambush setback to Colonel Barrett, who finally reached the front lines. The Texas Confederates were now "drawn up in line of battle on our front—on the edge of the chaparral," ready to contest the next Union advance.[100]

After learning of tactical developments and the failed ambush, Colonel Barrett by the afternoon decided to end the fight for the day. The unproduc-

tive Federal maneuvers had consumed the entire day, and most of that involved skirmishing. And by this time, the Yankees were worn out and hungry,
after marching and fighting in the scorching heat and high humidity. Lieutenant Jones, acting more like a battlefield commander than Colonel Barrett,
then asked the colonel if he had any particular objective in mind. "He said he
had not, only to drive them [toward Brownsville]."[101]

In no uncertain terms, Lieutenant Jones informed the colonel that he
should not advance any farther without specific orders. Eager to halt his
troops to sort out the tactical confusion as best he could, Colonel Barrett responded to Lieutenant Jones by saying, "Well, if you think best, we will return to the bluffs [the high ground along the river south and southwest of
Palmito Hill] and eat supper."[102]

Now, in the heat of early afternoon, Colonel Barrett ordered the 34th Indiana to return to Palmito Hill, where they were "to encamp and prepare for
their supper."[103] According to Colonel Branson, the 62nd had advanced a
mile and a half west of Palmito Hill.[104]

Following orders, the black regiment had just shifted ranks by this time.
With Enfield rifled muskets on shoulders, the African American troops began
to retire by the left flank. Inexplicably, "either Colonel Barrett or Colonel
Branson ordered a charge of the 62nd Regiment, on a run, over one of the
bush fences, and continued in that direction after getting over the fence until
they reached the top of one of the ridges, where they halted and fired three
volleys in the open prairie," wrote a disbelieving Lieutenant Jones, who was
then withdrawing his troops.[105]

The Texas Rebels were long gone from the immediate vicinity by this
time. Evidently, this unexpected offensive maneuver by the 62nd was a ruse
merely to demonstrate the Federals' strength to keep the Texans at bay. Now
the men of the 62nd were ordered to retire as well.

In deciding to break off the fight, Colonel Barrett summarized:

> I think it was about 2 o'clock in the afternoon [when] I ordered the
> 34th Indiana to stack their arms near the place where they had previ-
> ously been resting, under arms. There they prepared their meal [and]
> an hour and a half later the 62nd retired to the same camp and took
> their position to the right of the 34th by my orders [and] the [2nd
> Texas Cavalry] men also retired to the bluff [southwest of Palmito
> Hill] along the river and preparations were being made to rest there
> until night, with a view of moving camp at dark a short distance and
> marching in the morning at 3 o'clock in the direction of Port [Point]
> Isabel.

It was to be a withdrawal. Colonel Barrett had had enough of fighting the feisty Texas Rebels not only for this day but also for the rest of his life. The colonel's burning ambition to capture Brownsville and reap glory and riches was no more.[106]

Colonel Barrett at least ordered Lieutenant Colonel Branson to place "four or five men on high ground where they could overlook the surrounding country, in order to notify us of the approach of the enemy." This mere handful of pickets, unfortunately, was insufficient to cover a wide enough front to give advance warning to the Union encampment. Colonel Barrett made another serious error by not having established a regular picket or even a skirmish line to protect the camp, especially from cavalry attack. Here was an opportunity that would not go unnoticed by Colonel Ford.[107]

"OLD RIP" REACHES THE FIELD

Meanwhile, the long-awaited Confederate aid from Brownsville was finally reaching the field to reinforce Captain Robinson. Throughout the day, Robinson continued to hold firm because of Colonel Ford's earlier orders to "concentrate the command on the Brownsville and Brazos island road." The Southern reinforcements were late in arriving by about three hours thanks to the lack of harmony among Confederate leadership at headquarters. In addition, the poor quality of the horses, weak and undernourished as the result of drought and inactive service, slowed the pace in reaching the field of action.

Ready to move out at daylight, for hours Colonel Ford had waited in vain for General Slaughter and his men at Fort Brown, the designated rendezvous site. A new Mexican threat to Brownsville had attracted the general's attention, and Slaughter was not keen on Ford's plan to engage the Union invaders. But he failed to inform Colonel Ford of either the newly developed tactical situation or his decision to remain in town. Hence, the uniting of Colonel Ford's and General Slaughter's forces to reinforce Captain Robinson never took place at Brownsville as originally planned.

Knowing that time was of the essence and that Captain Robinson's horsemen were fighting against the odds to the east, "Old Rip" decided to move out at 11:00 A.M., May 13, after six pieces of artillery reached Brownsville after a long forced march. Despite his superior's failure to arrive or orders to advance on his own, Ford led his troopers eastward at a brisk pace. The Texas Rebels rode hard toward the escalating action. The caissons and limbers carrying the six artillery pieces bounded along the Brownsville Road, stirring up a cloud of dust that went unseen by the Federals.

For hours, Colonel Ford encouraged his cavalrymen onward across the flatlands of the Palo Alto plain. He was determined to rescue Captain Robin-

son's band before it was too late. Ford described the last-minute arrival of reinforcements on the field of Palmito Ranch, after an exhaustive three-hour
ride from Brownsville: "[O]n the morning of the 13th, Captain Robinson reported the enemy reinforced and again advancing. Steps were taken to meet
him at once. At 11 o'clock a.m. I made a forward movement with Capt.
O. G. Jones' light battery and a portion of the cavalry. Learning that Captain
Robinson was hard pressed and forced to give ground, I directed Lieutenant
[Jesse] Vineyard, commanding a detachment of Capt. A[llen] C[arter] Jones'
company to move briskly to Captain Robinson's support [and] the order was
executed with promptitude."[108]

Around 3:00 P.M., a dust-covered "Old Rip" and about one hundred of
his Texans reached the field about two miles west of Palmito Hill just as Lieutenant Jones had attempted to set up his ambush and Colonel Barrett was
hoping for the best. Arriving on the field, Colonel Ford was eager for the fray,
and his boys knew it. To face his last challenge of this war, the colonel
brought troopers of his own 2nd Texas Cavalry, additional companies of
Colonel Giddings's Battalion, the gray-clad Tejanos of Colonel Benavides's

regiment, a couple of independent horse companies, and an artillery battery of six guns and fifty men. In total, however, Colonel Ford still commanded fewer than 300 soldiers on the field.

The sight of Colonel Ford once again coming to the rescue inspired Captain Robinson's weary troopers. In their excitement, Captain Robinson's men raised the cry of "Hurrah for Old Rip!" These sweat-stained Texas Rebels, who had been fighting against the odds for days, suddenly came to life. They shouted and waved their hats, cheering "Old Rip" as never before. New confidence surged through the thinned ranks of the Texas Confederates. In contrast, no such enthusiasm or confidence existed among the worn out bluecoats under the bumbling Colonel Barrett.

Feeling the excitement of once more facing the Yankee invaders, Colonel Ford responded to the cheering with a smile. After savoring the moment, he then yelled to this troops, "Men, we have whipped the enemy in previous fights [and] we can do it again!" This was the fighting spirit that led the Texas Rebels to believe that the remaining bands of defenders of the Trans-Mississippi could yet "defy the combined powers of all Yankeedom."

Despite the large number of Yankees before him, which "somewhat unnerved" this savvy frontier commander, Colonel Ford, realizing that "this may be the last fight of the war," wanted to take the offensive and strike a blow. Not only were the Confederates determined to win victory but also to reap some revenge upon their opponents, especially the hated Texas Yankees.

Flying into action, Ford first placed his Rebel reinforcements in a "concentrate[d position] on the [road] in Captain Robinson's rear." As in the frontier way of waging war, Ford carefully positioned his soldiers under the cover of mesquite thickets, tangles of underbrush, and chaparral. By this means, he concealed his relatively small number of troops from the Federals, who still had no idea that Confederate reinforcements had arrived from Brownsville. Most important, Colonel Ford retained the element of surprise.

Here, just below the San Martin Ranch and between this position and the tree-covered La Tulosa Hill on Tulosa Ranch directly west of Palmito Hill, Captain Robinson and his men had established their final defensive position to block the Federal drive upon Brownsville. The thick brush and trees on Tulosa Hill hid the Confederates from Yankee view. Colonel Ford now "found Capt. Robinson [hotly engaged] in a heavy skirmish with Lieutenant Hancock's company, of the Second Texas and a company of Morton Rifles," wrote Captain Carrington.

As if fighting the Yankees was not enough on this sweltering day in mid-May, the Texas Rebels, ever individualistic and cantankerous, were also fighting among themselves. A hot-tempered Capt. O. G. Jones, commander of Jones's Company Texas Light Artillery, claimed seniority not only over Captain

Robinson, because of General Slaughter's orders, but also overall command on the field over Colonel Ford. And Captain Jones was adamantly arguing his point on the battlefield at a time when Colonel Ford needed to attend to the more serious business at hand, such as the development of a tactical plan.

Not surprisingly, Captain Jones was one of General Slaughter's cronies. He was aware that the popular ex–Texas Ranger possessed no official Confederate commission. In a showdown on the battlefield, Captain Jones attempted to take charge. The rivalry between Colonel Ford's and General Slaughter's troops and the long-simmering dispute between the frontier Texan, Colonel Ford, and the cavalier Virginian, General Slaughter, had once again resurfaced at a most inopportune time. An angry Ford, who could not be burdened with seniority issues with a battle brewing, immediately ordered Captain Jones arrested and placed under guard. This clash between strong frontier personalities in matters of rank was not surprising among the fiercely independent Texas Rebels. The feisty Captain Jones himself possessed a lengthy record of defiance to authority. When he did obey orders, it was often under protest.

After a few minutes Jones's temper cooled and he at last "abandoned his intention of commanding[, then] asked for permission to 'fight his battery'" in the upcoming fray. Colonel Ford respected the captain's return to reason because though hot-headed, Jones was a fine combat officer. Indeed, such combativeness would be needed on this day. Ford immediately restored Captain Jones to command of his Texas battery, while assuring him "there was nothing personal in the order of arrest." After solving the last remaining differences among themselves, the Texas Confederates prepared to square off against the Federals.

According to Captain Carrington, Captain Jones's decision to recognize Colonel Ford's authority and leadership was a wise choice. As Captain Carrington explained: "Capt. Jones was regarded as a very good captain of artillery, and in obedience to Ford's orders he [would today] manage his artillery well [and would do] good service. No one, however, regarded him in any other light than as a captain of artillery, and no captain on the field of battle would have received an order from him, because every captain on the battlefield, without exception, ranked him, and if he had assumed to command them, it is believed he would have been shot or immediately arrested": swift but necessary Texas frontier justice in the face of the enemy.

To ascertain the enemy's dispositions and exact tactical situation before him, "Old Rip" personally reconnoitered before the lines. As was his custom, the frontier commander ventured near the Federal lines to evaluate the situation, while hunting for a tactical weakness in the Union position. Colonel Ford was anything but the type of commander—like Colonel Barrett—who remained safely in the rear when the bullets began flying fast. His unorthodox style of personal reconnaissance made perfectly good sense to Ford. Indeed, he was one of the most experienced and reliable scouts in the entire Lower Rio Grande Valley.

As Colonel Ford described his risky solo reconnaissance before the lines: "I rode forward with a glass and made a reconnaissance of their force and position [and] I met with no interruption at that time." So many Federals now stood before his small Rebel force that it looked like a sea of blue had descended upon the land. Colonel Ford concluded initially that "this may be the last fight of the war and from the number of Union men I see before me, I am going to be whipped." He was, however, determined to formulate a shrewd tactical plan based upon the exploitation of some advantage.

After surveying the field and attempting to discover a weakness to exploit in the Yankees' dispositions, Colonel Ford ascertained that "the Federal lines [were] some half a mile lower down below the ranch of San Martin, cutting the road at right angles." Therefore, a well-conceived battle plan needed to be developed to exploit this opportunity.

Despite the odds, Colonel Ford once again rose to the occasion. Encouraged by the fact that his Texas soldiers were "in such good fighting trim . . . he made haste to put them to work." "Old Rip," consequently, was at once "determined to attack" the Yankees.

Colonel Ford had no way of knowing that on this very day the Texas governor, along with the chief executives of Arkansas, Missouri, and Louisiana, adopted a peace plan without surrender. In addition, they had already authorized Gen. Kirby Smith to disband, but not parole, his Rebel forces in the field to end the Trans-Mississippi war. The Confederate peace plan as formulated by the Trans-Mississippi governors was rejected out of hand.

Based upon his keen assessment of the situation, Colonel Ford redeployed his force of fewer than 300 men—both his reinforcements and Captain Robinson's troopers—for action. Ford positioned approximately 100 of his Rebels to reinforce Captain Robinson's less than 200 soldiers still holding their own in the foremost position. So as not to betray these moves to strengthen his thin battle line, Colonel Ford ordered his reinforcements to creep forward under cover of underbrush and mesquite to gain Captain Robinson's advanced position in small parties. This undetected movement of stealth paid dividends, disguising the reinforcements and allowing the overconfident Yankees to remain ignorant of the situation.

Moving swiftly into position, Col. Thomas Scott Anderson's Texas Cavalry battalion under Capt. David W. Wilson took position on the right, while Colonel Giddings's cavalry battalion formed on the left under Captain Robinson's command. Bestowing the main battle line to Captain Robinson was

Colonel Ford's reward for his captain's recent success in delaying the Union troops. Colonel Ford praised Captain Robinson, remarking that he "deserved to lead for the way he held the small force together" and delayed a superior opponent for two days. Captain Robinson now commanded the bulk of the cavalry on the field, both Colonel Anderson's battalion under Captain Wilson on the right and Colonel Giddings's horse soldiers on the left.

To anchor the weakest section of the Confederate battle line directly before the Yankees, a section of guns of Capt. O. G. Jones's battery, under Lt. J. Mayrant Smith, held the center. In guardian fashion, these cannons soon unlimbered across the Brownsville Road, after it looped southward west of Palmito Hill, to compensate for the wide bend in the river and to once again parallel the river in a west-east direction.

With precision and speed, the Texas artillery pieces wheeled into line, with the gunners ready for the hard work ahead. "Old Rip" expected much from Lieutenant Smith on this day. Another two-gun section of 12-pounder guns was held in reserve. Ford's orders, however, specified that the guns were to move "in advance of the line" once the Yankees were on the run. These Texas Rebel gunners and their four cannons, supported by the two-gun section, were ordered by Colonel Ford to play an aggressive tactical role much like that of the famous flying artillery of the Mexican-American War. Colonel Ford's careful positioning of the Texas guns in the line's center was a symbolic artillery deployment to these Texas frontiersmen. On that famous April 1836 day, which ensured Texas independence from Mexico, two 6-pounders known as the Twin Sisters, gifts of the citizens of Cincinnati, Ohio, had anchored the center of the Texas battle line at San Jacinto to play a key role in the decisive victory over General Santa Anna's army.

Relying on more than thirty years of military experience in contrast with Colonel Barrett's less than thirty months, Colonel Ford's tactical plan began to take shape. Ford laid the foundation of a battle plan to exploit both the advantages of terrain and the enemy's weaknesses, especially his overconfidence. Like an artist visualizing a masterpiece, "Old Rip" created a masterful plan to suit both the terrain and the hard-hitting capabilities of his Texas horse soldiers.

First and foremost, Ford knew that to compensate for the disparity in numbers he had to exploit his few available assets: mobility, the element of surprise, and speed. Consequently, he had to keep the Yankees in a fixed position without arousing their suspicion about the forthcoming counterpunch, while he stealthily maneuvered his troops. In addition, this was Colonel Ford's home turf, and he knew the ground well, unlike the Federals. And he did not take kindly to interlopers in blue on the Texas mainland, especially those from Texas, Missouri, and Indiana.

Colonel Ford judged that he could rely on Captains Robinson, Jones, and Wilson to occupy the Yankees' attention in front. Here, south of the road and the San Martin Ranch and barely more than two miles directly west and southwest of Palmito Ranch, the thin gray and butternut-hued line of Texas Rebels would have to stand firm, even if the Yankees attacked, to allow Colonel Ford time to set up the remainder of his tactical plan and to lay a foundation for the frontier formula for success.

Most of all, Colonel Ford planned to fully exploit his opponent's tactical mistakes. By sending his troops too far toward Brownsville and then along the course of the Rio Grande, he drew the Federals deeper into the trap that Colonel Ford was now laying. The Brownsville Road at the head of the river's bend was now two miles to the north.

Assisting Colonel Ford in setting the tactical stage were the natural advantages of the lay of the land. By sending the 34th Indiana southward a good distance below Palmito Ranch to march along the river, Colonel Barrett blocked his rear by the west edge of the wide bend of the Rio Grande. In fact, the west side of this wide bend, with Mios Ranch near its head and Palmito Ranch located farther south and lower down the bend, was a trap in itself. Here, the east-west flowing river turned north-south for nearly two miles and the bend's west side was perpendicular to the east-west running Brownsville Road at the head of the bend.

It was at this expansive bend, itself perpendicular to the river's general course both farther east and farther west, that the Rio Grande reached its farthest penetration both north, to nearly touch the road, and southward toward Mexico, while running through the level coastal plain east of Brownsville. Colonel Barrett had wasted precious time and effort in advancing along the river's meandering course and through the rugged countryside. In contrast, Colonel Ford's reinforcements had advanced swiftly across the open prairie from Brownsville along a relatively direct line.

Northward to the Federals' right stood a slight ridge covered with underbrush, and dense stands of yucca trees, cactus, and mesquite. Known as the Loma de la Jauja, this brushy patch of high ground slightly northwest of Palmito Ranch rose barely above sea level to a height of thirty to forty feet. This thin strip appeared almost like an Everglades-like hammock because the brush and tree-covered ridge was surrounded by the level, open ground of the coastal plain, which spanned eastward all the way to the sea. An expansive salt marsh covered the flat lands north of the ridge. Miles beyond the wide stretches of this level terrain could be seen the white lighthouse at Point Isabel. From here, the lighthouse appeared on the distant horizon like a lone tree standing tall amid the expansive stretches of flatland and salt water marshes and lagoons.

This unoccupied high ground presented an ideal position from which to launch a cavalry strike on Colonel Barrett's right flank or to intercept his line of retreat northward along the main road to reach the head of the river's bend. This opportunity was not lost to the perceptive Colonel Ford. He therefore devised his plan accordingly. Colonel Barrett not only failed to protect his exposed right flank and rear by dispatching a detail to occupy this key elevated position but he had also not bothered to make a reconnaissance of this commanding ground: a negligence to Colonel Ford's advantage. Colonel Barrett should have conducted such a reconnaissance the previous day because this slightly elevated position was near Captain Robinson's left flank, where the Rebels could earlier have been outflanked from the north.

So far, the Yankees erred tactically by attempting to strike the wrong Rebel flank. Instead of attempting to hit Captain Robinson's right amid the tangled and brush-choked bottoms along the river, Colonel Barrett would have been more successful in striking the Texans' more vulnerable left. Colonel Barrett would have also made his isolated force more secure by occupying the high ground of the Loma de la Jauja to protect his right flank, while keeping his line of retreat back along the Brownsville Road more secure and open.

By committing the mistake of advancing too far south and following the meandering course of the river for hours—first marching south and then west because of the river's wide bend—the bluecoats were now constricted along the high ground at the edge of the prairie, some two miles south of the Brownsville Road at the head of the river's bend.

Because of topography and with the leadership team of Captains Robinson, Wilson, and Jones blocking a renewed Federal advance upon Brownsville, the compressed Union force now only possessed a single, narrow passage of escape. This last avenue was now a slim bottleneck north of Palmito Ranch, at the head of the river's bend that jutted northward to nearly reach the Brownsville Road, and between the river and the eastern edge of the slight narrow ridge—which ran east-west for about one and three-quarter miles to roughly parallel the river—to the north and northwest of the Federals' position. This narrow passageway now offered the Yankees the only avenue of escape from Palmito Ranch and back north, to gain the road as it turned east toward the safety of "the Brazos."

To give the Yankees an additional false sense of security this early afternoon, meanwhile, Colonel Ford ordered Robinson, Jones, and Wilson to withdraw slowly westward to a small clump of brush and trees southwest of Palmito Hill and along the southern edge of the Palo Alto prairie. "Old Rip" instructed these veteran officers to conserve their full firepower so as not to betray the fact that Captain Robinson had been reinforced from Brownsville.

Here, to additionally disguise Ford's plan, the Rebels found good defensive positions amid heavy cover to delay any renewed Federal advance.

Meanwhile, the two-gun section of Texas light artillery under the quarrelsome Captain Jones also retired to redeploy under cover with the gray-clad troopers. But this was merely a clever ruse. Colonel Ford ordered these Texas gunners to concentrate their fire on the 34th Indiana in front once he gave the signal. This stealthy redeployment and concealment of artillery also paid dividends, masking Rebel strength and intentions. These silent maneuvers by Colonel Ford did nothing to break the ill-founded confidence among the Yankees. The bluecoats continued to prepare dinner and boil coffee without realizing either the extent or proximity of the Rebel threat.

To take advantage of the terrain, the good natural cover, and Colonel Barrett's overconfidence, Colonel Ford devised a plan that had so often proved successful against the Indians and Mexicans. While the forces of Captains Robinson, Jones, and Wilson served as a decoy to draw the Yankees' attention, Colonel Ford planned to launch a flanking movement northward beyond the unoccupied Loma de la Jauja. Once in position to the northeast, this Rebel force would then be poised to strike from the north to hit the Federals' exposed right flank.

Colonel Ford chose Lt. Jesse Vineyard, with a section of two guns of Captain Jones's Texas Light Artillery under Lt. William Gregory, "to move under cover of the hills [the slight ridge to the north] and chaparral, to flank the enemy's right, and if possible to get an enfilading fire" sweeping down from the high ground—the Loma de la Jauja. These Texas light guns would be supported by Lt. Jesse Vineyard's cavalry detachment consisting of Captain Jones's company.

Once unleashed, this Confederate enfilading fire was calculated to tear down the length of the right flank of the Union line from north to south, where the 62nd USCT was positioned. Directed by Colonel Ford to use swiftness and stealth, these Confederate flanking units were ordered to take position amid heavy cover for concealment. Towering above the sand flats and swept by the salty winds blowing westward from the Gulf of Mexico, this brush-choked high ground position overlooked the open prairie to the south and dominated the flatlands on all sides.

But Colonel Ford wanted to do much more than simply wreak havoc on the right flank of the Union line. He now planned to not only defeat but if possible to crush this force of invading bluecoats, who had violated the Wallace-Slaughter truce. Ford envisioned a final Confederate victory on Texas soil that completely eliminated the Union presence on the Texas mainland.

With this objective in mind, Colonel Ford also decided to dispatch yet another force of cavalry, north of the Loma de la Jauja and the Brownsville

Road to bolster the strength of Vineyard and Gregory's flank attack by creating what was in essence a flank force in depth. Ford correctly based his plan on the fact that the Loma de la Jauja would screen his flanking maneuver from prying Yankee eyes. Making a good choice, Colonel Ford picked Capt. John Gibbon, a former Texas Ranger who had fought beside "Old Rip" before the war, and another reliable officer, Capt. J. B. Cooke, to make the effort to apply the coup de grâce. Captain Cooke might also have been an ex–Texas Ranger who had served with Ford in the past.

The key assignment of Captains Gibbon and Cooke was to swing sufficiently wide northeastward and beyond the screen of the brushy Loma de la Jauja—and Lieutenants Vineyard and Gregory's units positioned on this slight ridge—with their horse companies, to gain the Federals' flank and rear, after they were positioned north of Lieutenants Vineyard and Gregory and the Loma de la Jauja. Indeed, Colonel Ford directed Gibbon and Cooke to swing "to the extreme left with orders to turn the enemy's right flank" at the head of the wide bend in the river that nearly reached the Brownsville Road.

While Lieutenants Vineyard and Gregory planned first to launch a flank attack from the north, the next phase of the Confederate flank attack would come farther northeast from Captains Cooke and Gibbon. Put simply, Colonel Ford's plan called for two staggered flank attacks from the north above the Federal position: a one-two knockout punch that was calculated to destroy Colonel Barrett's visions of glory and eliminate the threat to Brownsville.

Meanwhile, a line of Confederate skirmishers hurried forward to mask the stealthy flanking maneuvers of the Rebel troopers northeastward. Ford's bold plan was designed to trap and then destroy the entire Union force amid the wide bend of the Rio Grande. The area of the river's bend was an ideal place for Colonel Barrett and his Yankees to be cornered, captured, or annihilated. Colonel Ford placed the principal responsibility of delivering the killing blow on the dependable old Ranger whom Ford trusted completely, Captain Gibbon.

Gibbon had served as Ford's subordinate during the 1858 campaigns in which they defeated Iron Jacket's Comanches. The perfect choice for this assignment of closing the back door on the Yankees today, Captain Gibbon's tactical abilities were well-known. By 1858, for instance, Gibbon possessed a "fine reputation as a soldier," wrote a journalist of the *State Gazette* of Austin, Texas.

Colonel Ford's battle plan was fine-tuned to exploit Colonel Barrett's earlier tactical mistakes. Clearly, Barrett should have been wary of potential threats from the northeast, especially with the Rio Grande flowing to his left and rear. After the Federals encamped around Palmito Hill, they remained vulnerable and boxed-in, partly as a result of the topography but more importantly because of a false confidence in earlier seeing off Captain Robinson's

Rebels. By employing skillful delaying tactics, Captain Robinson had served as an effective decoy that drew the Yankees south and west along the Rio Grande and farther from Brazos Santiago and the section of the main road north of the bend: the Federal avenue of retreat. No one could more thoroughly capitalize on Yankee mistakes or more effectively close the back door on an opponent's retreat than "Old Rip."

By this time, an inexperienced Colonel Barrett had ventured too near to Brownsville, to the west, and to the Rio Grande, to the south, and too far from his base camp, to the northeast. And he had allowed his 34th Indiana to stray below the Brownsville Road, which was his only escape route to the coast around a dozen miles to the east.

Perhaps Colonel Ford and his Texans recalled the time when another confident and superior invader believed that he had Texas Rebels—or revolutionaries—beaten: General Santa Anna in April 1836. Gen. Sam Houston had launched a surprise attack when least expected and when Santa Anna's force was encamped and pinned against a swampy marsh and a lake. The Mexican army was smashed by the Texans' afternoon charge, paving the way for victory and Texas independence. And now Colonel Ford planned to repeat comparable offensive tactics to crush an invading force of Yankees against the Rio Grande. Here, on the southern rim of the Palo Alto prairie, where the Mexican-American War had started nearly two decades before, Colonel Ford was about to unleash another surprise attack on an unwary invader of Texas soil.

Ford's offensive tactics were bold considering the small number of soldiers that he had available—300 Texas Confederates on the field. This is a much smaller figure than some historians recognize. Some accounts estimate Confederate strength at Palmito Ranch as more than 1,000 soldiers. Other accounts have also overestimated the Confederate force's size, partly to rationalize the extent of the Union defeat. Not long after the battle, Colonel Ford recorded the most accurate figure, writing that "my force consisted of 275 cavalry and about twenty-five others, composed of artillery men and volunteers to man six pieces of artillery [and] this was my entire command[,]" which fought at Palmito Ranch.[109]

After the six Texas fieldpieces bounced to their respective positions behind the thin line of gray and butternut cavalrymen, the Rebel gunners then split off into three two-gun sections as ordered by Colonel Ford. Colonel Ford also commanded some French volunteers who manned at least one Imperialist gun. This French artillery was assigned to Colonel Ford by Comdr. A. Veron, the French naval commander at Matamoros. The French commander wanted Colonel Barrett and his U.S. troops, who were seen as potential allies of the Juaristas, repulsed and sent back to "the Brazos."[110]

Colonel Ford stated that he possessed only "artillery men and volunteers [enough] to man six pieces of artillery" at Palmito Ranch, without mentioning his timely French assistance. These were the only known French to serve as active Confederate allies on a Civil War battlefield.[111]

Later, the Texas colonel wrote that during the battle of Palmito Ranch: "[W]e had some volunteer French cannoneers [and] they had charge of the piece in front [and I] gave them a command to hurry up. After having gone two or three hundred yards, a [Texas] ranger came up at full speed and informed Ford that the Frenchmen had halted and unlimbered the piece [and I then] moved back at full speed and told the Frenchmen 'Allons!' They limbered up briskly and went forward with celerity."

Colonel Ford now needed every soldier that he could find. As could be expected, he "knew the French officers [for] about this time the military of France were expressing themselves much in favor of a war with the United States [and] if Louis Napoleon had made a war at the right time, it might have benefitted the Confederacy."

Meanwhile, Colonel Ford's thin line of skirmishers continued to slowly advance on the field of Palmito Ranch to allow him time to complete his dispositions and to keep the Yankees at bay. Outnumbered and on his own, Colonel Ford realized he must judiciously utilize the firepower of his six Confederate guns and at least one French cannon. Besides Rebel cavalrymen, artillery was Colonel Ford's only superiority at Palmito Ranch. In contrast, the Federals, in their haste to capture Brownsville, had ventured forth from Brazos Santiago without artillery.

Combined with the element of surprise, the skillful employment of these Texas fieldpieces might well tip the odds in Colonel Ford's favor. On such an open and flat battlefield, well-placed artillery might well determine the day. Coincidentally, as with the first battle of the Mexican War, Palo Alto, so now the last battle of the Civil War, fought only miles apart in Cameron County, might well be decided by artillery.[112]

Colonel Ford now carefully placed his trusty 12-pounders to maximize their firepower. Ford explained that "two pieces of artillery were [placed] on the right and on the road supported by our main body of cavalry [and] two pieces were [then unlimbered] in reserve . . . 300 yards in rear of that, two pieces on the extreme left of my line, supported by about fifty picked cavalry under my own immediate command."[113]

Colonel Ford had never been more eager for battle than on that hot afternoon of May 13. It did not matter that he could count on only a handful of Texas soldiers. What made up for numbers was Colonel Ford's decades of combat experience and his troops' fighting prowess. Ford also held an additional advantage by possessing an intimate knowledge of the terrain upon which he was about to fight. As Ford explained: "I am well acquainted with the country" in this remote corner of Cameron County.[114]

The Texas Rebel commander who probably deserved a general's rank, a veteran of more than thirty years of fighting along the borderlands of Texas-Mexico and the frontier, and the leading Confederate commander of the Lower Rio Grande Valley hardly looked the part. Now at age forty-nine—the same age that David Crockett met his own ill-fated destiny at the Alamo— and with his birthday in only thirteen days, Ford looked as rough as usual. He wore no fine, double-breasted colonel's uniform with three stars on the collar. He was dressed more like a Texas Ranger than a Confederate colonel. Such frontier apparel was much more suitable to the demands of border and frontier warfare than the regulation Confederate uniform. In practical terms, no gaudy Confederate colonel's uniform would betray his leadership role and exact location to Yankee marksmen. The Federals would be unable to concentrate their fire on Ford, who was about to have perhaps his finest day.[115]

Two traps were carefully laid at Palmito Ranch on May 13, one earlier by the Yankees and the other now by Colonel Ford. In trying his failed flanking attack, Lieutenant Jones had previously attempted to enfilade the Confederate right and gain their rear. Now, Colonel Ford planned to do the same to the Federals.

But while the superior number of Yankees had devised a tactical trap on a relatively small scale, the numerically inferior Confederates laid a much larger snare. In this way, "Old Rip" planned to capture or destroy the entire Union force with one blow if possible. Colonel Ford knew that his overconfident enemy was now unprepared to meet an attack. Not only were the bluecoats bivouacked for the day, but the smoke rising from the Yankees' cooking fires on the eastern horizon indicated to Colonel Ford that these soldiers no longer had fighting on their minds. What was almost unbelievable to Ford was that the Union commander had not thrown out a line of pickets or skirmishers to protect the encampment or to sound an early alarm if threatened. To this veteran frontier cavalry commander, the tactical vulnerabilities of the Union task force seemed almost too good to be true.

"In an explosion of daring," Colonel Ford now made last-minute preparations to launch his final assault. And when it came to laying tactical traps— as a good many Yankees, Mexicans, and Indians could attest—no one in this seemingly forsaken region of the Rio Grande Valley was more adept at snaring his quarry than Ford.

With well-founded confidence for success today, Colonel Ford watched the Rebel flanking cavalry column under Captain Gibbon, which included Captain Cooke's horse company, push northward on the double. At last, Colonel Ford was almost ready to hurl his Rebels forward in an attack. Both Texas leaders and soldiers knew that success would be theirs if Colonel Ford's instructions were followed precisely. At this time, "Lieutenant Gregory had orders to move under cover of the hills and chaparral to flank the enemy's right, and if possible to get in an enfilading fire [while] Captain Gibbons' and Cooke's companies were sent to the extreme left, with orders to turn the enemy's right flank."

Earlier Colonel Ford had faced what he believed was a potential threat along the Rio Grande. A steamboat heading toward Brownsville suddenly came into view. This might indicate the landing of Federal reinforcements from Brazos Santiago. In the colonel's words: "[O]ne of King and Kenedy's boats came steaming up the river [and] we could not satisfy ourselves as to the flag she bore[, consequently] two round balls were thrown at her from one of our cannons." Clearly, Colonel Ford was not taking any chances now that he had his prey cornered.

As the flanking force continued northeastward to ease behind the rising ground of the Loma de la Jauja and get into position, Colonel Ford remained not far from the Yankees.[116]

Confidence remained high among the Texas Rebels and for good reason. Colonel Ford's plan seemed destined for success. By this time, the Federals were more vulnerable than ever before. The Yankee command was weary and disorganized after a disjointed advance. To Ford's eyes, this was clear proof that an over-confident rookie commander had led the Federal task force too far from Brazos Santiago.

The Yankees were worn-out from the long march to Palmito Ranch, and the maneuvering and countermaneuvering through rough country. In laying his earlier ambush, Lieutenant Jones had advanced too far westward along the river. The overall advance had been disjointed with the 62nd USCT moving forward north of the 34th Indiana, which pushed too far to the east. Even worse, the Brownsville Road, now full of Rebel troops, ran between the 34th Indiana and a portion of the 62nd. The high ground of Palmito Hill also separated the two regiments. This Union force, then, was now ripe for the picking by a branch of the service that could inflict the maximum damage, the Texas Rebel cavalry.

But Colonel Ford was not solely responsible for gaining the tactical advantage on this day. Thanks to effective delaying tactics, Captain Robinson and his troopers had played the key role in setting up the opportunity that Colonel Ford was now about to exploit. Not only had Robinson regained the initiative before the arrivals of both Colonels Barrett and Ford but he had more than held his own for two days, impeding the Federals' advance mile after mile.

Indeed, Captain Robinson had accomplished a great deal in keeping the Yankees uncertain, off-balance, and tentative, while ensuring that the invaders would remain bottled up amid the wide bend of the Rio Grande. Because of the tactical skills of Captain Robinson and the hard fighting of his tough horse soldiers, Colonel Ford, despite having few troops at hand, was now prepared to deliver the lethal blow.

It was now around 5:00 P.M. during another hot and steamy day on the flat coastal plain of the Lower Rio Grande Valley. The Yankees were resting, attempting without much success to stay cool in the searing heat and humidity. Both officers and men, dusty and covered in sweat, were completely worn-out. Lieutenant Jones described that "being out there on the skirmish line six hours, I was somewhat fatigued and [lay] down" along with other Indiana soldiers.

These young men and boys from Indiana, Missouri, and Texas now only hoped for the sun to drop to cool the sun-baked land. Supper fires already burned in the Yankee bivouac, their smoke revealing the exact locations of Colonel Barrett's units to Colonel Ford. Many Federals now slept in an exhausted stupor, fatigued from the long day's marching and skirmishing. Without a trace of a need for vigilance, Colonel Barrett later described that "preparations were made to rest there until night, with a view of moving camp at dark, a short distance, and marching in the morning at 3 o'clock in the direction of Point Isabel."

No doubt, Colonel Barrett and his Union troops believed that they had already fought the last contest of the Civil War. It now seemed that the war was indeed finally over for them and that they would shortly be going home. After the hot skirmishes at Palmito Ranch, many Yankees took solace in the fact that they had survived the bloodiest war in American history. The prayers of both soldiers and families back home had seemingly been answered. Best of all, in the recent fighting around Palmito Ranch, not a single Yankee had won the dubious distinction of becoming the war's last fatality.[117]

Meanwhile, some Indiana soldiers of the detail left behind leisurely picked through the rubble of the destroyed buildings at the former Confederate outpost of Palmito Ranch. One Hoosier picked up a discarded Rebel letter left behind by one of Captain Robinson's Texans. Bored and with nothing to do, the curious Indiana Yankees read the Johnny Reb's letter with interest. One bluecoat described the amusing find made "at the [Palmito] ranche [*sic*] [when] a letter was picked up from a lady to her lover in the Confederate service [and] among other matters, she requested her soldier on his return home to bring her a pet Yankee. A number of our boys remarked that the young lady might tame some of our number, but she had given her lover a hard task." All the while, weariness—with both the war and this risky expedition deep in Confederate territory—dominated the complacent Union encampment during the early evening hours, as the sun-drenched land of Cameron County began to cool at last.[118]

Below the buildings of Palmito Ranch, meanwhile, other Federal soldiers discovered much more than discarded Rebel letters. To the west, an increased level of Confederate activity indicated to these veteran Indiana bluecoats that something was in the wind. Such Rebel movements usually meant that trouble was brewing, and it now began to look to some of Colonel Barrett's more perceptive veterans like this nightmarish war was not yet over after all.

The mysterious Confederate movements to the west mocked the folly of the Federals' general inactivity, over-confidence, and vulnerability. A thin line of gray skirmishers was now seen hurrying forward to the west. One Indiana soldier grew increasingly uneasy. He watched as the Rebels maneuvered for some unknown purpose, with "[their] mounted troopers galloping to and fro" toward where the sun would eventually set provided that he lived long enough to see it. Even the slanting rays of a dropping sun, which now shone in the Yankees' eyes, helped to disguise the increased Confederate activity, as Colonel Ford had planned.

Watching Rebel movements from Palmito Hill, a veteran officer of the 34th Indiana also realized that something was amiss and that more fighting lay ahead. He became so concerned about the impending menace to the west that he informed his troops in no uncertain terms: "I don't like the look of things over there." A number of Indiana soldiers now stood up and peered westward. These men now caught glimpses of the rapid Confederate movements for the first time. Most of the worn Hoosiers, however, remained oblivious of the escalating threat, while resting, sleeping, and wishing that they were back home in the cool of a late Indiana afternoon.

Colonel Barrett and most of his troops either simply ignored or never saw the mysterious Rebel movements to the west. The bluecoats continued to rest their weary feet and legs, after taking off their leather brogans. Aching shoulders got relief after these men finally gained an opportunity to discard the weight of cartridge boxes, knapsacks, and canteens. The suffocating heat along the Rio Grande had apparently sucked the life out of these Yankees at Palmito Ranch by the late afternoon of May 13. All the while, hundreds of stacked Union muskets, new Enfield rifles that sparkled in the sunlight, remained in neat rows and untouched as the Rebels steadily maneuvered into position.[119]

As could be expected with the sight of his dispositions unfolding before his eyes, Colonel Ford rejoiced at the Federals' continued complacency. All the

while, the Yankees continued to remain inactive, offering no response to the
Rebel movements. For whatever reason, the handful of Federal scouts failed to
alert the serene encampment. A patient Colonel Ford, meanwhile, waited for
these flanking forces to maneuver silently into their assigned positions. Some
two miles west of Palmito Hill and in a battle line perpendicular to the Rio
Grande to the south, Colonel Ford and his men were ready to strike.

A flurry of shots suddenly rang out. The firing shattered the late afternoon calm of the prairie lands along the Rio Grande. In Colonel Ford's
words: "[S]kirmish firing soon became brisk [and I] waited until [I] heard
[Captain Gibbon] and [Captain Cooke] open on [the] left." Then, the long-
awaited moment arrived. Colonel Ford galloped before his band of Rebels
who were poised and eager to strike a blow. Then, "Old Rip" suddenly raised
his six-shooter and screamed, "Charge!" With a "Rebel Yell" that rang across
the sweltering plain of the Rio Grande, the Texas Confederates, with Colonel
Ford leading the way, surged forward with battle flags flying.

Captain Carrington never forgot the moment when "the earnest voice of
every man [united and] . . . such a yell exploded on the air, and coalescing
into one combined sound, ha[d] been distinctly heard three miles across the
prairie, over the reports of the musketry and cannon of the raging battle."

Launching the last Confederate charge of the Civil War, the howling Texans swarmed forward in a scene reminiscent of Sam Houston's afternoon attack at San Jacinto. While Captain Robinson's troopers surged toward the
Federal left along the river and Colonel Giddings's horse soldiers charged toward the Union right north of the road, Colonel Ford led his cavalrymen eastward to smash into the Yankees' center.

To inflict maximum damage and to cause chaos, the Texas Rebel artillerymen now opened fire. The Confederate cannons sent shells screaming
through the air and toward the Federal encampments. With pride, Colonel
Ford described that the veteran cannoneers of the Texas "artillery opened fire
before the enemy were aware we had guns on the field" and [such experienced
officers as] Lieutenant [J. Mayrant] Smith threw several well-directed shells
and round shot into the enemy's lines."[120]

As Ford unleashed his attack, perhaps the most shocked Yankee in all
Cameron County was young Colonel Barrett. Hardly believing his eyes, he
suddenly now understood that he had been outfoxed by the former Texas
Ranger. Barrett only now began to realize the full extent of his predicament.
With the sun in their eyes and the river to their backs his command had been
caught by surprise by Colonel Ford's counterattack.[121]

Making his situation even more precarious, Colonel Barrett had not yet
ordered out a protective picket line to guard the encampment, making the
surprise more complete. Instead, Barrett had earlier ordered Lieutenant

Colonel Branson to position only "four or five men on high ground where they could overlook the surrounding country, in order to notify us of the approach of an enemy," wrote Lieutenant Colonel Branson later of the totally inadequate precautions.[122]

Clearly, this was an insufficient system of warning for an isolated expeditionary force deep in enemy country. As a result, the call failed to arrive in time to alert Colonel Barrett's idle soldiers. What came instead was a steamrolling Rebel attack of Texas horse soldiers and leapfrogging Confederate artillery sections that could not be stopped.[123]

To Colonel Ford, unleashing the surprise attack was sweet revenge for Captain Robinson's troops having been caught by surprise by Colonel Barrett's truce violation. Barrett's confidence and complacency were instantly dashed. The booming Texas light artillery "was [firing] about one mile distant [and] the number [of Rebels] in sight at the time [was put] at 500 to 600 cavalry, in addition to the artillery, [while] a portion of the enemy's cavalry was distant on the [right] flank about one third of a mile." Surgeon Corodan Allen of the 62nd Regiment never forgot the moment when the attack caught everyone by surprise, while the African Americans, the largest number of troops in the expedition, "were resting, and [their] arms were stacked."[124]

In a belated effort, the Yankees attempted to recover as best they could from the shock before the Texans reached them. Hectic activity swirled through the Union bivouac area.[125]

Beardless drummer boys and buglers, both black and white, sounded their calls to rally the troops to defend a position that had been tranquil only seconds before. The bluecoats raced to the stacked rows of guns, and then grabbed their muskets and strapped on gear. Then, the soldiers rushed into formation, without worrying if the lines were neat or not.[126]

Mingling with the high-pitched Rebel yells that erupted across the prairie, the first Rebels shells exploded overhead and around the Federal bivouac. The shells added to the initial confusion among the surprised Yankees. Lieutenant Colonel Branson described the shock among his regiment. "While resting, and with most of the men eating, the enemy's cavalry reappeared in considerable force from up the river, marching by a flank movement in a direction somewhat from and down the river, and in a direction to intercept our retreat to Boca Chica": a startling tactical development, which alone was sufficient to cause panic, especially among rookie troops.

After the first few minutes, the full extent of the danger became clear to the shaken Federal leadership. Colonel Barrett now began to realize that he should have remained on his safe haven of Brazos Santiago: "[W]ithin fifteen to thirty minutes after the 62nd had gone into camp, the enemy suddenly appeared in large force, in front, on our right flank, and was already attempting to gain our rear, being further down the river than ourselves on the left, having already flanked us." Equally alarmed by the sudden turn of events was Lieutenant Colonel Branson. Like other officers, he now knew that his black troops and the entire Union task force were in serious trouble.

But while Captain Robinson led his Rebels toward the Union right and Colonel Giddings's troopers converged on the Federal left, and Colonel Ford led his cavalrymen toward the center, the Rebel flanking units under Lieutenants Vineyard and Gregory suddenly rode into clearer view. Colonel Branson described that "the [Confederate] flanking party numbered from 100 to 200 of cavalry [and] were about three-fourths of a mile, and about as far down the river as we were [while] the ground between us was an open level plain [therefore] it was practicable for the enemy to out flank us."

Before the blue-clads recovered from the initial surprise, events quickly spun out of control. Like Comanches intent on wiping out the white interlopers of their ancestral homeland, the Texas Rebels charged with war yells, smashing into the Federal positions and "shooting at everything that moved."[127]

Never before had these Federals, veterans or rookies, been more unready for battle than now. Lieutenant Jones recalled the initial shock of the Rebel attack when he first "heard Lieutenant-Colonel Morrison's order to fall in, in line of battle [and shortly] the regiment moved off" eastward toward the highest ground of Palmito Hill to secure the best defensive position. Then, continued Lieutenant Jones, "as we moved up to the top of the Palmetto [sic] bluff," Lieutenant Colonel Morrison was greeted by a sweat-stained young lieutenant, the acting regimental adjutant, who carried new orders for him.[128]

Attempting to save his position, Colonel Barrett now ordered Lieutenant Colonel Morrison to throw out a skirmish line of two companies from his 34th Indiana in order "to cover" the vulnerable Hoosier regiment. Near Colonel Barrett, Corodan Allen recalled that Colonel Barrett barked out the orders in an excited tone that betrayed desperation, if not panic, in the midst of a confused situation: "Colonel Morrison, you will put out two companies to cover your front of your regiment."[129]

A young Indiana bugler put his musical instrument to his lips and blew with all his might. The notes of the bugle rang clear and loud, echoing eerily across the dry bottomlands. Blaring above the Texas cannon fire, the bugle blast signaled the men of Company B, 34th Indiana, forward. With the precision of a drill field maneuver, these battle-tested Yankees began to form a skirmish line as ordered. Shortly, a long line of Hoosier skirmishers spanned across the hot sand flats just north of the bluff.[130]

Realizing that a single company would not be enough to halt the onrushing Rebels, Barrett also ordered the 34th's Company E to align beside Company B on the skirmish line. On the double, the Company B soldiers hustled forward. Colonel Barrett now believed that his advanced skirmish line of only two companies was sufficient to thwart Colonel Ford and his Texas cavalrymen.[131]

To parry the Rebel threat, Colonel Barrett finally began to act decisively. He wisely ordered the 62nd to immediately form in line "obliquely to the rear" to face the flanking attack and prepare for action. Meanwhile, the two Indiana skirmish companies of around forty men took position out in front. Aligning to face northward along a line stretching west to east, the black troops formed in line parallel to the Rio Grande to the south. The left flank of the black regiment touched the western edge of Palmito Hill, while the remaining troops of the 62nd stretched in a line northeastward to cover the Brownsville Road. Meanwhile, the horseless troopers of the 2nd Texas protected the 62nd's left flank.[132]

The Yankees' situation, however, became even more confused when they were greeted with the first Rebel volley. As the first stream of bullets swept through the Hoosiers' ranks, Lieutenant Jones saw some men go down. He knew that the fight was now on in earnest. Corodan Allen recorded the sudden explosion when "firing became general along our entire line as well as that of the enemy."[133]

All the while, the disciplined veterans of Companies B and E, 34th Indiana, stood aligned in a lengthy skirmish line west of Palmito Hill under a hot fire. As could be expected, these men gamely held their ground before the attacking Texas Rebels.[134]

Among the skirmish ranks of Company B stood Pvt. John J. Williams. A strange destiny had brought Private Williams so far from home and to within sight of the Rio Grande River and Mexico only several hundred yards to the south. Already a staggering total of 360,000 Federals had been killed in action during this bloody war. And now no Indiana soldier desired the dubious distinction of becoming the war's last fatality.

Despite these pressing concerns, Private Williams and his comrades of Company B stood before the onrushing Texas Rebels with the discipline of veterans. Here, around fifty yards before the main line of the 34th, the lengthy blue line of skirmishers was stretched across the open, flat terrain of the Palo Alto prairie before the high ground of Palmito Hill.

To the north, the men of the 62nd maneuvered to face the threat to their right flank and to protect the rear of the task force. After Lieutenant Colonel Branson ordered his men "to form line obliquely to the rear, faced toward" the escalating Rebel threat, he then directed his black skirmishers to take an advanced position on slightly elevated terrain "in the chaparral, on the face of the hill [the western edge of Palmito Hill] farthest down the river" to protect the 62nd's left. At this time, the left of the 62nd USCT was aligned on the northwestern edge of Palmito Hill.[135]

Apparently, when Colonel Barrett first ordered the two companies of Indiana skirmishers forward to a point about fifty yards west of Palmito Hill, before the 34th Indiana, he planned to make a defensive stand on the high ground of Palmito Hill. But such a tactical maneuver in short order posed difficulties. Vulnerabilities existed not only in the present Union dispositions but also in the colonel's last-minute plan to redeploy on the highest ground in the area, which would expose tactical weaknesses that could be exploited. For instance, "the skirmish lines [of both regiments, the 34th and the 62nd] did not connect, and were upon opposite sides of the hill, the high ground between preventing them from seeing each other," wrote Lieutenant Colonel Branson later. In addition, a Union defense on the commanding ground of Palmito Hill would make the Federal infantrymen especially vulnerable to artillery fire from the six Rebel guns. Because there was no better alternative, however, the best tactical decision that Colonel Barrett could now have made was to stand and fight at Palmito Hill.[136]

Barrett and his fellow officers, therefore, began to patch together a last-minute defense on the crest of Palmito Hill as best they could. Lt. William T. Bryson, Company I, 34th Indiana, described that "after we had taken arms we moved [south] across the road on to the bluff," forming a battle line on the high ground of Palmito Hill. Lieutenant Jones recorded how the race of the 34th Indiana soldiers to gain the crest of Palmito Hill was not without incident. Confederate artillery continued to find the range, zeroing in on the fast-moving bluecoats with cannon fire. The lieutenant wrote: "[W]e moved to the top of the hill, but before the entire regiment had reached the top, a cannon shot struck on the right of the third company from the left of the 34th Indiana [and] at that time the enemy were firing cannon shot into us pretty rapidly, most of it passing over us."[137]

With senior officers like Barrett and Branson handicapped without combat experience, tried junior officers, like Lt. Charles Kantrener, Colonel Barrett's acting aide-de-camp and acting adjutant, now rose to the fore. This lieutenant of German ancestry was one of the most experienced officers in the 62nd. He not only possessed eight years of U.S. Army experience before the war, but most importantly had natural leadership ability.

Kantrener was granted Colonel Barrett's permission to request Lieutenant Colonel Morrison to "furnish men with a company of skirmishers or flankers."[138] Demonstrating tactical awareness during the crisis, the Indiana colonel, however, balked at the order. Morrison feared that the loss of yet another company would weaken his small command, which was already vulnerable, especially after he had dispatched Companies B and E forward and beyond the high ground of Palmito Hill as ordered.[139]

Kantrener reported that he patiently "waited about three minutes [but still] received no flankers or skirmishers from the [34th Indiana, therefore] I appealed to the men of a part of the 34th Regiment to help me to support their own flank by furnishing skirmishers, at which [time] about eighteen or twenty brave men stepped forward and helped me. I then placed them on the skirmish line, parallel with the 34th Indiana."[140]

After shifting by the flank, the 34th realigned across the high ground of Palmito Hill. Clearly, this elevated perch dominating the surrounding flat countryside to the north was a good defensive position to make a stand, especially against charging Rebel cavalry.[141]

Other problems developed, however, which began to weaken the Yankees' resolve to make a defiant stand on Palmito Hill. Shaken by Colonel Ford's four-pronged attack, Colonel Barrett began to lose his nerve. Finding himself in the midst of rapidly developing engagement and a confusing tactical situation, he suddenly changed his mind about the wisdom of defending Palmito Hill. Now, the colonel decided to forsake the high ground and abandon the Palmito Hill position. With the choice now to either fight or flee, Colonel Barrett ordered a general retreat from the best defensive position for miles around without consulting with any of his officers.[142]

In the colonel's words: "[W]ith the Rio Grande on our left, a superior force of the enemy in our front, and his flanking force on our right, our situation was at this time extremely critical." In addition, the booming of Confederate artillery and exploding shells on Palmito Hill caused Colonel Barrett to give up the fight.[143] Barrett now understood the folly of having advanced so far from Brazos Santiago without artillery. "Having no artillery to oppose the enemy's six 12-pounder field pieces[,] our position became untenable," Barrett wrote later.[144]

Colonel Barrett had completely lost control of the situation. Not long afterward in his offical report, he wrote that the "skirmishing commenced with considerable musketry firing [while] the enemy opened on us with artillery from the front and the body of Rebels on our flank pushed forward, attempting to gain our rear."[145] His decision to retreat was a blunder, opening the door to Union defeat at Palmito Ranch. Instead of holding firm and defending the commanding high ground of Palmito Hill to thwart the Texas cavalry attack, he now prepared to retreat across the open prairie with a slow-moving force of infantry. And after gaining some advantage by occupying Palmito Hill, the Federals would now have to turn and march under fire during what would be a lengthy retreat.[146]

In part, Colonel Barrett lost his will to resist Colonel Ford's attack after the Confederate artillery fire became more accurate and began pounding the slopes of Palmito Hill. Lieutenant Colonel Branson recalled that "as soon as [the men] formed, and while awaiting expected cavalry charge, the enemy from a hill up the river [the Loma de la Jauja] (one mile and a half farther on) opened with artillery."[147]

Then Colonel Barrett committed yet another mistake when he ordered a rapid retreat instead of a methodical retrograde movement to protect his withdrawal. Such a fast-paced retreat was certain to cause both confusion and some panic among the ranks, especially his rookie troops. Worst of all, the order for the 62nd USCT to retreat northeastward was issued while the Indiana regiment was redeploying in a battle line across Palmito Hill to receive the Rebels' cavalry attack.[148]

Lieutenant Jones, like his veteran Indiana soldiers, was shocked for "we were there in line of battle about three minutes, when I observed, on looking around, the [left of the] 62nd Regiment moving down the hill at the double-quick."[149] Incredibly, Lieutenant Colonel Morrison and his Indiana regiment had not been informed that a general retreat was now in progress as the 62nd retreated by the right flank.[150]

At best, Colonel Barrett's retreat order was premature. His directive to withdraw guaranteed additional confusion in the ranks and poor coordination among his junior officers and their commanders. As one Union officer complained, Colonel Barrett did the inexplicable when he suddenly ordered "480 well-armed and well-drilled infantry [to] retreat [off a commanding high ground defensive position] from 200 men in gray."[151]

To justify his hasty decision and his mistake, Colonel Barrett later explained his rationale for abandoning the commanding defensive terrain despite superior numbers: "I commenced to retreat in quick time [and] gave the command 'Double-quick' to get them out of the range of the artillery."[152] Indicating the degree of panic, Colonel Barrett gave the fateful order to double-quick after the 62nd had retreated northeastward only 100 yards.[153]

On a raging battlefield, the order for troops to double-quick was almost always used during an advance, not a retreat. In Captain Conklyn's opinion, Colonel Barrett's order to double-quick "was enough to frighten the bravest troops in the world," along with his contradictory "[Y]ou will get out of this yet; you will not be hurt" followed by "Hurry up then, you will not get out of this; you will surely be killed."[154] Conklyn later denounced Colonel Barrett's order to retreat at the double-quick as an "extraordinary and unheard of" directive issued to inexperienced troops during a confusing combat situation, and especially so given that it was only the engagement's beginning.[155]

Clearly, a retreat at the double-quick from high ground greatly increased the Yankees' vulnerability to both artillery and cavalry amid the wide open spaces of the coastal plain. Palmito Hill's abandonment only escalated the tactical dilemma for Colonel Barrett because his retreating force remained bottled-up inside the wide bend of the Rio Grande. The Yankees, consequently, would have to conduct a long, risky retreat northeastward to gain the head of the bend to escape Colonel Ford's trap.

Worst of all, the Federals' left flank would be exposed to the slashing cavalry strike of Captain Gibbons's flanking force during the long march northward. These dangers could have been avoided had Colonel Barrett not lost his nerve and only maintained a bold front with superior numbers on the good defensive ground of Palmito Hill. Despite their element of surprise, Colonel Ford's Texas horsemen could have inflicted relatively little damage to around 500 infantrymen in good defensive positions on high ground.[156]

To parry the escalating threat to the 62nd USCT, meanwhile, Lieutenant Colonel Branson, as ordered by Colonel Barrett, formed four skirmish companies of 140 soldiers to protect his vulnerable left flank. This deployment meant that nearly half of the 62nd now served as skirmishers. Commanding half of these black troops, Captain Dubois, who led Companies E and H, described that he encountered "little trouble in keeping the files dressed and the men in their proper places although two cannon balls passed through the rank."[157]

By this time, the skirmish line of African American troops extended from left to right near the river and the top of Palmito Hill to nearly three-quarters of a mile inland and into the expanse of the open prairie. Colonel Barrett made a good choice in selecting the men of the 62nd to go forward. Unlike the Indiana boys, these rookies did not yet know enough about warfare and tactics to realize how much trouble they were in. But the black troops had courage and had already demonstrated their reliability during this crisis. No rookie shakes affected the veterans of the 34th. Lieutenant Colonel Branson was proud to record in his official record after the battle that when the Confederate gunners first "opened with artillery, doing no damage and creating no panic in my command[,] the men did their duty nobly."[158]

With discipline and precision the main body of the 62nd retreated by the right flank as ordered. As Rebel cannons roared, the Union retreat off Palmito Hill gained momentum; in Lieutenant Colonel Branson's words, not long after it had "commenced near the top of the hill with the 34th being on the top of the hill it was continued until [the] regiment had gone far enough to get under cover of the hill from the artillery fire—a distance of about 200 paces."[159]

Colonel Barrett had initially delayed in sending the order to Lieutenant Colonel Morrison to retreat his men. The Indiana soldiers, consequently, now remained in a battle line on an increasingly isolated position on Palmito Hill, after the African Americans had retreated by the right flank on the double, leaving only a cloud of rising dust behind them.[160]

Colonel Barrett's order ensured that the "conducting of the retreat at such a pace [was] to needlessly weary the men."[161] Indeed, the Union soldiers were already exhausted, especially the Indiana men.

Lieutenant Colonel Morrison and most of his regiment, meanwhile, remained unaware of the latest order to retreat. He continued to know "nothing [of the retreat] until he discovered the 62nd at a double-quick 150 yards in advance of his regiment."[162]

Perhaps it was just as well that the Hoosier soldiers had not received orders to retreat. No doubt these Western veterans would have balked at such an unimaginable order as the battle was just beginning. Never before had these men of the 34th been ordered to retreat across open ground under artillery fire and before hard-riding Rebel cavalry. If some Indiana soldiers were now shaken it was only because they understood battlefield realities better than Colonel Barrett. The colonel's ill-advised decision to retreat only reconfirmed to the Hoosier troops that Barrett was simply the wrong man in command, at the wrong place.

After the 62nd had double-quicked northeastward, directly below, or south of, the buildings of Palmito Ranch, and then continued in the same direction, the Indiana bluecoats remained in position on top of Palmito Hill. Finally, the 34th received the belated order to retreat off their high ground position. Then, upon reaching the foot of Palmito Hill, the Indiana troops were suddenly directed to move by the left flank at the double-quick.[163]

Later Colonel Barrett explained the situation as best he understood it. The 62nd USCT "retreated by my order at a 'double-quick' from near the top of the hill, soon after the retreat commenced, to near the foot of the hill, where by my order, which was given to the whole command, it took the quick-step, and so continued during the retreat except when halted."[164]

Lieutenant Colonel Branson now took direct charge of his regiment's four companies of skirmishers after they "retreated across the hill, and got fairly out into the open bottom land."[165] Here, the African American skirmishers remained in line, firing away and protecting the regiment from cavalry attack as best they could. "Immediately at the foot of the hill, about 200 paces . . . from where the retreat commenced [the African American] skirmishers were already out to cover the command from the flanking forces," wrote Colonel Barrett of the black skirmishers' key role in delaying the Texas attackers and protecting the retreat.[166]

In position and prepared for the "expected cavalry charge," the skirmishers of the 62nd put up a bold front. Lieutenant Colonel Branson was proud of their conduct, writing that "they kept the enemy at a repectful distance": no small accomplishment under the circumstances.[167]

As the 62nd were continuing their withdrawal, the Hoosiers continued their own retreat by the left flank down Palmito Hill on the double-quick. By this time, Lieutenant Colonel Branson feared that "the nearest body of the enemy, 250 strong, with two pieces of artillery, were evidently trying to gain our rear and a favorable opportunity to charge."[168] The two Federal units continued to move rapidly rearward at an almost unsustainable rate. With some understatement, Lieutenant Jones described that "both regiments were at this at a double-quick," heading back the way they had come.[169]

A price now had to be paid for Colonel Barrett's decision to abandon the relative safety of the high ground of Palmito Hill. Barrett's spur-of-the-moment decision to retreat off the higher ground at the double-quick meant forsaking—or sacrificing—the two Indiana companies of skirmishers on the open ground west of the hill. Isolated and alone, the Hoosier skirmishers knew nothing of the retreat of the entire task force. These men from Indiana still believed that Colonel Barrett's entire command remained in defensive positions immediately to the rear and within easy supporting distance.

Aligned in the open prairie on both sides of the road west of Palmito Hill as the Federal retreat got under way, the Indiana skirmishers had just swung into an advanced position when they were hit by the Rebel cavalry attack. Here, with Company B positioned north of the road, and Company E aligned to the south, the Hoosiers did not stand a chance. At no time was any effort made by the Colonel Barrett to recall these men, sealing their doom. He simply abandoned the two Indiana skirmish companies to their fate.

Barrett had calculated that in order to save his command he would have to sacrifice the two Hoosier skirmish companies in a desperate attempt to slow the attacking Rebels. Partly because of the colonel's prejudice against the Indiana regiment and favoritism toward his black soldiers, he made a relatively easy decision to sacrifice the two Hoosier companies instead of any of his 62nd USCT, such as his pet skirmish unit, Company F. The colonel simply abandoned the Indianans, letting them fend for themselves as best they could against the odds. Colonel Barrett "never called them in."[170]

Colonel Barrett should not take all the blame for the Union flight from the field. As much as Barrett's bad tactics and poor decisions, the Union defeat was ordained because Colonel Ford "launched such a vicious assault that the battle developed into a long chase."[171]

Across the field of Palmito Ranch, Colonel Ford now "became once again the impulse Indian fighter of the 1850s." He urged his hard-hitting cavalrymen forward along both sides of the Brownsville Road to overrun the exposed Indiana skirmishers. At the head of his cavalrymen as usual, Ford could hardly believe his eyes. Before the onrushing Texas Confederates stood the men of two abandoned companies of the 34th Indiana far in front of the retreating bluecoats.

Colonel Ford described that "they had a [long] line of skirmishers [who] were stationed in open ground at the foot of the hill where I could see them plainly." With a killer instinct, Colonel Ford led the Texas troopers of his center onward to ride down the two Indiana companies. Colonel Ford knew that success was inevitable the moment he "saw the enemy's skirmishers, which were well-handled, left without support by the retreating main body."[172]

The forlorn skirmishers of Companies B and E, 34th Indiana, did not have a chance. Colonel Ford never forgot the moment "Captain Robinson charged with impetuosity" on his line's left, from the north. Despite the Texas troopers surging upon the lonely band of Yankees scattered across the open prairie, the Indiana veterans defiantly stood their ground. With bayonets fixed, the Indianans faced the sweeping cavalry attack without breaking or even shifting ranks. Colonel Ford, despite ordering the skirmishers' destruction, felt a sense of admiration for these tough Hoosiers who manfully faced him. Impressed by their brave stand against the odds, Colonel Ford explained that the Indiana men of Companies B and E "did their duty well [as] they stood" firm.

One member of Company B described that he saw Pvt. John Jefferson Williams shot in the head. Pvt. David Dix Harter, was horrified when he saw as the "ball struck [Williams] in the right temple and pass through his head." The bullet killed Private Williams instantly, and the young man dropped lifeless to the ground. He was the last Union soldier to be killed in battle during the war. Private Williams's death, the fall of additional Indiana soldiers, and the charging Texas cavalry failed to unnerve the Indiana skirmishers. Incredibly, the Hoosiers held firm, standing their ground to the bitter end. These courageous Indiana skirmishers could not imagine that they had been abandoned by not only the 62nd, but also by their own regiment because of Colonel Barrett's orders.[173]

Standing in line before the Rebel horsemen only ensured a swift demise for Companies B and E.[174] Respecting their valor in the face of a hopeless situation, Colonel Ford described that these blue-clad skirmishers "stood as long as they could, until many of them were run over by my cavalry, and nearly all of them were taken prisoners. They stood as long as the same number of men could resist such a force of cavalry opposed to them."

Along with Company E's ill-fated skirmishers, Capt. Abraham M. Templer's soldiers of Company B were also now eliminated by the Texas horse soldiers. The howling Rebels troops simultaneously struck the skirmishers' front and right flanks, while also gaining their rear to complete the encirclement. This envelopment sealed their fate as thoroughly as Colonel Barrett's failure to issue recall orders. With some bitterness, Captain Fussell described that the skirmish companies "were not relieved and being unsupported the rebel forces swept round their flank and they were surrounded and forced to surrender." Nearly fifty Indiana Yankees, besides the killed and wounded, were swooped up and captured by the Texas cavalrymen.

But the sacrifice of the two companies was not in vain. Even Colonel Barrett, as if out of a sense of guilt, described that the abandoned Hoosiers "did good service and did not surrender until completely surrounded by the enemy's cavalry." In the words of one Union officer, "[T]hese gallant men kept back the enemy forces until after they arrived at the Palmetto [*sic*] Ranch." The futile last stand of the Indiana companies played a vital role in saving Colonel Barrett's command from destruction because they "stood their ground and protected the retreating column two or three miles, and but for which the whole command would have been run over and captured."[175]

The initial success achieved in overwhelming the two Indiana companies only fueled Colonel Ford's desire to strike the main Union body a crushing blow. Sensing the kill, "Old Rip" described in his matter-of-fact manner: "[A]s we expected, the Yankee skirmishers were captured and the enemy troops were retreating at a run. Our guns pursued at the gallop [and] the shouting men pressed to the front" as the Rebels smelled a rout.

While the forces under Colonel Ford and Captain Robinson continued to apply pressure in front, the impact of the Rebel flanking force also struck the Yankees from the northeast. Lieutenant Vineyard's dismounted horsemen and Lieutenant Gregory's artillerymen, after "occupying the hills [of the Loma de la Jauja] adjacent to the road, [charged from the northwest after] fir[ing] in security from behind the crests" and then swarmed onto the open prairie, inflicting additional damage upon the retreating Federals.[176]

Meanwhile as the Indiana skirmishers were rounded up as prisoners, the 34th Indiana, the 2nd Texas cavalrymen, and the 62nd USCT continued the rapid retreat to gain the Brownsville Road at the head of the river bend. With shells exploding around them and the Texas horse soldiers close behind, the Hoosiers understood that, without either artillery or cavalry to slow the Texas cavalry attack, they were in serious trouble. These veterans realized that they had little chance of holding the attackers at bay or of surviving in an open fight on the prairie. One Indiana soldier explained that "it seemed useless slaughter" to stand and fight in the open and that "we were at the mercy of the enemy—they having light artillery while we had none." At this time, the veterans wished that they had remained in their good defensive positions on the high ground of Palmito Hill.[177]

By the left flank at the double, Colonel Barrett's soldiers continued the retreat the way they had come earlier with so much confidence.[178] In fact the Federals were forced to retire northeast toward the grave danger on their left flank. To reach the head of the river bend, the Yankees now retreated straight toward Colonel Ford's flanking force under Captain Gibbon, the experienced former Texas Ranger. During the rapid Union retreat northeastward, the Yankees' left flank became increasingly vulnerable to Captain Gibbon's cavalrymen who were sweeping down from the north.

The Texas light artillery continued to roar, hitting targets and causing more confusion among the retreating Yankees. During the Federal retreat, Lieutenant Colonel Branson described that "the enemy opened upon us with artillery from a distance of about one mile up the Telegraph [Brownsville] Road, and not far from the river [while another] fire from the enemy's artillery passed between the two regiments."[179] While not always on target, this fire from the Texas Light Artillery was effective in causing confusion among many bluecoats.[180]

The combined effect of Rebel artillery and cavalry was enough to alarm some Indiana veterans who knew full well the grim implications for them on such an open battlefield. Lieutenant Colonel Branson described that the Confederate artillery fire caused consternation among some men and they "increased their gait beyond the proper quick step, in which the battalion was marching, producing some confusion and disorder in the ranks of that regiment."[181]

In following behind the retreating African Americans who continued to double-quick northward, the Indiana soldiers remained within close range of the Rebel artillery. Consequently, the Hoosiers suffered more punishment from this cannon fire than the men of the 62nd. The increasingly accurate Confederate shell fire, the loss of two entire Indiana skirmish companies, and the sight of the 62nd doubling toward Palmito Ranch made the Hoosier veterans realize that they were in more trouble than they had previously imagined.[182]

The most confusion among the Indiana troops was caused by another ill-conceived order from Colonel Barrett. About two miles below Palmito Ranch, the colonel ordered the Indiana regiment to protect the wagons during the retreat. When the teamsters panicked under the shell fire, they whipped their teams to increase their speed and the men of the 34th were forced to keep up with the wagons' wild flight. Sgt. Aaron Weltz, Company H, described: "Colonel Barrett gave the order for the 34th Indiana to keep up with the wagons" below Palmito Ranch. This directive forced the Indiana soldiers to push onward through the heat and dust "at a pretty good gait, sometimes in a trot and sometimes in a run[; therefore] it was necessary for the regiment to double-quick to keep up with them," complained the sergeant.[183]

When not making poor decisions and playing into Colonel Ford's hands, Colonel Barrett was making no decisions at all. Either way, the repercussions of his own ill-conceived orders and indecisiveness only enhanced the likelihood of his force's destruction, while causing greater hardship and confusion among his men, especially the hard-luck Hoosiers. Lieutenant Jones complained bitterly that "Colonel Barrett's conduct was such as to cause distrust in the minds of the men by making request[s] of officers and men instead of giving orders" on the battlefield.[184]

For instance, Colonel Barrett rode up to the Indianans and said, "Lieutenant Jones, you have done well this afternoon, and [then] asked me if I would take my company and cover the retreat," Lieutenant Jones recalled of the abandonment of Companies B and E and the loss of these skirmishers. The Indiana lieutenant, consequently, balked at the colonel's directive. Jones defied Colonel Barrett on the battlefield. Using logic as a rationale, he maintained "that I would cover the retreat with any company but my own, as they had been on the march all night before and had been on the line all day, and their feet were blistered so that they could not go."[185]

Realizing his own leadership limitations by this point, Colonel Barrett rode off to look for another company. Lieutenant Jones must have breathed a sigh of relief with his commander's departure, feeling that he had escaped Colonel Barrett's mismanagement.[186]

Colonel Barrett's orders, especially to double-quick the 34th for nearly two miles to reach the bend of the river, broke down many Indiana soldiers. Already worn out and suffering in the heat and from the lack of water, these veterans "did all in their power to keep and remain in the ranks [but] Lieutenant Jones saw it was impossible for them to hold out longer [and] told them to swim the river, that they might not fall into the hands of the enemy."[187]

One Union officer concluded with anger that Colonel Barrett's "extraordinary and unheard of orders [to double-quick and keep pace with the wagons] were calculated to produce a panic among any troops but the effect was slight on the [34th, much like] the conduct of the two companies of [sacrificed] skirmishers."[188] The Hoosier soldiers, nevertheless, suffered so severely that some men could not continue.

More and more men fell out of the Hoosiers' ranks because of Colonel Barrett's "extraordinary" orders. Captain Fussell lamented that "the expedition was undertaken and [he never understood] why the retreat was ordered." Lieutenant Jones was sickened by these unnecessary losses—the regiment's first prisoners on a battlefield. He described that "as we passed through the chaparral many men had gone out into this chaparral from the 34th Indiana Regiment; many sat down by the road side and said that they could not go any further."[189]

During the confused retreat amid the tangled clumps of chaparral that choked the land, the color-bearer of the 34th Indiana, Pvt. John R. Smith of Company H, suddenly found himself in trouble. Like other exhausted Indiana soldiers, he dropped out of ranks near "a short bend in the road, near the edge of the chaparral."[190]

By this time, no Indiana soldier was immune to the fatigue and confusion. Lieutenant Colonel Branson saw "the national colors below Palmetto [sic] Ranch [and] the soldier carrying the national colors was seen going into the bushes on the bank of the river." In the words of Lieutenant Jones, the flag bearer who carried the U.S. colors "was a cripple in the right foot and not able to march well."[191] In following Lieutenant Jones's directive to escape by swimming across the river to reach the safety of Mexico, therefore, the handicapped Private Smith lost possession of the U.S. colors.[192]

The unfortunate Private Smith was forced to abandon the colors because even walking was difficult for him because of an earlier injury: "[T]he ball of my foot pains me when I walk on it much," explained the lame color-bearer.[193] As Private Smith described his dilemma during the rapid retreat to gain the Brownsville Road:

> In the first place, I was lame when I started and was very much fatigued from the march the night before, and when we started to retreat I was nearly give out at the time; we had some little rest [and] on the retreat I went just as far as I could [and] I fell out of the ranks about one half miles from [or south of] Palmetto [sic] Ranch [and] from there I tried to swim the river; I swam the river about halfway, when the Mexicans began to fire at me from the Mexican bank of the river [and] I then turned and swam back. About that time the Confederate Army was near me, and I hid the colors in the weeds close to the bank of the river to keep the Rebels from getting them [but] I was captured by the Rebels soon after.[194]

As if the loss of its U.S. flag was not sufficient humiliation for the 34th Indiana to suffer on this ill-fated day, Color Cpl. George Washington Burns, Company E, was also unable to protect the regimental colors during the chaotic retreat. Much like Sergeant Smith, a weary Corporal Burns could retreat no farther. He also fell to the ground in exhaustion, joining other fatigued comrades who lay prostrate.[195]

Then, the Indiana color corporal was captured when "the enemy filed across our front within musket shot to the amount of eighty-five or eighty-six men, and [all of] those eighty-five or eighty-six had fired" a close-range volley.[196] But fortunately before he was taken by the Texas cavalrymen, wrote Corporal Burns, "the sergeant took the regimental color from me, and went into the chaparral with it [and] that was the last I saw of it."[197] Colonel Barrett later reported the fate of the regimental colors, writing that "the 34th Indiana also lost its colors [but] the banner was returned two days afterward via Bagdad, Mexico [and] the national color fell into the hands of the enemy; it was reported to have been picked up the next day after the fight near the river bank. A number of men plunged into the Rio Grande and, crossing to Mexico," escaped the Texas Confederates.[198] Colonel Ford's attackers continued to capture Yankees, the more ground they gained.

Colonel Barrett, meanwhile, continued to lead his disorderly retreat to Palmito Ranch. Keeping up a bold front that fooled few of his veterans, he informed his troops in a low tone: "We will retreat in good order, and good order let it be. Men keep your ranks. They can't hurt you; we'll get out of this yet."[199] But in truth, Barrett was unnerved, and his tone and words implied as much. By this time, he incorrectly believed that he was greatly outnumbered by Colonel Ford's attackers. "I estimate the number in sight at the time to [be] 500 to 600 cavalry, in addition to the artillery [while] a portion of the enemy's cavalry was distant on the flank about one third of a mile," concluded the colonel.[200]

After the bluecoats had retreated hundreds of yards, and as if suddenly worrying about future political repercussions of the loss of two skirmish companies, Colonel Barrett made a belated attempt to reinforce them. But the effort came much too late. After Lieutenant Jones refused to send his exhausted company forward, Colonel Barrett then ordered the dismounted Texas cavalrymen to advance as skirmishers to protect the retreat. Colonel Barrett also directed two black companies under the command of Captain Miller, the skirmish commander, to form in a skirmish line behind the dismounted Texas Yankees, just in case the 2nd Texas Cavalry men were overwhelmed.[201]

After Colonel Barrett promised "to relieve them in a few minutes," the men of the 2nd Texas advanced, long after the Yankees had departed Palmito Hill and before they had reached the buildings of Palmito Ranch.[202] Like the Indiana skirmishers who were abandoned while the main force retreated, additional Union skirmishers would have to be sacrificed to buy time, compensating for Colonel Barrett's earlier tactical errors.

Like the sacrifice of the Indiana men of Companies B and E before them, the dismounted Lone Star State troopers, without support or even sufficient ammunition, now played the role of sacrificial lambs to buy time for the Federal retreat.

While the rookie Texas skirmishers pushed forward in the belief that their comrades behind them stood firm, the main body of Colonel Barrett's force hurriedly departed the field. Not surprisingly, the men of the 2nd Texas were soon in serious trouble. Rebels began swarming around the Texas Yankees like predators intent on the kill. In a repeat of events that had spelled the doom of the two Indiana skirmish companies, Colonel Barrett's abandonment brought a quick end for these isolated Texas Federals as well.

A Union surgeon never forgot that "as I started with the wounded from the field, the [Texas] skirmishers were falling back, and I could hear them complain of not having been relieved" until it was too late. The rout of the blue-clad Texans by Colonel Ford's Rebels bought precious time for the rapidly retreating Yankees. The surviving Texas Yankees escaped into the dense chaparral, where even the hard-riding Texas Rebel cavalrymen could not go.[203]

Having ensured their demise, Colonel Barrett summarized the sad plight of the 2nd Texas: "[T]his detachment, consisting of less than fifty men under Lieutenants Hancock and James, fought bravely, but having been on picket the night previous and also on the skirmish line during the day were much fatigued previous to the retreat, and being new troops, without discipline, soon became disorganized. Allowing themselves to seek shelter from the enemy's fire under the bluff at Palmetto [sic] Ranch, they were soon surrounded and cut off."[204]

Among other officers, Lieutenant Jones was angered by Colonel Barrett's abandonment of the Texas skirmishers. He described the quick end of the dismounted Texas cavalry company: "[B]efore we reach[ed] Palmetto [sic] Ranch, however, the 2nd Texas Cavalry was thrown out to cover the retreat [and] I heard Lieutenant Hancock tell Colonel Barrett that he had not more than two rounds of ammunition per man. He told him to get out, and he would relieve him in a few minutes [but] the 2nd Texas Cavalry did not return and were taken prisoners."[205]

Here, amid the dense stands of chaparral, some black soldiers were also cut off and captured by the Rebels. One of these African Americans was Sgt. David Clark, Company C. Clark was taken prisoner in the chaparral along the riverbank and feared a repeat of the slaughter of the surrendered blacks at Fort Pillow. He would be spared by the Texas Rebels on this day, however. Clark never forgot the moment when "there was a cheering behind me [and] I was sick; it caused me to look round [and] I saw a United States flag—the Stars and Stripes, very ragged" in the hands of the victorious Texas Rebels.[206]

As the Federal retreat continued, capable leaders like Lieutenant Colonel Morrison maintained control of a chaotic situation as best they could. Along the route of retreat, the lieutenant colonel of the Indiana regiment remained active and highly visible to his troops. Natural leaders such as Lieutenant Kantrener, of the 62nd, also demonstrated leadership ability to encourage the inexperienced troops in this chaotic situation.[207]

All the while, the 62nd skirmishers continued to rise to the challenge on this day. Maintaining a heavy fire on their Rebel pursuers, the black soldiers continued to protect the retreat, buying precious time. Lieutenant Colonel Branson described how his men kept the Texans "at a respectful distance at all times and did their duty in the best possible manner [and every Rebel attempt to gain the rear] was each time prevented by halting my command and coming to a front, thus facing him with the river at our backs."[208]

But this thin line of protection was simply not enough. Colonel Barrett summarized the tactical adjustments that he made out of desperation, if not panic, in the attempt to gain the head of the river's bend. He explained that his force had been "attacked in front previous to the retreat[, then] we retreated by the flank[, and] then our front was changed [and] the front of the battalion at that time, being halted, would front toward the enemy—the back toward the river—the [Confederate] artillery playing from up the river, and the forces would be on our flank and rear."[209]

But the grave tactical situation was exacting a heavy toll on the retreating Federals. Lieutenant Colonel Branson described the increasing trouble the hard-fighting black skirmishers faced. "Owing to [the] flanking force of the enemy, our skirmish line could not be relieved without exposing the men and our colors to capture while rallying," recalled Branson. Therefore, the skirmishers of the 62nd held firm but risked greater danger the longer they thwarted the relentless Texans. With the utmost understatement, Lieutenant Colonel Branson wrote that the skirmishers fought "under very trying circumstances."[210]

By this time, the Yankees were on the run across the open prairie. Survivors feared the fate of being caught out in the open by the Texas horse soldiers and cut to pieces. All the while, the bluecoats raced to escape the pursuing Rebel horsemen, dashing northward to gain the head of the river's bend before it was too late. To escape from the cavalry and keep up with the fast-moving wagons, the Indiana soldiers proved the swiftest runners on this hot day in Cameron County.[211]

The Union retreat became more confused. Lieutenant Colonel Branson described that "a more rapid gait was kept up by the 34th Indiana Regiment, only portions of it, thus going upon and crowding against my regiment" on the narrow, sandy roadbed that ran through Palmito Ranch.[212] Despite the drubbing that they had taken on their most brutal day, the Indiana soldiers still possessed enough lingering pride to not only race the Rebels but also the black regiment as well.

Lieutenant Jones described that "the 62nd Regiment slacked their time and the 34th Indiana Regiment, continuing their double-quick, came alongside the 62nd Regiment [and] I heard Colonel Barrett order the 62nd Regiment to take 'quick time' and we gained on them."[213]

Clearly, the Union retreat was dissolving into a wild footrace that bordered on panic, and the worst was yet to come. With the Rebels close behind, the two fast-moving infantry regiments were on a collision course.

Here, just before reaching the small cluster of buildings at Palmito Ranch, Colonel Barrett committed yet another mistake. He now ordered the African American regiment to shift with the "head of column to the left."[214] Lieutenant Jones described the disastrous consequences of Colonel Barrett's ill-timed order: "[T]he 62nd Regiment being on our right, the 62nd Regiment broke the ranks of the 34th Regiment by marching through it."[215] Already amid chaos, this collision between the two rapidly moving Union regiments below Palmito Ranch caused more confusion among the ranks. Unable to adjust to the fast-transpiring developments, which were swirling out of control around him, Colonel Barrett could only react belatedly. He now pleaded to his exhausted and beaten troops: "For God's sake, men, don't break my ranks!"[216]

But Colonel Barrett's order led to yet more chaos, if that was possible, when the Indiana regiment caught up and then collided with the black regiment. This development resulted partly because the slower-moving 62nd USCT retreated by a longer but more direct route, while the faster-moving Indiana regiment, wrote Lieutenant Colonel Branson, "went a greater distance marching in the arc of a circle" along a shorter route parallel to the Rebels.[217] Setting the stage, Lieutenant Bryson described that before reaching the buildings of "Palmetto [sic] Ranch, the 34th Regiment took a road leading to the right and next to the river, the 62nd taking the road on our left."[218]

Angry over the collision and the resulting confusion that slowed the retreat, Sergeant Weltz, 34th Indiana, explained that "both regiments were marching side by side—the 62nd Regiment on the right [when suddenly] the 62nd Regiment filed through the 34th Regiment, cutting Lieutenant Jones' company off."[219] Viewing a shocking sight, a seething Lieutenant Jones, leading what little remained of the Indiana color company, described that "the 62nd broke through [the] ranks" of the Indiana regiment and succeeded in "cutting off the companies on the left, which halted to let the 62nd pass through."[220]

Along with other Indiana company commanders, Lieutenant Jones halted his men to allow the fast-moving African American soldiers pass by them, after "the 34th Indiana [had already] double-quicked one mile [when] the 62nd Regiment ran through it."[221] In an attempt to restore order among the Indianans' ranks, Colonel Barrett galloped up. He then "promised them that they would stop at Palmito Ranch [and] that he would fight the enemy there, make a stand there [and] the men pulled off their hats and cheered him," recalled Lieutenant Jones.[222]

Colonel Barrett's promise to make a stand and fight acted like a tonic to these hardy veterans from Indiana. In tactical terms, the decision to fight in the open now also indicated the folly of earlier abandoning the good defensive ground of Palmito Hill. Despite having been badly used up during this expedition, the 34th Indiana still retained plenty of fighting spirit.

Much like Colonel Barrett's earlier broken promises, however, there would be no defensive stand at Palmito Ranch. Only a continued retreat on the double and a dogged Rebel pursuit lay in store for the Yankees of this ill-fated invasion force.[223]

Lieutenant Jones felt the disillusionment among the veteran Indianans who missed this opportunity to make a defensive stand to face the surging Texas cavalrymen: "[A]rriving at Palmetto [*sic*] Ranch the 62nd Regiment was one fourth of a mile to our left, and Colonel Barrett at this time ordered Lieutenant-Colonel Morrison to double-quick his regiment around the bend, after we had passed Palmetto [*sic*] Ranch [and] we double-quicked at this time about one and a half miles."[224]

Finally, with a skirmish line of African Americans deployed at the ranch to protect the retreating Federals, Lieutenant Colonel Branson halted his black regiment to realign ranks. This respite allowed his troops to catch their breath in preparation for the additional challenges that lay ahead. On this scorching day, the halt by the African American troops allowed the double-quicking Hoosier soldiers to finally pass the black regiment.[225]

Meanwhile to the rear, the skirmish line of the 62nd held firm before the ever-aggressive swarm of Texans, opening a heavy fire upon their tormentors. Maintaining a bold front, the black skirmishers fought with spirit under the steadying influence of two experienced leaders, Captain Durkee and Lieutenant Kantrener, who commanded in Colonel Barrett's absence. Perhaps here, thirty-five-year-old Capt. Allen Carter Jones who now led "as fine a company of cavalry as the Confederate service could boast," was wounded. Jones was described as a "gallant and capable officer."[226]

To stabilize the lines, these experienced officers knew that they now needed as many battle-hardened veterans in the ranks as possible to ensure that the skirmish line would hold firm. Captain Durkee requested reinforcement from only Indiana soldiers who were volunteers, not drafted men. But the suspicious Indiana soldiers were wary of 62nd officers, who wanted Hoosier volunteers to skirmish before the task force during a rapid retreat: a bitter lesson learned from the sacrifice of Companies B and E, and the skirmish company of the 2nd Texas Cavalry.

The stand of the 62nd was timely because the 34th Indiana was in bad shape by this time. The battered state of the Indiana regiment minimized the wisdom of employing these Indiana veterans for skirmish duty. But the poor condition of the regiment was not the Hoosiers' fault. The wearing-out of the 34th partly resulted because the 62nd USCT had initially advanced too far ahead of the Indiana regiment. Consequently, Colonel Barrett had earlier ordered the 34th Indiana "to double-quick around the bend below the [Palmito] Ranch for the distance of half a mile, in order that the [34th Indiana then] might take the advance." Colonel Barrett's directive had resulted in additional straggling in the 34th's ranks. This was only the latest in a series of orders that eroded the Hoosier unit's effectiveness.[227]

At this point, the greatest danger for Colonel Barrett's task force was if they failed to reach the head of the river's bend before the Rebels' flank attack. Here, as Colonel Ford envisioned, was the best point to block the Federal retreat. Captain Miller deployed his skirmishers of Company F in time, however, protecting the retreat and denying the Rebels the chance to cut off the Federals. The chase and running fight, nevertheless, continued across the open Palo Alto prairie.[228]

After finally reaching the head of the bend, the 34th Indiana troops now led the retreat, with the 62nd USCT following behind them. The African Americans acted as a rearguard, holding the Rebel pursuit at a respectful distance. Lieutenant Bryson, 34th Indiana, described that "the 62nd Regiment kept [the lead in] the advance [retreat] until they reached Palmetto [sic] Ranch, a distance of nearly three miles [and] then the 34th Regiment took the advance," or retreat, toward the Gulf Coast.[229]

Like other officers, Lieutenant Kantrener, leading Company K of the 62nd, was upset because the 34th Indiana's retreat "was rather hasty [and the Hoosier regiment] marched . . . on [to] the bend of the road to the right of the Telegraph [Brownsville] Road."[230]

On the Mios Ranch, northeast of Palmito Ranch and just east of the head of the river bend, the 62nd USCT again aligned along a slight ridge in an attempt to keep the ever-aggressive Texans at bay. After racing across a long stretch of barren prairie without trees or underbrush, the African Americans and their white officers placed themselves in good defensive positions. Here, the worn blue-clads threw up a wall of resistance, holding firm before the Texas Rebels. A stand by the black troops at this point was calculated to buy more time for Colonel Barrett and his retreating command.[231] Here, in Captain Fussell's words, "the officers and men of the 34th begged to be allowed to halt and make a stand, but no halt was made and the headlong retreat continued."

This defensive position was situated at the edge of another hammock-like, narrow ridge, the Loma de la Estrella. Much like the Loma de la Jauja, this brush-lined and tree-covered elevation ran north-south rather than east-west. Most important in tactical terms, the defensive position along the Loma de la Estrella, located several miles east of the Loma de la Jauja, commanded the Brownsville Road for a good distance to protect the line of retreat.[232]

Taking advantage of the natural cover and the slight elevation, the black soldiers fought well until they were outflanked by Captain Gibbon's force. The 62nd then had no choice but to rapidly withdraw. With muskets on shoulders, the black soldiers followed on the heels of the fast-moving Hoosiers. Hour after hour, Colonel Ford continued the pursuit in his hunt-like chase of the fleeing Yankees.[233]

With Colonel Ford and his Texans keeping up the pressure, the Federal retreat degenerated into a rout of the worst kind. With understatement, Colonel Barrett later presented for the record a sanitized version of the race for the coast: "[W]e retreated by the [left] flank because there was [the enemy] upon our left, as we were faced to the rear, a heavy body of cavalry and indications of artillery masked, which they had behind their horses, attempting to flank us [and] they followed us several miles in that way."[234]

Continuing to push forward with the cavalry and providing support for the attack, the Texas Light Artillery battery under Captain Jones kept up the pace. Unable to strike back at the leapfrogging Rebel guns, Colonel Barrett could offer no checkmate to this successful "long arm" tactic. The young colonel described with some amazement that "they continued [to advance their guns and fire for] about six miles [while] they used round shot, spherical & shell" to pound his retreat. Proud of his ragged Texas artillerymen on this day, Colonel Ford never forgot how his gray-clad artillerymen and how their "guns pursued at a gallop [and] the shouting men pressed to the front."

All the time, the fighting continued to rage on the field. Colonel Barrett summarized the nature of the struggle, which now became little more than a series of stubborn Union rearguard actions, first at Mios Ranch and then White's Ranch, to keep the Texas Rebels at a distance: "[T]he line of skirmishers was never broken so as to allow the enemy to get to the main body . . . [and] it was to avoid capture by them . . . and because we could by halting and fronting, present a line of battle to the flanking party, that we retreated by the flank."

A sergeant of the 62nd USCT recorded with pride that the "retreat was saved from being an utter rout by the steadiness of the 62nd USCT and a part of the 34th Indiana." Indeed, the African Americans played a key role in saving the day for Colonel Barrett and his force. The Federals, nevertheless, were outflanked at every defensive position they established. Throughout the day, Colonel Ford was determined to keep up the pressure and not allow the hard-hit Yankees time to regroup and rally.

Most of all, with the Yankees on the run, "Old Rip" knew that the initiative and momentum could not be allowed to slip away. Therefore, the attacking Rebels, like the fleeing Yankees, were not allowed to rest during the long-running fight across the coastal plain. Delivering blows that could not be parried, Colonel Ford described that "the enemy endeavored to hold various points, but were driven from them" each time. And Captain Carrington wrote without exaggeration that Colonel "Ford's fierce cavalry charges harassed them exceedingly [while] the artillery moved at a gallop [and,] three times, lines of skirmishers were thrown out to check the pursuit [but] these lines were roughly handled."

More Rebels fell during these hot rearguard actions. Some of the last Confederate casualties of the war went down, falling upon the soil of Cameron County, Texas. Symbolically, these fallen Texas Rebels, seen as defenders of slavery, were probably hit by the fire of ex-slaves. Most ironic, these troops of the 62nd struggled within sight of a foreign land—Mexico—that no longer was tainted by slavery, while battling on U.S. soil where slavery still lingered like a cancer.

As the retreat went on, Indiana soldiers continued to straggle and fall out of ranks amid the sweltering heat and choking dust. Some Hoosier soldiers threw down arms and equipment out of exhaustion. Other Indiana men collapsed along the dusty road to rise no more until their capture, when the war for them ended at last. Even Capt. James M. Butler, originally commanding the Indiana color company, broke down in exhaustion and near sunstroke, after retreating three miles and completely "giving out at that time."

Like the Indiana soldiers, the men of the 62nd continued to labor rearward but under relatively fewer disadvantages than the Hoosiers. Captain Durkee recalled that "the 34th Indiana Volunteer Regiment in advance [was] considerably disorganized, many of the men being fallen out of ranks." Lieutenant Jones and his Western troops suffered more severely than any other Yankees on the field. He described: "[M]y feet were very sore and it was all I could do to take care of and keep up with my company [and] I had to take off my boots and go barefooted." Even Lieutenant Colonel Branson was sympathetic to the Indiana troops' sad plight. He lamented that the weary Hoosiers were forced to march "further and more irregularly than the 62nd Regiment, there being more confusion in their ranks[, which] wearied the men more."

Lieutenant Colonel Morrison, always rising to the occasion, restored some order amid the chaos. He reminded his Indiana soldiers, "Men, don't go so fast; take it steady." On this ill-fated day, Morrison was one of the most active officers on the field, "riding backward and forward, endeavoring to keep his men in the ranks, and telling them there was no danger of their being captured, that he would not leave them, and that if they were captured, he would be also[, he was other times,] walking on foot, ordering and encouraging his soldiers" under trying circumstances.[235]

Such inspired leadership as demonstrated by Lieutenant Colonel Morrison during the Indiana regiment's worst crisis restored some order and confidence among these Yankees. In the words of one bluecoat survivor: "[I]n some of the largest companies of the 34th there was but little or no straggling, and [what straggling] there was, was attributable to the sore feet and fatigue of the men."[236]

The 34th Indiana's condition, nevertheless, worsened with each passing hour, with the Hoosiers continuing to suffer more than the black troops. Indeed, "the white troops [were] more fatigued than the colored, notwithstanding the 62nd Colored Infantry had enjoyed a comfortable sleep and rest on the night of May 12, while the 34th had been on the march and without sleep from 10 o'clock until the next morning at daylight, over sand and bogs."[237]

The primary culprit that most thoroughly wore down the 34th Indiana was the extra effort and confusion brought about by the ill-advised "double-quick" order from Colonel Barrett. Captain Conklyn pinpointed the guilty party: "[W]hat produced this panic [was] the extraordinary and unheard of orders which were given by the commanding officer; these were calculated to produce a panic among any troops, but the effect was slight on the 34th."[238]

The fast-paced Union retreat continued across the coastal plain, with the Yankees fleeing northeastward to reach the relative safety of the coast. Here, among the tidal flats, sand dunes, salt marshes, and brackish saltwater of the alluvial plain of the Rio Grande country, which gradually descended toward the sea, the running fight between blue and gray continued for miles. This ordeal must have seemed like an eternity to the hard-pressed Yankees.[239]

Despite all his tireless efforts, Colonel Ford was unable to deliver a killing blow. It is not known, but perhaps one of Ford's orders was misunderstood and not carried out by a subordinate as directed. Or perhaps the shell fire from the Rebel cannons only hastened the Union retreat to such a degree or endangered the attackers that Colonel Ford was not able to either capture or destroy the entire Federal force.

Hour after hour, Colonel Ford continued to encourage both his cavalry and artillery forward in pursuit. One Rebel artillerymen scribbled in a letter with delight that "Captain O. G. Jones, of Jones battery . . . charged the Federal foot [soldiers] with artillery and kept up a running fight for nine miles." This tactical innovation on the battlefield hastened the Federal retreat, though it eventually exhausted the Confederate artillery horses, which were simply unable to keep up the rapid pace.

With his fighting blood up, Colonel Ford described that during the hot "pursuit[, which] lasted for nearly seven miles, the artillery horses were greatly fatigued (some of them had given out), the cavalry horses were jaded" as well. Ford continued: "[T]he horses of the men had shown signs of failing [altogether]." Captain Carrington lamented that during the height of the Palmito Ranch races "the artillery for the time was, by reason of broken-down horses, comparatively useless [and] many of the horses of the troopers were also broken down." These factors explain in part why Ford was unable to deliver a lethal blow.

Finally, during the lengthy pursuit in the day's heat, the inevitable occurred and the pursuers became as exhausted as the pursued. In addition, the tactical situation had changed by this time. Because Colonel Ford "was convinced the enemy would be reinforced at or near the White House [White's Ranch, he now] ordered the officers to withdraw the men." With the bluecoats defeated and with his pursuers now closer to the Union reinforcements at Brazos Santiago, Colonel Ford finally called a halt to his relentless pursuit. At this time, he simply informed his soldiers, "Boys, we have done finely [and] we will let well enough alone and retire."

A complete victory escaped Colonel Ford only by the narrowest of margins at Palmito Ranch but at no fault of his own. Captain Carrington explained that "if Ford had more troops he would doubtless have placed himself between the enemy and Brazos Island, but with his small force of less than three hundred men, he said 'the undertaking would be too hazardous.'" The Yankees' rapid retreat and the worn-out horses of the artillery and the cavalry mounts of their pursuers had combined to eliminate any chance of achieving a complete Rebel success.

In addition, when Ford initially caught Colonel Barrett by surprise, the Federals were widely dispersed and under the impression that the day's fighting was at an end. Striking a widely scattered force actually worked to the Yankees' advantage by minimizing the full impact of Colonel Ford's blows, which then came at staggered intervals during the pursuit. Lieutenant Colonel Branson stated that "the entire line which Colonel Barrett commanded during the retreat was more than one mile in length."

Other factors explain why Colonel Ford narrowly missed destroying the Union task force. The Federals had moved swiftly off the field on the double not long after his attack. This allowed the Union troops to minimize the damage that would have been inflicted had the Rebels' surprise assault hit them while they were concentrated. Also, the sacrificed Union companies—the unfortunate Indiana and Texas skirmishers—more than once bought precious time during the retreat. Even the rounding up of Union prisoners took time and momentum away from the pursuit, sapping the impact of the Rebel attack. Finally, the setting sun and the day's conclusion ended Colonel Ford's ambition of completely destroying Colonel Barrett's expedition on the Texas mainland.

Some time elapsed before Colonel Ford's orders to cease fighting spread across the field to his various scattered commands, which were still in fast pursuit. Lt. J. Mayrant Smith and his cannon was one of the few gun crews blessed with good horses. With the Yankees on the run Lieutenant Smith continued to encourage his cannoneers forward in pursuit. Colonel Ford described Lieutenant Smith as "a promising young officer." As demonstrated repeatedly at Palmito Ranch, "Old Rip's" confidence in Lieutenant Smith was well-founded.

Throughout the fighting at Palmito Ranch, Lieutenant Smith showed inspired leadership as Captain Jones's "right arm." After all, this was a personal fight for Lieutenant Smith, who was battling on home soil to repulse an invader. Smith's hometown of Galveston, Texas, had been captured by the Federals. Eager for revenge, this Texas officer was determined to drive the hated Yankee invader into the sea on May 13.

Lieutenant Smith and his gunners of the Texas Light Artillery punished the Federals for a long distance across an extensive stretch of the coastal plain. The lieutenant was determined to keep on hammering the retreating bluecoats with shell fire as long as possible. Most of all, these Texas artillerymen wanted to punish the Yankees before they either rallied or received reinforcements from Brazos Santiago.

After chasing the blue-clads for miles and knowing that the victory was won, Lieutenant Smith inflicted final punishment upon the retreating Federals. After loading the gun with what was to be the final Confederate artillery shell of the war, and upon sighting his 12-pounder on the fleeing Yankees, Lieutenant Smith was ready for one last shot. With his artillery piece facing eastward toward the sea, the lone cannon of Captain Jones's Texas Light Artillery was primed and ready.

As hundreds of times in the past, Lieutenant Smith grabbed the lanyard to fire the gun. He then jerked the lanyard of the 12-pounder. Here, on the field of Palmito Ranch, Lieutenant Smith fired the final Rebel artillery shell of the war's land battles. The last Confederate artillery round unleashed in a Civil War land engagement echoed over the coastal plain nearly five weeks after the haunting stillness at Appomattox.

The Rebel shell screamed over the sand dunes and tidal flats of Cameron County and toward the sea. Lieutenant Smith's shot sounded the last clap of thunder from a Southern "long arm" unit during the war. But Lieutenant

Smith and his Texas gunners did not believe this Confederate cannon shot was fired in vain. Unleashing this shot merely meant sealing an unexpected victory—the Confederacy's final battlefield success on American soil—along the Rio Grande, for the elusive dream of independence that would never come true for these young men and boys in gray.

To this day, the result of Lieutenant Smith's final shot remains unknown. Perhaps it caused the final Union casualty of the war. After Lieutenant Smith's final act of defiance, Captain Jones received Colonel Ford's directive to cease fighting. Captain Jones then informed Lieutenant Smith that all pursuit and firing were to immediately cease.[240]

Symbolically, the final Confederate artillery shot during a land battle of the Civil War was fired in much the same way as the war's first shot: an artillery piece firing eastward toward an enemy occupying Southern soil and toward the sea. It was perhaps an appropriate end.

In many ways, it was also symbolic that Lieutenant Smith's shot was fired along the Rio Grande. The consequences of an earlier conflict along the river had now finally come full circle. The first large-scale armed clash of the Mexican-American War in 1846—which led to the U.S. acquisition of a vast tract of Western lands, helping to pave the way for the expansion of slavery—and the last land battle of the Civil War were fought only a few miles apart in Cameron County, Texas.

With the day drawing to a close, the running fight between blue and gray continued across the sandy prairie. Before the Rebel pursuit finally ceased, the Yankees were driven northeastward to Cobb's Ranch, within two miles of Brazos Santiago. At this point, Union reinforcements awaited their hard-luck comrades of Colonel Barrett's ill-fated command. Upon gaining the position, the first Federals to arrive halted and aligned to make their final stand of the day.

Here, Lieutenant Colonel Branson ordered Capt. Fred B. Coffin and his Company K, 62nd USCT, forward as skirmishers to protect his retreating troops. Meanwhile, Colonel Barrett's remaining forces continued to labor eastward during the last trek of the race for the safety of "the Brazos."

One officer of Colonel Giddings's Battalion, twenty-six-year-old Summerfield H. Barton from Victoria County, Texas, who had raised a cavalry company for Colonel Ford, was in the forefront of the chase. He was active on the field, despite poor health from months of confinement in an Illinois prison camp. Barton, a Mississippi native who had migrated to Texas with his family in 1854, was yet leading his cavalrymen forward near the close of the fighting.

Along with Pvt. Ferdinand Gerring, a German Confederate of Giddings's Battalion, these two soldiers, as it was believed after the war, "fired the last two shots of the war on this field." From Clinton, Texas, north of Corpus Christi,

Private Gerring had originally enlisted in the horse company of Capt. W. J. Weisiger, another German Rebel, of Colonel Giddings's Battalion.

Near the conclusion of the pursuit, a final volley from the Yankees unleashed a stream of bullets that hit both Captain Barton and Private Gerring. Captain Barton was only slightly wounded and remained in the saddle. He was destined to recover from his injuries and live to see old age.

The fortunes of war were less kind to Private Gerring, however. The Texas private suffered a severe wound. He was destined to become a tragic counterpart to Pvt. John Jefferson Williams, 34th Indiana, as the last fatality of the Rebel side in the final land battle of the Civil War.[241]

During the lengthy running fight and chase across the prairies and despite their rookie status, the 62nd continued to maintain discipline to provide invaluable service. The black troops might well have saved Colonel Barrett's force from destruction. Indeed, "every attempt of the enemy's cavalry to break this line was repulsed with loss to him, and the entire regiment fell back with precision and perfect order, under circumstances that would have tested the discipline of the best troops."[242]

Not long thereafter, not long before sunset, the last concentrated volley of the war was fired by the troops of the 62nd U.S. Colored Infantry. Aligned in neat ranks across the flat coastal plain at some point between White's Ranch and Brazos Santiago and maintaining poise as if on a parade ground at Benton Barracks, these African Americans unleashed a crashing volley from their .577 caliber Enfield rifles, with their backs practically to the Gulf of Mexico. The final volley, however, was not fired at a swarm of Rebel pursuers. Motivated solely by a desire to claim that he was the one to order the war's last volley, Colonel Barrett "ordered the 62nd Regiment to charge at a run over a brush fence to a ridge, where the 62nd fired their volleys."

In the words of an amused Lieutenant Jones, the black soldiers "did not fire at the enemy, nor in the direction of the enemy [as] the fire was into the open prairie." Knowing that the end had come at last, Lieutenant Colonel Branson then turned to a company commander. With dramatic affect, he then "sententiously and with an animation he can never feel again, remarked, 'That winds up the war.'"[243]

In many ways, this final concentrated fire by the troops of the 62nd was perhaps one of the most symbolic volleys of the entire conflict. Absent from the history books is the fact that this last organized volley of the Civil War was fired by black soldiers who were former slaves. Additionally, this gunfire unleashed by the 62nd USCT also symbolized the conflict's new realities. After all, this was now a struggle on behalf of human freedom for all Americans.

As could be expected, more than one officer of the 62nd took credit for ordering the final volley, including both Colonel Branson and Lt. R. B. Foster, who led Company I. Lieutenant Foster claimed to have given the "last command to fire at Confederate troops in this last battle of the war." Years after the conflict, Lieutenant Colonel Branson claimed the distinction of having ordered the final volley, "with probably deeper feeling than [I] ever before gave a military order."

Under the veil of near-darkness, the beaten Federals now continued retreating toward the sea. These survivors felt fortunate that they had escaped the Texans' wrath on this unforgettable day at Palmito Ranch. At last and after a three-hour retreat, the Hoosier troops were the first to reach the waters of the Boca Chica. These men instantly "rushed into the water to get into boats to get across the Boca," wrote Captain Durkee, who was shocked by the extent of the unseemly rout.

Thereafter, the remaining Indiana bluecoats reaching the Boca Chica did so in a more organized fashion. But vestiges of the Palmito Ranch rout remained to haunt the Union bid to reap glory by capturing Brownsville. All the while, Lieutenant Colonel Morrison sat on his horse beside the dark waters of the Boca Chica in protective fashion. After this badly managed affair, he ensured that all of his Indiana boys crossed safely. Clearly, this was an ill-fated day, which the Indiana soldiers felt had left a stain on their distinguished record of past accomplishments.

Then, around 8:00 P.M., with muskets on shoulders, the 62nd USCT reached the Boca Chica in good order, after a hard day's work. With pride, Lieutenant Colonel Branson described that the African Americans gained the coast. The African American soldiers then formed up rank. Here, they made a stand to allow the remaining Indiana soldiers to reach safety. Providing stability and inspiration, the troops of the 62nd remained until 4:00 A.M., maintaining discipline as they had done throughout the day. Then, the regiment would finally retire across the Boca Chica to Brazos Santiago, after a job well-done from beginning to end.

Lieutenant Colonel Branson emphasized how well his black troops had performed on this day. They "marched over nearly the same ground [in retreat as in advance] in good order, leaving four men behind only (two of these were captured and were returned afterward), having four men wounded, all of whom were brought in, losing seven guns only [and] they came in, too, with colors flying and music playing."

With no Yankees left to fight and after having withdrawn his troops with the victory won, Colonel Ford once again resumed his personal fight with his superior, General Slaughter. As might be expected, the general had belatedly reached the field with a cavalry battalion long after Colonel Ford had already won his lopsided victory. General Slaughter, as inexperienced in combat as the vanquished Colonel Barrett, now ordered the Confederate pursuit continued.

Defiant as usual, "Old Rip" refused to obey the order, "unless he could first see General Slaughter and explain to him the fatigued condition of the horses in his command [and because] we were then too near Brazos Island not to expect Union reinforcements to be hastened to meet their retiring troops."

Meanwhile, General Slaughter and his fresh troopers briefly resumed skirmishing with the last of the retreating Yankees. The Virginia general then retired his battalion, after having missed all but the last flurry of fighting. He ordered Captain Carrington and his troopers "to press the rear guard of the enemy and cut if off [but] the enemy gained the high ground" and formed a battle line "among the sand hills" near the coast, wrote Capt. Luther Conyer.

Now that the fight with the Yankees had ended, the two leading Confederate officers of the valley met near Palmito Ranch and clashed once again. When General Slaughter demanded that Colonel Ford encamp his troops around the ranch, Ford angrily exploded at the general's lack of military insight. Not a man to take orders, especially if they made no sense, Colonel Ford declared in loud tones, "I am not going to stop here in reach of the infantry forces on Brazos Island, and allow them a chance to 'gobble' me up before daylight." He had fought too long on the border and frontier to make such a foolish tactical mistake.

Once again, Colonel Ford's commonsense arguments paid dividends, convincing the general to change his mind. Thereafter, Ford and his Texas cavalrymen "moved about 8 miles higher up [the river] and encamped" safely out of harm's way. In typical frontier style, Colonel Ford was not going to risk a single soldier's loss if possible.

Early the next morning, on May 14, Colonel Ford would order Captain Carrington to take a detail to collect Federal weapons left on the field and to bury the dead. To his surprise, Carrington would only then learn that a surviving "body of Federals was [still] in a bend of the river near the old Palmetto [*sic*] Rancho." Captain Carrington would then direct a sergeant and a squad of Texas Rebels to round up the last remaining Yankees who had been cut off during the rapid retreat.

In one final act, Captain Carrington's Rebels "captured about a score of Hancock's [Texas Cavalry] company[, and] Lieut. James [Hancock] and Hancock's brother were numbered among the prisoners thus captured [while] several who attempted to swim the river to escape capture were drowned [or perhaps shot]. Several swam across and were immediately slain and stripped by Mexican bandits, and then thrown into the river." Later, Colonel Barrett reported that "both [2nd Texas Cavalry] lieutenants and a portion of their men [more than twenty troopers] were picked up . . . by the enemy, having in vain endeavored to escape their destruction by secreting their colors in the chaparral."

A host of similarities and symbolisms distinguished the final land battle of the Civil War. The first and last land battle of the war both ended in Confederate victory during the first and last springtimes of the Southern nation. Even the first and last Rebel artillery rounds of the war in a land engagement were fired in the same direction and toward an ocean during the first and last Confederate victories of the war. Also, at both Fort Sumter and Palmito Ranch, not one Southern soldier lost his life during the fighting. And during the first and last clashes of the war, the Union lost its first and last national flag.

With the victory, "Old Rip" Ford, the longtime defender of the Rio Grande Valley, gave thanks to a merciful providence that had spared him and his Texas soldiers for so long. Acting more like a frontier parson than a Confederate commander, he gave his blessings: "[W]e must return to the Almighty for this victory, though small it may be, gained against great odds and over a veteran foe [in] this . . . the last land fight in the war."

After around four hours of fighting at Palmito Ranch, Colonel Ford had won yet another victory on Texas soil, adding to a long list of successes. According to the Yankees, Ford fought one last battle because he wanted one final opportunity to face the enemy in the last engagement of the war. The Texas Rebels had believed that "the war was played out, but felt that this was a good opportunity to give us a whipping," reported one paroled Yankee, who was captured by Colonel Ford's men.

Captain Carrington praised the former Texas Ranger who worked his tactical skill with precision at Palmito Ranch to achieve yet another surprising victory: "[T]he battle was precipitated upon Ford and won by him; and whatever of honor resulted from winning the last battle of the war and inflicting a heavy loss upon the enemy, who outnumbered his troops more than five to one, without the loss of a man, properly belongs to Ford and his poorly armed troopers." In typical Ford fashion, at Palmito Ranch he had unleashed a "charge which no infantry line formed on the Rio Grande could withstand."

The losses suffered by both sides during the battle of Palmito Ranch have always been a subject of controversy. But the Confederates suffered far less during the four-hour battle. Colonel Ford summarized that, during the battle,

the enemy lost twenty-five or thirty killed and wounded, and 113 prisoners [and] some were killed while swimming the river [and] a great many escaped to Mexico. In killed, wounded, and missing their loss approximated two hundred [and] they lost two battle flags, one of which belonged to the 34th Indiana (the Morton Rifles) [and] they abandoned many stands of arms, threw others into the Rio

Grande, and left clothing scattered on their whole line of retreat. . . . Colonel Barrett and his command ran from about 300 cavalry, and they were swift of foot, went like men who had important business at some other place[; these bluecoats] proved themselves long-winded and swift-footed.

In a letter, one Texas artilleryman summarized the extent of the Rebel victory by writing that "the Federals were defeated and completely routed, many of them jumping into the Rio Grande and swimming to the Mexican side," the Confederates capturing many Yankees.

For an attacking force during a lengthy action, Confederate losses were surprisingly light at Palmito Ranch. Colonel Ford answered the question as to the exact number of his casualties not long after the battle: "I think it was five or six, wounded." Later, he wrote: "[O]ur loss was five wounded, none of them supposed to be dangerous."

At least ten Texas Rebels fell wounded and another three Confederates were captured during the fighting at Palmito Ranch. A Texas historian, however, concluded that "although Ford reported only five men wounded, the number of Texans killed and wounded was probably about the same as the Federals," around 30 men. The latter estimation was probably correct. It is not known if any of the "French volunteers" who fought on the Rebel side were either killed or wounded, while serving the French cannons or perhaps even the Confederate artillery beside Rebel gunners.

Likewise, the 62nd USCT suffered light casualties, despite repeatedly acting as skirmishers and keeping the Texas Rebels at bay. The 62nd only lost five men wounded, and another three soldiers captured. Two other African Americans were captured but managed to escape in the running fight across the Palo Alto prairie. One of these men who fell mortally wounded was Pvt. Bill Redmon. At Palmito Ranch, he fought in the ranks of Company H, the primary regimental skirmish company. Private Redmon was the last Union soldier and African American to die as the result of a battle wound during the Civil War. He would die on June 4, 1865, in a Brazos Santiago hospital, nearly two months after General Lee's surrender at Appomattox.[244]

The other Federal units were less fortunate than the 62nd. The dismounted company of the 2nd Texas cavalry was virtually wiped out at Palmito Ranch, and all but ceased to exist. Of the fifty-man company, twenty-two Texas Yankees were captured by the Rebels, and three soldiers fell wounded during the fighting. No lengthy captivity was in store for either these Texas "renegades" or any other soldiers in Colonel Barrett's ill-fated expedition.

Colonel Ford explained that

> the prisoners . . . were conducted to Fort Brown [at Brownsville] and
> treated with kindness [and] several of them were from Texas [but]
> this made no difference in their treatment [and] some were taken
> who had deserted from [Ford's] command on the lower Rio Grande.
> The most of these were allowed to escape on the march up to
> Brownsville [and] the Confederate soldiers were unwilling to see
> them tried as deserters. Some of the 62nd Colored Regiment [in-
> cluding Pvt. Allen Stale of Company I and Sgt. David Clark] were
> also taken by the victors. They had been led to believe that if cap-
> tured they would either be shot or returned to slavery. They were
> agreeably surprised when they were paroled and permitted to depart
> with the white prisoners [and] there was no disposition to visit upon
> them a mean spirit of revenge [as] all seemed to feel that, although
> engaged in terrible warfare, they were still brothers, still free-born
> Americans.

Carrying a tinge of racism and certainly hyperbole, Captain Carrington's explanation as to why more African American soldiers were not captured at
Palmito Ranch was because "they outran our cavalry horses."

The heaviest loss suffered by either side at Palmito Ranch was sustained
by the 34th Indiana. In the words of one Union officer, the Indiana Regiment
"suffered almost the entire loss on the expedition." Later, in 1865, the adjutant general of Indiana reported that the loss of Lieutenant Colonel Morrison's regiment consisted of eighty-two men who were either killed, wounded,
or captured. But the real loss among the 34th Indiana was in fact higher, as
was Colonel Barrett's total number of casualties.

For instance, one account has stated that in total, the Union task force
"lost four officers and 111 men, 30 of whom were killed and some drowned
in attempting to swim the river into Mexico." Renowned historian Stephen
Oates wrote that the "Federal losses out of about 800 engaged were probably
30 killed and wounded and 113 taken prisoner."

Another modern historian, T. R. Fehrenbach, has summarized that "the
victory was staggering: no Confederates were dead, although there were a number of wounded men. By comparison, the 34th Indiana had lost 220 out of the
300 soldiers on its rolls. Union dead lay all over the battlefield and strung over
the seven miles to the sea. Other bodies floated in the Rio Grande; they were
drowned Union infantry who had tried to swim the river to escape the terrible
charging horse. Ford had also taken 111 men and 4 officers as prisoners of

war." Yet another historian emphasized the heavy losses suffered by Colonel Barrett's forces: "a sad trail of blue-coated corpses led from Palmito Hill to the sea, where still more bobbed in the surf."

It is not known, but perhaps the Indianans' losses might have been deliberately underestimated in order to help to save Lieutenant Colonel Morrison from court-martial when Colonel Barrett attempted to transform him into the scapegoat for the Palmito Ranch defeat. Indeed, one of Colonel Barrett's charges against the commander of the 34th Indiana was that Lieutenant Colonel Morrison was solely responsible for the Hoosier regiment's disproportionate high losses in the battle.

Numerous Union accounts stating higher losses suffered by Colonel Barrett's command at Palmito Ranch also seemed to indicate that Federal casualties were perhaps miscounted to downplay the full extent of what was described at the time as the terrible Union "disaster" and "stampede" at Palmito Ranch. To this day, some historians, relic hunters, and those familiar with the remote battlefield of Palmito Ranch still uncover the remains of skeletons of Union soldiers identified by U.S. buttons and buckles. If these reports are true, then quite possibly a larger number of dead on both sides—but primarily on the Union side—lay on the field of Palmito Ranch. Here, known only to God, they rest today either in unmarked graves or in the brush-choked thickets, chaparral, and tangled mesquite, where their bodies were never recovered.

Captain Carrington was ordered back to the battlefield on May 14 to "bury the dead" but his Rebel detail probably was anything but thorough in the disagreeable task in hot weather. In addition, chances might have been slim that these Texas Rebels would bury the bodies of the hated Texas "renegade" Yankees, especially at the war's end. Historian Louis J. Schuler, in his work on the battle, described the Federals, some "thirty of whom were killed" on May 13. Perhaps because of a possible Union whitewash to minimize the full extent of the "disaster" at Palmito Ranch, some Yankees were not listed as killed in action.

Quite possibly, these overlooked fatalities might well have included African Americans of the 62nd USCT. Since these ex-slaves' next of kin were probably unknown, and, therefore, since their disappearances would not raise great concern compared with white soldiers with families, quite likely some soldiers of the 62nd were among the unaccounted Union dead at Palmito Ranch. And with Reconstruction on the horizon and the Republican administration preparing to assimilate ex-slaves into American society, any negative publicity concerning the black troops' conduct or higher casualty rate in an already controversial battle after the war's end might have needed to be kept quiet for political reasons, including Colonel Barrett's political aspirations, and for the proposed Union-Confederate alliance against the French in Mexico after the war.

Perhaps some Northern politicians or generals had encouraged Colonel Barrett to launch his ill-fated attempt to capture Brownsville to either add laurels to the black soldiers' battlefield performance or to secure cotton riches, or perhaps both. Whatever the reasons, many details and usually easily accessible facts of what exactly occurred on the field of Palmito Ranch, including an accurate count of casualties, might have been deliberately obscured, if not covered up, by either military commanders or the civil authorities.[245]

In addition, the story of Palmito Ranch might well have been obscured for another reason: the possibility of forgotten atrocities that might have been committed by Rebel troops on the battlefield. If so, then such a factor would also explain the relatively low number of reported fatalities during a lengthy engagement and running fight across miles of open country. Indeed, numerous Confederate accounts indicate that a "great" many Federals either escaped to Mexico or drowned in attempting to swim the Rio Grande—a shallow, narrow, and placid stream that would have been relatively easy to swim across especially during a long period of drought that had reduced the river to wading levels—and that a number of Yankees had been killed by Mexican bandits on the south bank.

The majority of Rebel accounts, including Colonel Ford's, also emphasized that almost all of the Federal prisoners failed to reach Brownsville because they were allowed to desert. According to such accounts, these Yankees simply vanished mysteriously across the Rio Grande into the great unknown of Mexico. A host of discrepancies exist in Confederate accounts, however. One exception to the generally accepted Rebel version of the Yankee desertion stories came from General Slaughter. He maintained: "[A]fter the battle I told my prisoners they were at liberty to return to Brazos Santiago, or go with me to Brownsville, and they elected to accompany me. I had regular rolls made of my prisoners, and sent them back on a steamer[,] I really did not consider them as captives, as we passed a very pleasant time together."

Indeed, some Union soldiers signed paroles at Brownsville, and thanks to the efforts of two 34th Indiana officers under a flag of truce, they were then transported to Brazos Santiago. It is hard to imagine how captured Union soldiers, particularly African Americans, would have willingly decided to accompany their captors, who were well-known for exacting revenge on both black and white Yankees, to Brownsville instead of freely returning to their Brazos Santiago base, especially with the Confederacy disintegrating into chaos and the Trans-Mississippi Rebels still under arms.

According to most accounts, many Union soldiers simply disappeared either into the remoteness of the Texas countryside, or into the depths of Mexico, or to the bottom of the Rio Grande. Obviously by way of explanation, a larger number of Yankees—more than indicated in official reports—seem to have been killed at Palmito Ranch on May 13. If so, then what could possibly explain the mystery of the disappearances of a larger number of Federals on the battlefield?

Quite possibly, the real forgotten story of Palmito Ranch was that the Texas Rebels took bloody revenge on the Yankees, especially those of Hispanic or African American descent. One modern historian, Jerry Don Thompson, certainly was convinced as much. He explained that "many of the [captured] Texans were executed after they had surrendered" at Palmito Ranch. Clearly, opportunities existed for atrocities on the battlefield, either during the confusion of the running fight or afterward, when the Confederates flushed many weary Indiana and Texas soldiers, including unarmed men, from the chaparral thickets along the remote border. With the war over, any repercussions for executing prisoners would certainly not be forthcoming. In this sense, the Texas Rebels might well have had a license to kill and settle old scores because they knew that they would not be accountable. If so, then was the time spent in rounding up and allegedly killing prisoners one reason to explain why the Rebels failed to capture or destroy Colonel Barrett's entire force?

By May 1865, the Texas Yankees were aware of the possibility of a no-quarter policy because they had seen it before. The Texas Yankees were the prime targets of the Texas Rebels' wrath for years, and this no-quarter warfare was demonstrated most recently in the fight at Las Rucias. Such an emotion-charged situation on the battlefield may help to explain why so many blue-clad "renegades"—as the Texas Rebels called them—remained hidden in the chaparral instead of making the attempt to rejoin the retreating column in order to escape. These Union Texas soldiers refused to risk their lives by getting caught on the open prairie by Texas Rebel horsemen who were after revenge.

According to one Yankee who survived his brief capture at Palmito Ranch, and later reported to his unit at Brazos Santiago on May 17: "[T]here was one company of Texans, made up mostly of deserters from the rebels [and] as fast as these were captured they were shot down. Neither would the deserters surrender for they knew it would be death, and so died fighting." Colonel Barrett himself reported days after the battle that "a few men [of the Texas Cavalry] are still missing from this detachment."

The possible cover-up of what was perhaps the last atrocity of the Civil War also explains in part why the battle has been so long buried in mystery and has been obscured for generations. The skeletons that are still discovered on the field of Palmito Ranch provide some clues of higher fatalities from a possible no-quarter policy. In addition, a discrepancy exists between the reports as published in the official records, which minimized the number of fatalities, and other more reliable primary documentation. Because Palmito Ranch was the last land battle of the Civil War, perhaps the final atrocity of that conflict needed to be ignored if the American nation was to bind its wounds on the road to recovery. Quite possibly, the untold story of Palmito Ranch remained so obscure partly because of a battlefield atrocity.

In fact, the controversies surrounding the battle began almost as soon as the last shot was fired. To tarnish the image of both Lieutenant Colonel Morrison and his Indiana regiment, in part to influence the opinions of the upcoming court-martial proceedings against Morrison, Colonel Barrett overly promoted the fighting prowess of his 62nd U.S. Colored Regiment at the expense of the veteran 34th Indiana in his official report after the battle. Throughout the engagement, Colonel Barrett acted in a manner that indicated his desire to sacrifice the Indiana soldiers in order to preserve his own regiment as much as possible. As has been seen, animosity between the Indiana troops and the white officers of the black regiment had festered to new levels by the time of the battle.

In regard to the performance of his African American troops, Lieutenant Colonel Branson described in his official report that "the entire operation demonstrated the fact that the negro soldiers can march [while] this regiment can keep order in the ranks and be depended upon under trying circumstances."

The results of the court-martial proceedings against Lieutenant Colonel Morrison brought high praise for the 62nd at the expense of the Indiana troops: "the 62nd Regiment [U.S.] Colored Troops, which had seen much less service and experience, suffered no such losses [as the 34th Indiana] and had no panic or stragglers, although nearest the enemy most of the time."[246]

Lieutenant Colonel Morrison, the Missourian far from home support and political clout, unlike Colonel Barrett, became a natural scapegoat for the Union defeat at Palmito Ranch, therefore Colonel Barrett attempted to shift the blame for the Union defeat on him by ordering a court-martial. From the beginning, the ever-ambitious and image-conscious Colonel Barrett falsely charged Lieutenant Colonel Morrison with the primary responsibility for the Union defeat. He unfairly stated: "[H]ad it not been for [a needless panic] on the part of the 34th Indiana, our loss would have been comparatively nothing." Morrison and Barrett had clashed from the beginning. Morrison had been arrested on February 28, 1865, only four days after Colonel Barrett's arrival at Brazos Santiago. Colonel Barrett seemed to have old scores to settle.[247]

While Lieutenant Colonel Morrison was serving as a convenient scapegoat, Union losses and the full magnitude of the Federal defeat at Palmito Ranch might have been downplayed because of the intended joint Union-Confederate operations against the French in Mexico. The publicity of the unexpected clash between blue and gray at Palmito Ranch on May 13, 1865, might well have sabotaged such a unified effort south of the border. For this reason, Union losses might well have also been understated by headquarters and Washington, D.C., in order to deal with the perceived imminent threat of a strong European power in Mexico. Again, this sensitive political and military situation along the Rio Grande border might have also explained the cover-up of possible battlefield atrocities. By this time, the last publicity that the war-weary American nation needed was that of a war atrocity committed during the war's final days and weeks after Appomattox.

With the future joint Union-Confederate effort foremost in his mind, Colonel Ford may well have minimized the total number of acknowledged Rebel casualties for the same reason. Under these circumstances, perhaps a whitewash took place both in regard to the number of casualties of both sides and the possible massacre of captured Union troops. Most likely, such a cover-up, if it occurred, was initiated for the benefit of future cooperation between Union and Confederate forces during the joint expedition against the French in northern Mexico. Pressing geopolitical and domestic requirements of the day might well have obscured the full sacrifice and real price paid by the men in blue and gray who fought at Palmito Ranch on May 13, 1865.[248]

EPILOGUE

At long last, the land battles of the Civil War finally came to a merciful conclusion when the fighting closed at Palmito Ranch. The Civil War sputtered to an inglorious end in a remote section of Cameron County, Texas, where the last land battle was fought in the most obscure corner of the dying Confederacy. Here, at Palmito Ranch in one of the southernmost points of the U.S. mainland, the North suffered its last defeat.

In the words of Colonel Ford, who would take his family across the Rio Grande to Matamoros for safekeeping before the end of May, this final victory on Texas soil was won because "the Confederate soldiers on the lower Rio Grande would submit to nothing implicating their honor and manhood [as] they considered the advance of the Union troops as a violation of the terms of nonaction, as specified by General Lew Wallace, and they fought" one last time against an invader of their homeland.[1]

Today, the remote, isolated battlefield of Palmito Ranch lies all but forgotten. Appearing almost exactly as it did almost 140 years ago, the obscure field of battle remains undisturbed, basking in an eerie silence. The field of Palmito Ranch remains unmarked today except for a single modest stone monument along the main highway—not the same route as the old Brownsville Road—far from the scene of the initial combat along the Rio Grande to the south. Although the opening guns of Fort Sumter have been immortalized, the final fury at Palmito Ranch, which closed the final chapter on the bloodiest war in American history, has been forgotten.

While Fort Sumter is visited annually by thousands, the forgotten field of Palmito Ranch remains undisturbed, ignored, and left in isolated peace as if to honor the young men and boys who lost their lives there. In many ways, Palmito Ranch seems almost to be suspended in time. Surprisingly little of the battlefield has changed since that hot day in May 1865, when "Old Rip" Ford won the Confederacy's final success along the Rio Grande border. Neither museums, guided tours, nor gaudy statues commemorate the scene of this final clash of blue and gray. Likewise forgotten were the brave men—Anglo, black, Irish, Mexican, German, Tejano, French, and Hispanic—who fought and died at Palmito Ranch for what they believed to be right.

While the major Civil War battlefields in the East have become shrines decorated with seemingly countless monuments and markers to ensure that their historical legacy will endure for generations, the young men and boys on both sides who fought with valor at Palmito Ranch have faded from memory as completely as the battlefield itself. In the popular memory, the Civil War ended when General Lee surrendered to General Grant at Appomattox Court House, relegating what happened at Palmito Ranch to a mere historical footnote in even the most respected histories of the war.

But to the hundreds of soldiers who fought at Palmito Ranch, the battle was as challenging as Miller's cornfield at Antietam, the stone wall of Fredericksburg, or Little Round Top at Gettysburg. Here, on May 13, 1865, these men in blue and gray launched the last charge, fired the last volley, swung the last saber, flew the last flag, unleashed the final "Rebel Yell," and fell for the last time after four years of conflict. Most of all, it is the overlooked chapter of sacrifices, heroics, and accomplishments by the young soldiers of Palmito Ranch that should not be forgotten, even though the battle was fought nearly a month and a half after the surrender at Appomattox Court House.

ENDNOTES

CHAPTER 1

1. James Cooper Nisbet, *Four Years on the Firing Line* (Jackson: McCowat-Mercer, 1963), 237.
2. Chris M. Calkins, *The Battles of Appomattox Station and Appomattox Court House, April 8–9, 1865* (Lynchburg: Howard, 1987), 100–109, 191; Noah Andre Trudeau, *Out of the Storm: The End of the Civil War, April–June 1865* (New York: Little, Brown, 1994), 3–74, 79, 83–84; C. Vann Woodward, *Mary Chesnut's Civil War* (New Haven: Yale University Press, 1981), 771, 782.
3. John B. Gordon, *Reminiscences of the Civil War* (New York: Charles Scribner's Sons, 1904), 445–54; Trudeau, *Out of the Storm*, 118, 142–43.
4. Gary W. Gallagher, ed., *Fighting for the Confederacy: The Personal Recollections of General Edward Porter Alexander* (Chapel Hill: University of North Carolina Press, 1989), 531.
5. Arthur W. Bergeron, Jr., *Confederate Mobile* (Jackson: University Press of Mississippi, 1991), 196–97; Woodward, ed., *Mary Chesnut's Civil War*, 790.
6. Trudeau, *Out of the Storm*, 208–19, 237–44; Jefferson Davis, *The Rise and Fall of the Confederate Government* (New York: Collier, 1961), 530.
7. Ibid., 277–82; 291–98.
8. Ibid., 145–50; Craig L. Symonds, *Joseph E. Johnston: A Civil War Biography* (New York: Norton, 1992), 355–57.

9. Ralph A. Wooster, *Texas and Texans in the Civil War* (Austin: Eakin, 1995), 179.

10. Stephen B. Oates, ed., *Rip Ford's Texas* (Austin: University of Texas Press, 1994), 388; *War of the Rebellion: A Compilation of the Official Records of the Union and Confederate Armies* (128 vols., Washington D.C.: Government Printing Office, 1880–1901, vol. 48, ser. 1. pt. 1, 1275–80 (hereafter cited as *OR*); Mark Mayo Boatner, *The Civil War Dictionary* (New York: David McKay, 1959), 887; Robert L. Kerby, *Kirby Smith's Confederacy: The Trans-Mississippi South, 1863–1865* (Tuscaloosa: University of Alabama Press, 1972), 372.

11. *OR*, vol. 48, ser. 1, pt. 1, 1277.

12. Ibid.

13. Ibid.; Boatner, *The Civil War Dictionary*, 887; O. M. Roberts, *Confederate Military History: Texas* (Atlanta: Confederate Publishing Company, 1899), 11: 126 (hereafter cited as *CMH*); Oates, ed., *Rip Ford's Texas*, 388.

14. *OR*, vol. 48, ser. 1, pt. 1, 1277; Oates, ed., *Rip Ford's Texas*, 388.

15. *OR*, vol. 48, ser. 1, pt. 1, 1277.

16. Ibid., 1277–80; Oates, ed., *Rip Ford's Texas*, 389; Kerby, *Kirby Smith's Confederacy*, 372.

17. *OR*, vol. 48, ser. 1, pt. 1, 1275–76; John C. Moore, *Confederate Military History: Missouri* (Atlanta: Confederate Publishing Company, 1899), 12: 223–25; Kerby, *Kirby Smith's Confederacy*, 372–73.

18. *OR*, vol. 48, ser. 1, pt. 1, 1279.

19. Ibid., 1276.

20. Ibid., 1166–67.

21. Ibid.

22. Ibid., 1167; Joseph H. Parks, *General Edmund Kirby Smith, C.S.A.* (Baton Rouge: Louisiana State University Press, 1992), 451.

23. Ronnie C. Tyler, *Santiago Vidaurri and the Southern Confederacy* (Austin: Texas State Historical Association, 1973), 56–57.

24. Roberts, *CMH*, 126.

25. Frank W. Johnson, *A History of Texas and Texans* (Chicago: American Historical Society, 1914), vol. 2, 613.

26. Ibid.; 1860 Cameron County, Texas, Census Records from the Seventh Census of the United States; *OR*, vol. 48, ser. 1, pt. 1, 1278; Oates, ed., *Rip Ford's Texas*, 32–33, 214–15; Randolph B. Campbell, *An Empire for Slavery: The Peculiar Institution in Texas, 1821–1865* (Baton Rouge: Louisiana State University Press, 1989), 231; Robert Selph Henry, *The Story of the Mexican War* (New York: Da Capo Press, 1961), 54–61.

27. *OR*, vol. 48, ser. 1, pt. 1, 1167; Marshall DeBruhl, *Sword of San Jacinto: A Life of Sam Houston* (New York: Random House, 1993), 208–13.
28. T. Michael Parrish, *Richard Taylor: Soldier Prince of Dixie* (Chapel Hill: University of North Carolina Press, 1992), 8, 10, 441–43; Trudeau, *Out of the Storm*, 259–60; Woodward, ed., *Mary Chesnut's Civil War*, 812.
29. Parks, *General Smith*, 456–62.
30. Ibid., 460–69; Kerby, *Kirby Smith's Confederacy*, 430–23.

CHAPTER 2
1. Oates, ed., *Rip Ford's Texas*, xvii–xxii, 5–6, 9–10, 15–19; Virgil E. Baugh, *Rendezvous at the Alamo: Highlights in the Lives of Bowie, Crockett, and Travis* (Lincoln: University of Nebraska Press, 1985), 142–48; Ralph Widener, "John S. 'Rip' Ford, Colonel, CSA," *Confederate Veteran* (May–June 1993): 15 (hereafter cited as *CV*).
2. Oates, ed., *Rip Ford's Texas*, pp. xx–xxiii, 23–24, 26–30, 34–37, 44, 60–62; Widener, "John S. 'Rip' Ford, Colonel, C.S.A.," 15.
3. Oates, ed., *Rip Ford's Texas*, 66–68; Widener, "John S. 'Rip' Ford, Colonel, CSA," 15.
4. Oates, ed., *Rip Ford's Texas*, 73.
5. Ibid., 73–82.
6. Ibid., 86–98, 103.
7. Ibid., 141–47.
8. Ibid., 141–89.
9. Ibid., xxxii, 219–40; Stephen Hardin and Richard Hook, *The Texas Rangers* (London: Osprey Books, 1991), 22–23.
10. Oates, ed., *Rip Ford's Texas*, xxxiv, xxxv, 260–89; Thomas W. Cutrer, *Ben McCullock and the Frontier Military Tradition* (Chapel Hill: University of North Carolina Press, 1993), 169.
11. Oates, ed., *Rip Ford's Texas*, 290–309; Alvin M. Josephy, Jr., *The Civil War in the American West* (New York: Knopf, 1991), 25; Cutrer, *Ben McCulloch*, 169; Widener, "John S. 'Rip' Ford, Colonel, CSA," 16.
12. Oates, ed., *Rip Ford's Texas*, xxxv–xxxvii, 316–17; Josephy, *The Civil War in the American West*, 21–22; John Salmon Ford Papers, Archives Division, University of Texas Library, Austin.
13. Stephen B. Oates, *Confederate Cavalry West of the River* (Austin: University of Texas, 1961), 3–5, 8; Kerby, *Kirby Smith's Confederacy*, xxxvii, 15, 318; Josephy, *The Civil War in the American West*, 24, 27; Widener, "John S. 'Rip' Ford, Colonel, CSA," 17.
14. Josephy, *The Civil War in the American West*, 20–21, 26.

15. Oates, ed., *Rip Ford's Texas*, 317.

16. Ibid., 15, 62, 318; Josephy, *The Civil War in the American West*, 28; James A. Irby, "Backdoor at Bagdad: The Civil War on the Rio Grande," Monograph no. 53, *Southwestern Studies* (1977): 18 (hereafter cited as *SS*).

17. Oates, ed., *Rip Ford's Texas*, 8, 320–21; Irby, "Backdoor at Bagdad," 18.

18. Oates, ed., Rip Ford's Texas, pp. xxxv, xxxvii, 8, 324; Irby, "Backdoor At Bagdad," 18–19; Widener, "John S. 'Rip' Ford, Colonel, CSA," 17.

19. Oates, ed., *Rip Ford's Texas*, 8, 66.

20. Arthur James Lyon Fremantle, *The Fremantle Diary* (Boston: Little, Brown, 1954), 7; Thomas North, *Five Years in Texas* (Cincinnati: Elm Street, 1871), 104.

21. Oates, ed., *Rip Ford's Texas*, xxxvii, 322–26; Stephen L. Hardin, *Texian Illiad: A Military History of the Texas Revolution, 1835–1836* (Austin: University of Texas Press, 1994), 28, 42, 57.

22. Oates, ed., *Rip Ford's Texas*, 324–32; Stephen B. Oates, "John S. 'Rip' Ford, Prudent Cavalryman, C.S.A.," *Southwestern Historical Quarterly* 64, no. 3 (January 1961): 293–97 (hereafter cited as *SWHQ*); Widener, "John S. 'Rip' Ford, Colonel, CSA," 18.

23. Kerby, *Kirby Smith's Confederacy*, 191; Michael A. Mullins, *The Fremont Rifles: A History of the 37th Illinois Veteran Volunteer Infantry* (Wilmington: Broadfoot, 1990), 233–34; Josephy, *The Civil War in the American West*, 161, 179–84.

24. Kerby, *Kirby Smith's Confederacy*, 191; Josephy, *The Civil War in the American West*, 161, 186–87.

25. Kerby, *Kirby Smith's Confederacy*, 191; Capt. Edward Gee Miller, Diary, November 1, 1863, Washington County Historical Society, Fayetteville, Arkansas; Ludwell H. Johnson, *Red River Campaign: Politics and Cotton in the Civil War* (Kent: Kent State University Press, 1993), 39–43; Josephy, *The Civil War in the American West*, 186–87.

26. Kerby, *Kirby Smith's Confederacy*, 191–93; Mullins, *The Fremont Rifles*, 236–44; Josephy, *The Civil War in the American West*, 186–87.

27. Kerby, *Kirby Smith's Confederacy*, 192–94; Oates, ed., *Rip Ford's Texas*, 343; W. J. Hughes, *Rebellious Ranger: Rip Ford and the Old Southwest* (Norman: University of Oklahoma Press, 1964), 212; Irby, "Backdoor at Bagdad," 30–31; Widener, "John S. 'Rip' Ford, Colonel, CSA," 19; Roberts, *CMH*, 11: 122–23.

28. Kerby, *Kirby Smith's Confederacy*, 194–95; Johnson, *Red River Campaign*, 39–44; Josephy, *The Civil War in the American West*, 188–89.

29. Oates, ed., *Rip Ford's Texas*, 343; *OR*, vol. 26, ser. 1, pt. 1, 534–35; Kerby, *Kirby Smith's Confederacy*, 364–66; Oates, "John S. 'Rip' Ford," 298–99; Roberts, *CMH*, 11: 122.
30. Oates, ed., *Rip Ford's Texas*, 344; Hughes, *Rebellious Ranger*, 214–15.
31. Oates, ed., *Rip Ford's Texas*, 345; Hughes, *Rebellious Ranger*, 213; Alwyn Barr, *Texans in Revolt: The Battle for San Antonio, 1835* (Austin: University of Texas Press, 1990), 30, 49, 70; Paul Horgan, *Great River: The Rio Grande in North American History* (Hanover, NH: University Press of New England, 1984), 510, 529–30.
32. Josephy, *The Civil War in the American West*, 41.
33. Oates, ed., *Rip Ford's Texas*, 349; Bruce Marshall, "Santos Benavides: The Confederacy on the Rio Grande," *Civil War* 8, no. 3 (May–June 1990): 18–20; Jerry D. Thompson, *Mexican Texans in the Union Army* (El Paso: University of Texas at El Paso Press, 1986), vii-viii; Hardin, *Texian Illiad*, 28; Jerry D. Thompson, *Vaqueros in Blue and Gray* (Austin: Presidial, 1976), 8–10.
34. Albert A. Nofi, *The Alamo and the Texas War for Independence, September 30, 1835–April 21, 1836* (Conshocken, PA: Combined, 1992), 176.
35. Hughes, *Rebellious Ranger*, 213–15.
36. Oates, ed., *Rip Ford's Texas*, 350; Hughes, *Rebellious Ranger*, 214; Roberts, *CMH*, 11: 123.
37. Oates, ed., *Rip Ford's Texas*, 352–53; *Houston Daily Telegraph*, February 13, 1864; Hughes, *Rebellious Ranger*, 212, 216; Anne Fears Crawford, *The Eagle: The Autobiography of Santa Anna* (Austin: State House Press, 1988), 49–52, 216; Kerby, *Kirby Smith's Confederacy*, 366–67; Oates, "John S. 'Rip' Ford," 303; Roberts, *CMH*, 11: 122.
38. Oates, ed., *Rip Ford's Texas*, 358–59; Kerby, *Kirby Smith's Confederacy*, 366–67; Hughes, *Rebellious Ranger*, 213.
39. Roberts, *CMH*, 11: 125.
40. Emmie Giddings W. Mahon and Chester V. Kielman, "George H. Giddings and the San Antonio–San Diego Mail Line," *SWHQ* (October 1957): 220; Oates, ed., *Rip Ford's Texas*, 301.
41. Mahon and Kielman, "George H. Giddings and the San Antonio-San Diego Mail Line," 221.
42. Ibid., 222–23.
43. Ibid., 224–25.
44. Anne J. Bailey, *Between the Enemy and Texas: Parsons's Texas Cavalry in the Civil War* (Fort Worth: Texas Christian University Press, 1989), 88–91, 119.

45. Hughes, *Rebellious Ranger*, 216–17; Oates, ed., *Rip Ford's Texas*, 359; Kerby, *Kirby Smith's Confederacy*, 366–67.

46. Hughes, *Rebellious Ranger*, 218–21; Oates, ed., *Rip Ford's Texas*, 362–63; Kerby, *Kirby Smith's Confederacy*, 367–68; Irby, "Backdoor at Bagdad," 32–34; Oates, "John S. 'Rip' Ford," 304; Frank C. Pierce, *A Brief History of the Lower Rio Grande Valley* (Menasha, WI: George Banta, 1917), 49.

47. Hughes, *Rebellious Ranger*, 221–22; Kerby, *Kirby Smith's Confederacy*, 368–69; Oates, ed., *Rip Ford's Texas*, 363–64.

48. Hughes, *Rebellious Ranger*, 222–24; Kerby, *Kirby Smith's Confederacy*, 369; Oates, "John S. 'Rip' Ford," 305; Oates, ed., *Rip Ford's Texas*, 364–65.

49. Hughes, *Rebellious Ranger*, 224–29; Kerby, *Kirby Smith's Confederacy*, 369–70; Oates, "John S. 'Rip' Ford," 307.

50. Hughes, *Rebellious Ranger*, 228–29; Kerby, *Kirby Smith's Confederacy*, 370–71; *San Antonio Weekly Herald*, March 19, 1864; Oates, "John S. 'Rip' Ford," 309–310; Oates, ed., *Rip Ford's Texas*, 367.

51. Kerby, *Kirby Smith's Confederacy*, 371; Oates, ed., *Rip Ford's Texas*, 367; Oates, "John S. 'Rip' Ford," 309–10.

CHAPTER THREE

1. James M. McPherson, *The Negro's Civil War: How American Negroes Felt and Acted During the War for the Union* (New York: Vintage, 1965), 20, 173–92; Phillip Thomas Tucker, *From Auction Block to Glory: The African American Experience* (New York: Friedman, 1997), 1–76.

2. *OR*, vol. 48, ser. 1, pt. 1, 1023; Tucker, *From Auction Block to Glory*, 1–95.

3. William A. Gladstone, *United States Colored Troops, 1863–1867* (Gettysburg: Thomas, 1990), 104, 109; William C. Winter, *The Civil War in St. Louis: A Guided Tour* (St. Louis: Missouri Historical Society Press, 1994), 73–75; Noah Andre Trudeau, *Like Men of War: Black Troops in the Civil War 1862–1865* (New York: Little, Brown, 1998), 435–38.

4. Trudeau, *Like Men of War*, 437; Dudley Taylor Cornish, *The Sable Arm: Negro Troops in the Union Army, 1861–1865* (Lawrence: University Press of Kansas, 1987), 100.

5. Trudeau, *Like Men of War*, 440; Boatner, *The Civil War Dictionary*, 653.

6. Trudeau, *Like Men of War*, 396–408, 439–40.

7. R. Douglas Hurt, *Agriculture and Slavery in Missouri's Little Dixie* (Columbia: University of Missouri Press, 1992), xi–xii, 80–81, 103.

8. Joseph T. Glatthaar, *Forged in Battle: The Civil War Alliance of Black Soldiers and White Officers* (New York: Meridian, 1991), 114.

9. Trudeau, *Like Men of War*, 436.

10. Ibid., 234.

11. Thomas Wentworth Higginson, *Army Life in a Black Regiment* (New York: Collier, 1962), 237.

12. Edwin S. Redkey, ed., *A Grand Army of Black Men: Letters from African-American Soldiers in the Union Army, 1861–1865* (Cambridge: Cambridge University Press, 1992), 18.

13. Ibid., 219.

14. James M. McPherson, *Battle Cry of Freedom: The Civil War Era* (New York: Oxford University Press, 1988), 566.

15. Redkey, ed., *A Grand Army of Black Men*, 68; McPherson, *The Negro's Civil War*, 216–22.

16. Campbell, *An Empire for Slavery*, 239–40, 248; Hardin, *Texian Illiad*, 14–17, 59, 68, 79; Tucker, *From Auction Block to Glory*, 25–87.

17. Trudeau, *Like Men of War*, 436; Proceedings, Findings, and Opinions of the Court-Martial convened by order of the U.S. Army in Special Orders No. 36, Headquarters of the Army of the Rio Grande, Brownsville, Texas, July 19, 1865, in the case of Robert G. Morrison, RG 153, Records of the Judge Advocate General, National Archives, Washington, D.C. (hereafter cited as Morrison Court-Martial).

18. Trudeau, *Like Men of War*, 436.

19. Ibid.

20. Ibid., 437.

21. Ibid., 436–38; Morrison Court-Martial.

22. Trudeau, *Like Men of War*, 439.

23. Oates, ed., *Rip Ford's Texas*, 344.

24. Mullins, *The Fremont Rifles*, 236.

25. Trudeau, *Out of the Storm*, 299.

26. McPherson, *The Negro's Civil War*, 222.

27. Personnel and Regimental Records of Civil War Soldiers from Indiana, Indiana State Archives, Indianapolis; Compiled Service Records of Troops Who Served from the State of Indiana, National Archives, Washington, D.C. (hereafter cited as NA).

28. Personnel and Regimental Records of Civil War Soldiers from Indiana; Edwin C. Bearss, *Grant Strikes a Fatal Blow: The Campaign for Vicksburg* (Dayton, OH: Morningside Bookshop, 1986), 2: 378–81.

29. Personnel and Regimental Records of Civil War Soldiers from Indiana; Bearss, *Grant Strikes a Fatal Blow*, 2: 613–16.

30. Personnel and Regimental Records of Civil War Soldiers from Indiana.

31. Mark Warren, letter to author, March 20, 2000; Bobby Roberts and Carl Moneyhon, *Portraits of Conflict: A Photographic History of Missis-*

sippi in the Civil War (Fayetteville: University of Arkansas Press, 1993), 244; Personnel and Regimental Records of Civil War Soldiers from Indiana; Morrison Court-Martial.

32. Morrison Court-Martial.

33. Ibid.

34. Ibid; Boatner, *The Civil War Dictionary*, 412.

35. Personnel and Regimental Records; Bruce Aiken, "Civil War's Last Death Lives Again by Cold Records, Warm Memories," *Brownsville Herald Plus*, March 27, 1993.

36. Morrison Court-Martial.

37. Ibid.

38. Frank H. Smyrl, "Texans in the Union Army, 1861–1865," *SWHQ*, 65, no. 2 (October 1961): 234; Oates, ed., *Rip Ford's Texas*, 344; Kerby, *Kirby Smith's Confederacy*, 16; James Marten, "Texans in the U.S. Army: True to the Union," *North and South*, 3, no. 1 (November 1999): 79–80.

39. Smyrl, "Texans in the Union Army, 1861–1865," 234–43; Thompson, *Mexican Texans in the Union Army*, 10–16; Mullins, *The Fremont Rifles*, 244–46; Thompson, *Vaqueros in Blue and Gray*, 82; Marten, "Texans in the U.S. Army," 79, 81.

40. Smyrl, "Texans in the Union Army, 1861–1865," 243; Thompson, *Mexican Texans in the Union Army*, 13–17; Thompson, *Vaqueros in Blue and Gray*, 85–89; Marten, "Texans in the U.S. Army," 80, 82.

41. Smyrl, "Texans in the Union Army, 1861–1865," 243; Oates, ed., *Rip Ford's Texas*, 344; Thompson, *Mexican Texans in the Union Army*, vii, viii, 50, 70, 73.

42. Smyrl, "Texans in the Union Army, 1861–1865," 245; Thompson, *Mexican Texans in the Union Army*, 28; Thompson, *Vaqueros in Blue and Gray*, 88–92.

43. Smyrl, "Texans in the Union Army, 1861–1865," 246–47; Thompson, *Vaqueros in Blue and Gray*, 93.

44. Smyrl, "Texans in the Union Army, 1861–1865," 248–49; Thompson, *Mexican Texans in the Union Army*, 31–34; Thompson, *Vaqueros in Blue and Gray*, 93–94.

45. Thompson, *Mexican Texans in the Union Army*, 35; Thompson, *Vaqueros in Blue and Gray*, 95.

46. Oates, ed., *Rip Ford's Texas*, 344; Hughes, *Rebellious Ranger*, 220–21; Thompson, *Mexican Texans in the Union Army*, 30; Thompson, *Vaqueros in Blue and Gray*, 92–93.

CHAPTER 4

1. Josephy, *The Civil War in the American West*, 223; Oates, ed., *Rip Ford's Texas*, 331–32, 336, 347.

2. Louis J. Schuler, *The Last Battle in the War between the States, May 13, 1865* (Brownsville, TX: Springman-King, 1960), 20; Ronnie C. Tyler, ed., *The New Handbook of Texas* (Austin: Texas State Historical Association, 1996), 5: 25; Dr. Tony Zavaleta, University of Texas, Brownsville, and present owner of Palmito Ranch property, letter to author, March 4, 1998.

3. Schuler, *The Last Battle in the War between the States*, 20; Oates, ed., *Rip Ford's Texas*, 326–27.

4. Trudeau, *Out of the Storm*, 299; Thompson, *Mexican Texans in the Union Army*, 60; I. L. Fussell, *History of the 34th Regiment*, (Indianapolis: n.p., n.d.), 50.

5. Trudeau, *Out of the Storm*, 299; Mullins, *The Fremont Rifles*, 244–45; Trudeau, *Like Men of War*, 437–38.

6. Schuler, *The Last Battle in the War between the States*, 24.

7. Oates, ed., *Rip Ford's Texas*, 344; Hughes, *Rebellious Ranger*, 237.

8. Mullins, *The Fremont Rifles*, 236; John Lofton, *Denmark Vesey's Revolt* (Kent, OH: Kent State University Press, 1983), 144–89; Horgan, *Great River*, 486; Hardin, *Texian Illiad*, 16–17.

9. Horgan, *Great River*, vii–5; Ulysses S. Grant, *Personal Memoirs of U. S. Grant* (New York: C. M. Webster, 1885–86), 1: 93.

10. Horgan, *Great River*, 5–6, 505.

11. Irby, "Backdoor at Bagdad," 5–10; Tyler, *Santiago Vidaurri*, 51–55, 97–156; Ronnie C. Tyler, "Cotton on the Border, 1861–1865," *SWHQ* 73, no. 4 (April 1970): 456–77; Robert W. Delaney, "Matamoros, Port for Texas during the Civil War," *SWHQ*, 58, no. 4 (April 1955): 473–487; Horgan, *Great River*, 840–41; Milo Kearny and Anthony Knapp, *Boom and Bust: The Historical Cycles of Matamoros and Brownsville* (Austin: Eakin, 1991), 138–40.

12. Oates, ed., *Rip Ford's Texas*, 388–89; Trudeau, *Out of the Storm*, 299–300; Robert J. Casey, *The Texas Border and Some Borderliners* (Indianapolis: Bobbs-Merrill, 1950), 389; Milo Kearney, ed., *Still More Studies in Brownsville History* (Brownsville, TX: University of Texas Press, 1991), 7–8; Tyler, ed., *The New Handbook of Texas*, 5: 25; Trudeau, *Like Men of War*, 439–40, 442; Fussell, *History of the 34th Regiment*, 51.

13. W. C. Nunn, ed., *Ten More Texans in Gray* (Hillsboro, TX: Hill Junior College Press, 1980), 14.

14. Trudeau, *Out of the Storm*, 300; Tyler, "Cotton on the Border, 1861–1865," 476; Kerby, *Kirby Smith's Confederacy*, 399, 413, 419; Hughes, *Rebellious Ranger*, 238; T. R. Fehrenbach, *Lone Star: A History of Texas and the Texans* (New York: American Legacy, 1983), 389; Fussell, *History of the 34th Regiment*, 51.

15. Morrison Court-Martial; Oates, *Confederate Cavalry West of the River*, 156; Trudeau, *Out of the Storm*, 299–302; *OR*, vol. 48, ser. 1, pt. 1, 267; Pierce, *A Brief History of the Lower Rio Grande Valley*, 52–53; Henry N. Ferguson, *The Port of Brownsville: A Maritime History of the Rio Grande Valley* (Brownsville, TX: Springman-King, 1976), 173; Compiled Service Records of Troops Who Served from the State of Minnesota, NA; Irby, "Backdoor at Bagdad," 47; Trudeau, *Like Men of War*, 436, 438, 440–42.

16. Morrison Court-Martial; Oates, *Confederate Cavalry West of the River*, 156; Trudeau, *Out of the Storm*, 301; *OR*, vol. 48, ser. 1, pt. 1, 267; Missouri Civil War Service Records, Missouri State Archives, Jefferson City; Oates, ed., *Rip Ford's Texas*, 389; Trudeau, *Like Men of War*, 442.

17. Hardin, *Texian Illiad*, 109, 187.

18. Trudeau, *Like Men of War*, 442–43.

19. Ibid.

20. Morrison Court-Martial; Trudeau, *Like Men of War*, 443.

21. Oates, *Confederate Cavalry West of the River*, 156; Trudeau, *Out of the Storm*, 302; *OR*, vol. 48, ser. 1, no. 1, 267–68; Pierce, *A Brief History of the Lower Rio Grande Valley*, 53; Ralph Widener, "The Last Land Battle of the War between the States, May 13, 1865," 1, Texas State Library, Austin; Trudeau, *Like Men of War*, 442–43; Bill Winsor, *Texas in the Confederacy: Military Installations, Economy and People* (Hillsboro, TX: Hill Junior College Press, 1978), 34; Roberts, *CMH*, 11: 126; Zavaleta, letter to author.

22. Trudeau, *Like Men of War*, 443; Morrison Court-Martial.

23. Oates, *Confederate Cavalry West of the River*, 156; Trudeau, *Out of the Storm*, 302; Oates, ed., *Rip Ford's Texas*, 389; Morrison Court-Martial; Raphael Cowen, "The Last Battle of the Civil War: Its Causes and Afterwards," in Brownsville Historical Association, *A Blast from the Past: 50th Anniversary, 1947–1997* (Brownsville, TX: Border, 1996), 16; Roberts, *CMH*, 11: 126; Widener, *The Last Battle in the War between the States*, 1, 5; Trudeau, *Like Men of War*, 443–44; Fussell, *History of the 34th Regiment*, 52.

24. Oates, *Confederate Cavalry West of the River*, 156; Trudeau, *Out of the Storm*, 302–3; Oates, ed., *Rip Ford's Texas*, 389; *OR*, vol. 24, ser. 1., no.

1, 1354–55, 1358, 1456; Cowen, "The Last Battle of the Civil War," 16; Roberts, *CMH*, 11: 126.

25. Trudeau, *Out of the Storm*, 303; Oates, *Confederate Cavalry West of the River*, 156; Oates, ed., *Rip Ford's Texas*, 389–90; Cowen, "The Last Battle of the Civil War," 16; W. C. West, "The Last Battle of the War," *Southern Historical Society Papers*, 21 (1893): 227 (hereafter cited as *SHSP*); Trudeau, *Like Men of War*, 445; Wooster, *Texas and Texans in the Civil War*, 179.

26. Oates, ed., *Rip Ford's Texas*, 389.

27. Oates, *Confederate Cavalry West of the River*, 389; Trudeau, *Out of the Storm*, 300–302; Trudeau, *Like Men of War*, 443–44; Morrison Court-Martial.

28. Trudeau, *Out of the Storm*, 301–2; West, "The Last Battle of the War," 227.

CHAPTER FIVE

1. Morrison Court-Martial; Civil War Service Records, Missouri State Archives, Jefferson City.

2. Morrison Court-Martial.

3. Ibid.; Trudeau, *Like Men of War*, 444.

4. Morrison Court-Martial; Trudeau, *Like Men of War*, 444.

5. Morrison Court-Martial; Fussell, *History of the 34th Regiment*, 51–52.

6. Morrison Court-Martial.

7. Ibid.

8. Ibid; Trudeau, *Like Men of War*, 444.

9. Morrison Court-Martial.

10. Morrison Court-Martial; Trudeau, *Like Men of War*, 444.

11. Morrison Court-Martial.

12–17. Ibid.

18. Ibid.; Aiken, "Civil War's Last Death Lives Again in Cold Records, Warm Memories," *Brownsville Herald Plus*, March 27, 1993; Trudeau, *Out of the Storm*, 303–4.

19. Morrison Court-Martial; Trudeau, *Like Men of War*, 444.

20. Morrison Court-Martial; Trudeau, *Like Men of War*, 444.

21. Morrison Court-Martial.

22. Ibid.

23. Ibid.; Fussell, *History of the 34th Regiment*, 52.

24. Morrison Court-Martial.

25. Ibid.

26. Ibid.; Trudeau, *Like Men of War*, 444.

27. Morrison Court-Martial.

28. Ibid.; Trudeau, *Like Men of War*, p. 444.

29. Zavaleta, letter to author; Leandra Costilla, "County's Oldest Ranches Honored," *Harlingen Texas Valley Morning Star*, n.d.

30. Morrison Court-Martial; Trudeau, *Like Men of War*, 445.

31. Morrison Court-Martial; Trudeau, *Like Men of War*, 444.

32. Trudeau, *Like Men of War*, 445.

33. Morrison Court-Martial.

34–46. Ibid.

47. Ibid.; Oates, *Confederate Cavalry West of the River*, 156.

48. Morrison Court-Martial; Trudeau, *Like Men of War*, p. 445.

49. Morrison Court-Martial.

50–64. Ibid.

65. Ibid.; Zavaleta, letter to author.

66. Morrison Court-Martial.

67–69. Ibid.

70. Trudeau, *Like Men of War*, 446.

71. Ibid.; Morrison Court-Martial.

72. Morrison Court-Martial.

73–77. Ibid.

78. Ibid.; Trudeau, *Like Men of War*, 446.

79. Morrison Court-Martial.

80–85. Ibid.

86. Morrison Court-Martial; Trudeau, *Like Men of War*, 446.

87. Morrison Court-Martial; Trudeau, *Like Men of War*, 446.

88. Morrison Court-Martial; Schuler, *The Last Battle in the War between the States*, 21; Trudeau, *Like Men of War*, 446.

89. Morrison Court-Martial.

90–97. Ibid.

98. Ibid.; Trudeau, *Like Men of War*, 450.

99. Morrison Court-Martial.

100. Ibid.; Trudeau, *Out of the Storm*, 306.

101–103. Ibid.

104. *OR*, vol. 48, ser. 1, pt. 1, 268.

105. Morrison Court-Martial; Trudeau, *Like Men of War*, 446.

106. Morrsion Court-Martial; *OR*, vol. 48, ser. 1, pt. 1, 268; Trudeau, *Out of the Storm*, 306.

107. Morrison Court-Martial; Trudeau, *Like Men of War*, 446.

108. Roberts, *CMH*, 11: 126–127; Oates, ed., Rip Ford's Texas, 390; Trudeau, Out of the Storm, 306; Hughes, Rebellious Ranger, 238; Trudeau, *Like Men of War*, 445.

109. Kerby, *Kirby Smith's Confederacy*, 419; Morrison Court-Martial; Oates, *Confederate Cavalry West of the River*, 156–59, 178; James W. Pohl, *The Battle of San Jacinto* (Austin: Texas State Historical Association, 1989), 21, 29–45; Trudeau, *Out of the Storm*, 306–7; Roberts, *CMH*, 11: 126–27; Oates, ed., *Rip Ford's Texas*, 242, 247, 390; Schuler, *The Last Battle in the War between the States*, 21, 24–25; Widener, "John S. 'Rip' Ford, Colonel, CSA," 21; Hughes, *Rebellious Ranger*, 238; Tyler, ed., *The New Handbook of Texas*, 5: 26; Fehrenbach, *Lone Star*, 389; for O. G. Jones see Compiled Service Records of Troops Who Served, NA; Irby, "Backdoor to Bagdad," 48; Widener, *The Last Land Battle of the War Between The States*, 7; for J. M. Smith see Compiled Service Records of Troops Who Served, NA; Luther Conyer, "Last Battle of the War," *SHSP* 24 (1896): 310; Trudeau, *Like Men of War*, 445–47.

110. Morrison Court-Martial.

111. Ibid.

112. Ibid.; John S. D. Eisenhower, *So Far from God: The U.S. War with Mexico, 1846–1848* (New York: Doubleday, 1989), 76–80; Roberts, *CMH*, 11: 126–27; Hughes, *Rebellious Ranger*, 238; Oates, ed., *Rip Ford's Texas*, 391, 397; Widener, *The Last Land Battle Of The War between the States*, 5.

113. Morrison Court-Martial.

114–115. Ibid.

116. Ibid.; Roberts, *CMH*, 11: 127; Schuler, *The Last Battle in the War between the States*, 21; Stephen Oates, "Texas under the Secessionists," in *Texas Vistas: Selections from the* Southwest Historical Quarterly, compiled by Ralph A. Wooster and Robert A. Calvert (Austin: University of Texas Press, 1987), 165; Compiled Service Records of Troops Who Served, NA; Oates, ed., *Rip Ford's Texas*, 390–91; Trudeau, *Like Men of War*, 448.

117. Morrison Court-Martial; Trudeau, *Out of the Storm*, 307.

118. Trudeau, *Out of the Storm*, 307.

119. Ibid.; Morrison Court-Martial.

120. Trudeau, *Out of the Storm*, 307; Morrison Court-Martial; Oates, *Confederate Cavalry West of the River*, 157; Hughes, *Rebellious Ranger*, 238–39; Oates, ed., *Rip Ford's Texas*, 391; Trudeau, *Like Men of War*, 447.

121. Morrison Court-Martial.

122. Ibid.; Trudeau, *Like Men of War*, 446.

123. Morrison Court-Martial.

124. Ibid.; Trudeau, *Out of the Storm*, 307.

125. Morrison Court-Martial.

126. Ibid.

127. Ibid.; Trudeau, *Out of the Storm*, 307; Oates, *Confederate Cavalry West of the River*, 157.

128. Morrison Court-Martial.

129. Ibid.; Trudeau, *Like Men of War*, 447.

130. Morrison Court-Martial.

131. Ibid.

132. Ibid.; Trudeau, *Like Men of War*, 447–48; *OR*, vol. 48, ser. 1, pt. 1, 268; Fussell, *History of the 34th Regiment*, 52.

133. Morrison Court-Martial.

134. Ibid.; Fussell, *History of the 34th Regiment*, 52.

135. Morrison Court-Martial; Compiled Service Records of Troops Who Served from the State of Indiana.

136. Morrison Court-Martial.

137–142. Ibid.

143. Ibid; Trudeau, *Like Men of War*, 447.

144. *OR*, vol. 48, ser. 1, pt. 1, 266; Trudeau, *Like Men of War*, 447.

145. Morrison Court-Martial.

146. Ibid.

147. *OR*, vol. 48, ser. 1, pt. 1, 267.

148. Morrison Court-Martial.

149–156. Ibid.

157. Morrison Court-Martial; *OR*, vol. 48, ser. 1, pt. 1, 268.

158. Morrison Court-Martial; *OR*, vol. 48, ser. 1, pt. 1, 268.

159. Morrison Court-Martial; *OR*, vol. 48, ser. 1, pt. 1, 268.

160. Morrison Court-Martial; *OR*, vol. 48, ser. 1, pt. 1, 268.

161. Morrison Court-Martial.

162–164. Ibid.

165. Morrison Court-Martial; *OR*, vol. 48, ser. 1, pt. 1, 268.

166. Morrison Court-Martial; *OR*, vol. 48, ser. 1, pt. 1, 268.

167. *OR*, vol. 48, ser. 1, pt. 1, 268.

168. Morrison Court-Martial; *OR*, vol. 48, ser. 1, pt. 1, 268.

169. Morrison Court-Martial.

170. Morrison Court-Martial; Trudeau, *Out of the Storm*, 307–8; Personnel and Regimental Records of Civil War Soldiers from Indiana; Author in-

terview with Mr. Bruce Aiken, Executive Director of the Historic Brownsville Museum, Brownsville, Texas, January 6, 1997; Hughes, *Rebellious Ranger*, 239; *OR*, vol. 48, ser. 1, pt. 1, 268.

171. James Farber, *Texas, C.S.A.: A Spotlight on Disaster* (New York: Jackson, 1947), 241.

172. Oates, "John S. 'Rip' Ford," 312; Morrison Court-Martial; Oates, ed., *Rip Ford's Texas*, 391.

173. Morrison Court-Martial; Bruce Aiken, "Civil War's Last Death Lives Again in Cold Records, Warm Memories," *Brownsville Herald Plus*, March 27, 1993; Oates, ed., *Rip Ford's Texas*, 391; Fussell, *History of the 34th Regiment*, 53.

174. Morrison Court-Martial.

175. Ibid.; Fussell, *History of the 34th Regiment*, 52.

176. Oates, ed., *Rip Ford's Texas*, 391; Morrison Court-Martial.

177. Morrison Court-Martial; Trudeau, *Out of the Storm*, 308.

178. Morrison Court-Martial.

179. Ibid.; Trudeau, *Out of the Storm*, 308.

180. Morrison Court-Martial.

181. Ibid.; *OR*, vol. 48, ser. 1, pt. 1, 268.

182. Morrison Court-Martial.

183–188. Ibid.

189. Ibid.; Fussell, *History of the 34th Regiment*, 53.

190. Morrison Court-Martial.

191–202. Ibid.

203. Morrison Court-Martial; Trudeau, *Out of the Storm*, 308; Schuler, *The Last Battle in the War between the States*, 21.

204. Morrison Court-Martial.

205–207. Ibid.

208. *OR*, vol. 48, ser. 1, pt. 1, 268.

209. Morrison Court-Martial.

210. *OR*, vol. 48, ser. 1, pt. 1, 268.

211. Morrison Court-Martial.

212–225. Ibid.

226. Morrison Court-Martial; *OR*, vol. 48, ser. 1, pt. 1, 268; Roberts, *CMH*, 484.

227. Morrison Court-Martial; Trudeau, *Out of the Storm*, 308.

228. Morrison Court-Martial; Trudeau, *Like Men of War*, 308.

229. Morrison Court-Martial.

230. Ibid.

231. Morrison Court-Martial; Fussell, *History of the 34th Regiment*, 53.

232. Morrison Court-Martial.

233–234. Ibid.

235. Morrison Court-Martial; Roberts, *CMH*, 11: 127; Trudeau, *Out of the Storm*, 308; Oates, ed., *Rip Ford's Texas*, 391; Schuler, *The Last Battle in the War between the States*, 21; Widener, *The Last Land Battle of the War between the States*, 7–9.

236. Morrison Court-Martial.

237–239. Ibid.

240. Verna Jackson McKenna, *Old Point Lighthouse: Beacon of Brazos Santiago* (Harlingen, TX: private printing, 1956), 16; Oates, ed., *Rip Ford's Texas*, 391; Schuler, *The Last Battle in the War between the States*, 21, 23; Morrison Court-Martial.

241. Morrison Court-Martial; Roberts, *CMH*, 289–90; "Captain Summerfield H. Barton," *CV* 25 (January 1917–December 1917): 322; Private Ferdinand Gerring Service Record, Harold B. Simpson History College, Hillsboro, Texas.

242. Morrison Court-Martial; Trudeau, *Like Men of War*, 450; *OR*, vol. 48, ser. 1, pt. 1, 268.

243. Morrison Court-Martial; Schuler, *The Last Battle in the War between the States*, 21; Trudeau, *Out of the Storm*, 360; Trudeau, *Like Men of War*, 450.

244. Trudeau, *Out of the Storm*, 309–10; Schuler, *The Last Battle in the War between the States*, 22–24; Trudeau, *Like Men of War*, 450–51; *OR*, vol. 48, ser. 1, pt. 1, 269; Aiken, interview; Oates, ed., *Rip Ford's Texas*, 391–93; Morrison Court-Martial; Hughes, *Rebellious Ranger*, 241; Widener, *The Last Land Battle of the War between the States*, 8; Conyer, "Last Battle of the War," 314; Wooster, *Texas and Texans in the Civil War*, 181.

245. Trudeau, *Out of the Storm*, 309–10; Personnel and Regimental Records of Civil War Soldiers from Indiana; Pierce, *A Brief History of the Lower Rio Grande Valley*, 54; Morrison Court-Martial; Steve Hathcock, interview with author, South Padre Island, Texas, January 4, 1997; Fehrenbach, *Lone Star*, 390; Oates, *Confederate Cavalry West of the River*, 158; Oates, ed., *Rip Ford's Texas*, 395–96; Schuler, *The Last Battle in the War between the States*, 22–25; Pierre Comtois, "War's Last Battle," *America's Civil War* 5, no. 2 (July 1992): 53; Trudeau, *Like Men of War*, 450.

246. Morrison Court-Martial; Fussell, *History of the 34th Regiment*, 53; Irby, "Backdoor to Bagdad," 49; Hughes, *Rebellious Ranger*, 240–41; *OR*, vol. 48, ser. 1, pt. 1, 269; West, "The Last Battle of the War," 227; Trudeau, *Like Men of War*, 452.

247. Compiled Service Records of Troops Who Served from the State of Indiana.
248. Oates, *Confederate Cavalry West of the River*, 158; Thompson, *Vaqueros in Blue and Gray*, 396, 401.

EPILOGUE

1. Oates, ed., *Rip Ford's Texas*, 396, 401.

BIBLIOGRAPHY

PRIMARY SOURCES

Cameron County, Texas, Census Records from the Seventh Census of the United States.

Compiled Service Records of Troops Who Served from the State of Indiana. National Archives, Washington, D.C.

Compiled Service Records of Troops Who Served from the State of Minnesota. National Archives, Washington, D.C.

Compiled Service Records of Troops Who Served from the State of Missouri. National Archives, Washington, D.C.

Compiled Service Records of Troops Who Served from the State of Texas. National Archives, Washington, D.C.

Ford, John S. Papers. Archives Division, University of Texas Library, Austin.

Missouri Civil War Service Records. Missouri State Archives, Jefferson City.

Gerring, Private Ferdinand. Service Record. Harold B. Simpson History College, Hillsboro, Texas.

Miller, Capt. Edward Gee. Diary. Washington County Historical Society, Fayetteville, Arkansas.

Personnel and Regimental Records of Civil War Soldiers from Indiana. Indiana State Archives, Indianapolis.

Proceedings, Findings, and Opinions of the Court-Martial convened by order of the U.S. Army in Special Orders No. 36, Headquarters of the Army of the Rio Grande, July 19, 1865, in the case of Robert G. Morrison. RG 153, Records of the Judge Advocate General. National Archives, Washington, D.C.

Texas Military Service Records. Harold B. Simpson History Complex, Hillsboro, Texas.

Widener, Ralph W. "The Last Land Battle of the War between the States, May 13, 1865." Texas State Library, Austin.

NEWSPAPERS
Brownsville (Texas) Herald Plus.
Houston Daily Telegraph.
New York Herald.
Harlingen (Texas) Valley Morning Star.
San Antonio Weekly Herald.

CORRESPONDENCE AND INTERVIEWS
Aiken, Bruce, Executive Director of the Historic Brownsville (Texas) Museum. Conversation with author, January 6, 1997.

Hathcock, Steve. Conversation with author, South Padre, Texas, January 4, 1997.

Warren, Mark. Letter to author, March 20, 2000.

Zavaleta, Dr. Tony, Vice President for External Affairs, University of Texas, Brownsville. Letter to author, March 4, 1998.

BOOKS
Bailey, Anne J. *Between the Enemy and Texas: Parsons's Texas Cavalry in the Civil War*. Fort Worth: Texas Christian University Press, 1989.

Barr, Alwyn. *Texans in Revolt: The Battle for San Antonio, 1835*. Austin: University of Texas Press, 1990.

Baugh, Virgil E. *Rendezvous at the Alamo: Highlights in the Lives of Bowie, Crockett, and Travis*. Lincoln: University of Nebraska Press, 1985.

Bearss, Edwin C. *Grant Strikes a Fatal Blow: The Campaign for Vicksburg*. 3 vols. Dayton, OH: Morningside Bookshop, 1986.

Bergeron, Arthur W., Jr. *Confederate Mobile*. Jackson: University Press of Mississippi, 1991.

Boatner, Mark Mayo. *The Civil War Dictionary*. New York: David McKay, 1959.

Calkins, Chris M. *The Battles of Appomattox Station and Appomattox Court House, April 8–9, 1865*. Lynchburg, VA: Howard, 1987.

Campbell, Randolph B. *An Empire for Slavery: The Peculiar Institution in Texas, 1821–1865*. Baton Rouge: Louisiana State University Press, 1989.

Casey, Robert J. *The Texas Border and Some Borderliners*. New York: Bobbs-Merill, 1950.

Cornish, Dudley Taylor. *The Sable Arm: Black Troops in the Union Army, 1861–1865.* Lawrence: University Press of Kansas, 1987.

Cowen, Raphael. "The Last Battle of the Civil War: Its Causes and Afterwards." In Brownsville Historical Association. *A Blast from the Past: 50th Anniversary, 1947–1997.* Brownsville, TX: Border, 1996.

Crawford, Anne Fears. *The Eagle: The Autobiography of Santa Anna.* Austin: State House, 1988.

Cutrer, Thomas W. *Ben McCullock and the Frontier Military Tradition.* Chapel Hill: University of North Carolina Press, 1993.

Davis, Jefferson. *The Rise and Fall of the Confederate Government.* New York: Collier, 1961.

DeBruhl, Marshall. *Sword of San Jacinto: A Life of Sam Houston.* New York: Random House, 1993.

Eisenhower, John S. D. *So Far from God: The U.S. War with Mexico, 1846–1848.* New York: Doubleday, 1989.

Farber, James. *Texas, C.S.A.: A Spotlight on Disaster.* New York: Jackson, 1947.

Fehrenbach, T. R. *Lone Star: A History of Texas and the Texans.* New York: American Legacy, 1983.

Ferguson, Henry N. *The Port of Brownsville: A Maritime History of the Rio Grande Valley.* Brownsville: Spring-King, 1976.

Fremantle, Arthur James Lyon. *The Fremantle Diary.* Boston: Little, Brown, 1954.

Fussell, I. L. *History of the 34th Regiment.* Indianapolis: N.p., n.d.

Gallagher, Gary W., ed. *Fighting for the Confederacy: The Personal Recollections of General Edward Porter Alexander.* Chapel Hill: University of North Carolina Press, 1989.

Gladstone, William A. *United States Colored Troops, 1863–1867.* Gettysburg, PA: Thomas, 1990.

Glatthaar, Joseph T. *Forged in Battle: The Civil War Alliance of Black Soldiers and White Officers.* New York: Meridian, 1991.

Gordon, John B. *Reminiscences of the Civil War.* New York: Charles Scribner's Sons, 1904.

Grant, Ulysses S. *Personal Memoirs of U. S. Grant.* 2 vols. New York: C. M. Webster, 1885–86.

Hardin, Stephen L. *Texian Illiad: A Military History of the Texas Revolution, 1835–1836.* Austin: University of Texas Press, 1994.

Hardin, Stephen, and Richard Hook. *The Texas Rangers.* London: Osprey, 1991.

Henry, Robert Selph. *The Story of the Mexican War.* New York: Da Capo, 1961.

Higginson, Thomas Wentworth. *Army Life in a Black Regiment.* New York: Collier, 1962.

History of Minnesota. Chicago: Lewis Publishing, 1915.

Horgan, Paul. *Great River: The Rio Grande in North American History.* Hanover, NH: University Press of New England, 1984.

Hughes, W. J. *Rebellious Ranger: Rip Ford and the Old Southwest.* Norman: University of Oklahoma Press, 1964.

Hurt, R. Douglas. *Agriculture and Slavery in Missouri's Little Dixie.* Columbia: University of Missouri Press, 1992.

Johnson, Frank W. *A History of Texas and Texans.* 2 vols. Chicago: American Historical Society, 1914.

Johnson, Ludwell H. *Red River Campaign: Politics and Cotton in the Civil War.* Kent, OH: Kent State University Press, 1993.

Josephy, Alvin M. Jr. *The Civil War in the American West.* New York: Knopf, 1991.

Kearny, Milo and Anthony Knapp. *Boom and Bust: The Historical Cycles of Matamoros and Brownsville.* Austin: Eakin, 1991.

Kearny, Milo, ed. *Still More Studies in Brownsville History.* Brownsville: University of Texas Press, 1991.

Kerby, Robert L. *Kirby Smith's Confederacy: The Trans-Mississippi South, 1863–1865.* Tuscaloosa: University of Alabama Press, 1972.

Lofton, John. *Denmark Vesey's Revolt.* Kent, OH: Kent State University Press, 1983.

McKenna, Verna Jackson. *Old Point Lighthouse: Beacon of Brazos Santiago.* Harlingen, TX: private printing, 1956.

McPherson, James M. *Battle Cry of Freedom: The Civil War Era.* Oxford: Oxford University Press, 1988.

———. *The Negro's Civil War: How American Negroes Felt and Acted during the War for the Union.* New York: Vintage, 1965.

Moore, John C. *Confederate Military History: Missouri.* 12 vols. Atlanta: Confederate, 1899.

Mullins, Michael A. *The Fremont Rifles: A History of the 37th Illinois Veteran Volunteer Infantry.* Wilmington, NC: Broadfoot, 1990.

Nisbet, James Cooper. *Four Years on the Firing Line.* Jackson, TN: McCowat-Mercer, 1963.

Nofi, Albert A. *The Alamo and the Texas War for Independence, September 30, 1835–April 21, 1836.* Conshohocken, PA: Combined, 1992.

North, Thomas. *Five Years in Texas.* Cincinnati: Elm Street, 1871.

Nunn, W. C., ed. *Ten More Texans in Gray.* Hillsboro, TX: Hill Junior College Press, 1980.

Oates, Stephen B. *Confederate Cavalry West of the River*. Austin: University of Texas Press, 1961.

———., ed. *Rip Ford's Texas*. Austin: University of Texas Press, 1994.

Parks, Joseph H. *General Edmund Kirby Smith, C.S.A.* Baton Rouge: Louisiana State University Press, 1992.

Parrish, T. Michael. *Richard Taylor: Soldier Prince of Dixie*. Chapel Hill: University of North Carolina Press, 1992.

Pierce, Frank C. *A Brief History of the Lower Rio Grande Valley*. Menasha, WI: George Banta, 1917.

Pohl, James W. *The Battle of San Jacinto*. Austin: Texas State Historical Association, 1989.

Redkey, Edwin S. *A Grand Army of Black Men: Letters from African-American Soldiers in the Union Army, 1861–1865*. Cambridge: Cambridge University Press, 1992.

Roberts, Bobby and Carl Moneyhon. *Portaits of Conflict: A Photographic History of Mississippi in the Civil War*. Fayetteville: University of Arkansas Press, 1993.

Roberts, O. M. *Confederate Military History: Texas*. 12 vols. Atlanta: Confederate, 1899.

Schuler, Louis J. *The Last Battle in the War Between the States, May 13, 1865*. Brownsville: Springman-King, 1960.

Symonds, Craig L. *Joseph E. Johnston: A Civil War Biography*. New York: Norton, 1992.

Thompson, Jerry D. *Mexican Texans in the Union Army*. El Paso: University of Texas at El Paso, 1986.

———. *Vaqueros in Blue and Gray*. Austin: Presidial, 1976.

Trudeau, Noah Andre. *Like Men of War: Black Troops in the Civil War, 1862–1865*. New York: Little, Brown, 1998.

———. *Out of the Storm: The End of the Civil War, April–June 1865*. New York: Little, Brown, 1994.

Tucker, Phillip Thomas. *From Auction Block to Glory: The African American Experience*. New York: Friedman, 1997.

Tyler, Ronnie C. *Santiago Vidaurri and the Southern Confederacy*. Austin: Texas State Historical Association, 1973.

———., ed. *The New Handbook of Texas*. 6 vols. Austin: Texas State Historical Association, 1996.

War of the Rebellion: A Compilation of the Official Records of the Union and Confederate Armies. 128 vols. Washington, D.C.: Government Printing Office, 1880–1901.

Winsor, Bill. *Texas in the Confederacy: Military Installations, Economy, and People*. Hillsboro, TX: Hill Junior College Press, 1978.

Winter, William C. *The Civil War in St. Louis: A Guided Tour.* St. Louis: Missouri Historical Society Press, 1994.

Woodward, C. Vann. *Mary Chesnut's Civil War.* New Haven, CT: Yale University Press, 1981.

Wooster, Ralph A. *Texas and Texans in the Civil War.* Austin: Eakin, 1995.

———. *Texas Vistas: Selections from the* Southerwest Historical Quarterly. Austin: University of Texas Press, 1987.

ARTICLES

"Captain Summerfield H. Barton." *Confederate Veteran* (January 1917–December 1917): 322.

Comtois, Pierre. "War's Last Battle." *America's Civil War* 5, no. 2 (July 1992): 46–53.

Conyer, Luther. "Last Battle of the War." *Southern Historical Society Papers* (1896): 309–15.

Delaney, Robert W. "Matamoros: Port for Texas during the Civil War." *Southwestern Historical Quarterly* (April 1955): 473–87.

Irby, James A. "Backdoor at Bagdad: The Civil War on the Rio Grande." Monograph no. 53. *Southwestern Studies* (1977): 5–50.

Mahon, Emmie Giddings W. and Chester V. Kielman. "George H. Giddings and the San Antonio-San Diego Mail Line." *Southwestern Historical Quarterly* (October 1957): 220–39.

Marshall, Bruce. "Santos Benavides: 'The Confederacy on the Rio Grande.'" *Civil War* 8 no. 3 (May–June 1990): 18–20.

Marten, James. "Texans in the U.S. Army: True to the Union." *North and South* (November 1999): 79–87.

Oates, Stephen B. "John S. 'Rip' Ford: Prudent Cavalryman, C.S.A." *Southwestern Historical Quarterly* (January 1961): 289–314.

———. "Texas under the Secessionists." In *Texas Vistas: Selections from the* Southwest Historical Quarterly. Compiled by Ralph A. Wooster and Robert A. Calvert. Austin: University of Texas Press, 1987.

Smyrl, Frank H. "Texans in the Union Army, 1861–1865." *Southwestern Historical Quarterly* (October 1961): 234–50.

Tyler, Ronnie C. "Cotton on the Border, 1861–1865." *Southwestern Historical Quarterly* (April 1970): 456–477.

West, W. C. "The Last Battle of the War." *Southern Historical Society Papers.* 226–227.

Widener, Ralph. "John S. 'Rip' Ford, Colonel, CSA." *Confederate Veteran* (May–June 1993): 14–21.

INDEX

Note: Page references in boldface type indicate
photographs or illustrations. The denotation "ph." indicates
a photograph in the plates between pp. 86 and 87.